INDIA: ECONOMIC, POLITICAL AND SOCIAL ISSUES

URLAH B. NISSAM
EDITOR

Nova Science Publishers, Inc.
New York

LIBRARY OF CONGRESS CATALOGING-IN-PUBLICATION DATA

India : economic, political and social issues / Urlah B. Nissam (editor).
    p. cm.
 Includes bibliographical references and index.
 ISBN 978-1-60456-509-6 (hardcover : alk. paper)
 1. India--Foreign relations--1984- 2. India--Economic conditions--1991- 3. India--Social conditions--1947- 4. India--Politics and government--1977- 5. India--Foreign relations--United States. 6. United States--Foreign relations--India. 7. East Indians--Australia--Melbourne (Vic.) 8. Medical care--India. 9. India--Commerce--Indonesia--Bali (Province) 10. Bali (Indonesia : Province)--Commerce--India. I. Nissam, Urlah B.
 DS449.I63 2008
 954.05'2--dc22
               2008012146

Published by Nova Science Publishers, Inc. ✛ *New York*

£ 65-99

172237

UNIVERSITY COLLEGE BIRMINGHAM
COLLEGE LIBRARY, SUMMER ROW
BIRMINGHAM. B3 1JB
Tel: (0121) 243 0055

DATE OF RETURN		
5/10/09		

Please remember to return on time or pay the fine

INDIA: ECONOMIC, POLITICAL AND SOCIAL ISSUES

CONTENTS

PREFACE

India is the world's twelfth largest economy at market exchange rates and the third largest in purchasing power. Economic reforms have transformed it into the second fastest growing large economy; however, it still suffers from high levels of poverty, illiteracy, malnutrition and environmental degradation. A pluralistic, multilingual, and multiethnic society, India is also home to a diversity of wildlife in a variety of protected habitats. This new book presents recent important issues dealing with India.

Chapter 1 – India is profiled.

Chapter 2 - India's foreign policy today is characterised by unprecedented pragmatism as well as cautious idealism. The pragmatism is rather visible in the growing realisation that, as the twenty-first century unfolds, mediated by the hegemony of trans-national liberalism, the conventional 'commonsense' understanding of the apparently fixed geographical location of India and its 'neighbourhood' (the manner in which 'regions' as well as regional groupings tend to acquire, over a period of time, a sense of territoriality and hence an image of immutability) are due for a thorough revision. As pointed out perceptively by C. Raja Mohan, 'it is not often that a country finds itself on the verge of multiple breakthroughs on foreign policy. India is at one of those rare moments'. India appears far more confident than ever before to take on the challenge posed by the complex interplay between geopolitics and geoeconomics. The normative thrust of India's foreign policy relates to a critical reassessment of the country's role in global affairs, while working towards the goal of Asian (even Afro-Asian) solidarity through inter-cultural dialogue and co-operative economic diplomacy. Of late, a serious and systematic pursuit by India of its economic-energy security, at regional as well as sub-regional levels, is a good example of how normative and pragmatic considerations are being combined in innovative policy frameworks and alliance-making.

Chapter 3 - Globalization has thrown many challenges as well as opened several opportunities for the SMEs. Today, SMEs need to network more intensely with the academic and R&D institutions and among themselves for their very survival. Since contribution of SMEs to economic and industrial development, worldwide is substantial, a pro-SME policy becomes necessary. Growing performance of high technology users in sectors such as auto-components and pharmaceuticals in India underlines the importance of technology transfer to SMEs. SMEs in India number more than 11 million, employ more than 28 million people, contribute to around 40% of industrial production and 35% of exports. SME sector in India is undergoing reforms to enable the units to take on the increased competition in the globalizing economy.

The Government of India has many schemes and programmes that support acquisition, management, development and commercialization of technology by the SMEs. Specialized agencies and mechanisms have been established that transfer the technology from laboratories to industry and facilitate their commercialization. The FDI policy is being further liberalized that is conducive to foreign investment and technology inflow in the country. Many venture capital mechanisms that support technology transfer exist in the country. Among the infrastructure facilities for technology transfer, a number of Science and Technology Entrepreneurship parks (STEPs) and Technology Business Incubators (TBIs) have been set-up in the vicinity of institutions and industry clusters. Policies and infrastructure facilities for technology transfer to SMEs should be aimed at enhancing their competitiveness in the globalized economy. Besides this, the policies and mechanisms should be innovative that encourage the SMEs to participate aggressively in the technology transfer process. Easier access to foreign technologies, internationalization, and encouragement to generate intellectual property and promote innovation clusters, start ups etc. are needed, besides innovative financing including venture capital.

Chapter 4 - The U.S. goods trade deficit with India was $11.7 billion in 2006, an increase of $920 million from $10.8 billion in 2005. U.S. goods exports in 2006 were $10.1 billion, up 26.3 percent from the previous year. Corresponding U.S. imports from India were $21.8 billion, up 16.1 percent. India is currently the twenty-first largest export market for U.S. goods.

Chapter 5 - The Indian community, a minority distinguishable from the Anglo-Australian majority, has the opportunity to articulate its ethnic and cultural identity through this process of mothering. Mothers and mothers-in-law play important roles in their daughters' and daughters'-in-law mothering, in the retention of cultural knowledge, and in the reaffirmation of identity. Daughters will be expected to do the same eventually for the following generation, as illustrated for daughters of Indian immigrants in the United States, who maintain ethnic or cultural identity by retaining certain values and behaviours. In this chapter, the author outlines the research among the Indian diaspora in Australia.

Chapter 6 - The Trade Agreements between India and Indonesia in 1978, followed by many other Agreements between various bilateral organizations like FICCI, CII, ASSOCHAM, have strengthened the economic relations between India and Indonesia,

Chapter 7 - It has been increasingly recognised that apart from medical inputs, a wide range of socio-economic factors plays an important role in determining health. The objective of the study has been to ascertain the impact of predominantly medical inputs on health status of individuals and simultaneously capture the influence of such socio-economic variables on the (in) efficiency prevalent in the production process (of health). A stochastic production frontier with inefficiency effects has been estimated based on data drawn from the fourteen major states of India over the time frame of 1986 to 1995. The frontier estimates throw light on some conflicting issues facing the policy-makers. Most importantly the results revealed that the beneficial impact of economic growth is not large enough to supersede that of medical services. Consequently greater priority ought to be given to the enhancement of health sector and utilisation of medical services. Finally the index of efficiency, generated by the frontier model, highlights the blatant regional disparity prevalent in India and draws attention to the need for pursuing policies directed towards eradication of this existing regional imbalance.

Chapter 8 - Long considered a "strategic backwater"from Washington's perspective, South Asia has emerged in the 21st century as increasingly vital to core U.S. foreign policy interests. India, the region's dominant actor with more than one billion citizens, is now recognized as a nascent major power and "natural partner" of the United States, one that many analysts view as a potential counterweight to China's growing clout. Washington and New Delhi have since 2004 been pursuing a "strategic partnership" based on shared values such as democracy, multi-culturalism, and rule of law. Numerous economic, security, and global initiatives, including plans for "full civilian nuclear energy cooperation," are underway. This latter initiative, launched by President Bush in July 2005 and provisionally endorsed by the 109th Congress in late 2006 (P.L. 109-401), reverses three decades of U.S. nonproliferation policy. It would require, among other steps, conclusion of a peaceful nuclear agreement between the United States and India, which would itself enter into force only after a Joint Resolution of Approval by Congress. Also in 2005, the United States and India signed a ten-year defense framework agreement that calls for expanding bilateral security cooperation. Since 2002, the two countries have engaged in numerous and unprecedented combined military exercises. The issue of major U.S. arms sales to India may come before the 110th Congress. The influence of a growing and relatively wealthy Indian-American community of more than two million is reflected in Congress's largest country-specific caucus.

Further U.S. interest in South Asia focuses on ongoing tensions between India and Pakistan, a problem rooted in unfinished business from the 1947 Partition, competing claims to the Kashmir region, and, in more recent years, "cross-border terrorism" in both Kashmir and major Indian cities. In the interests of regional stability, the United States strongly encourages an ongoing India-Pakistan peace initiative and remains concerned about the potential for conflict over Kashmiri sovereignty to cause open hostilities between these two nuclear-armed countries. The United States seeks to curtail the proliferation of nuclear weapons and ballistic missiles in South Asia. Both India and Pakistan have resisted external pressure to sign the major nonproliferation treaties. In 1998, the two countries conducted nuclear tests that evoked international condemnation. Proliferation-related restrictions on U.S. aid were triggered, then later lifted through congressional-executive cooperation from 1998 to 2000. Remaining sanctions on India (and Pakistan) were removed in October 2001.

India is in the midst of major and rapid economic expansion. Many U.S. business interests view India as a lucrative market and candidate for foreign investment. The United States supports India's efforts to transform its once quasi-socialist economy through fiscal reform and market opening. Since 1991, India has taken steps in this direction, with coalition governments keeping the country on a general path of reform. Yet there is U.S. concern that such movement remains slow and inconsistent. Congress also continues to have concerns about abuses of human rights, including caste- and gender-based discrimination, and religious freedoms in India. Moreover, the spread of HIV/AIDS in India has attracted congressional attention as a serious development.

Chapter 9 - In March 2006, the Bush Administration proposed legislation to create an exception for India from certain provisions of the Atomic Energy Act to facilitate a future nuclear cooperation agreement. After hearings in April and May, the House International Relations Committee and the Senate Foreign Relations Committee considered bills in late June 2006 to provide an exception for India to certain provisions of the Atomic Energy Act related to a peaceful nuclear cooperation agreement. On July 26, 2006, the House passed its version of the legislation, H.R. 5682, by a vote of 359 to 68. On November 16, 2006, the Senate incorporated the text of S. 3709, as amended, into H.R. 5682 and passed that bill by a vote of 85 to 12. The Senate insisted on its amendment, and a conference committee produced a conference report on December 7, 2006. The House agreed to the conference report (H.Rept. 109-721) on December 8 in a 330-59 vote; the Senate agreed by unanimous consent to the conference report on December 9. The President signed the bill into law (P.L. 109-401) on December 18, 2006.

The Senate and House versions of the India bill contained similar provisions, with four differences. The Senate version contained an additional requirement for the President to execute his waiver authority, an amendment introduced by Senator Harkin and adopted by unanimous consent that the President determine that India is "fully and actively participating in U.S. and international efforts to dissuade, sanction and contain Iran for its nuclear program." This provision was watered down into a reporting requirement in the conference report. The Senate version also had two unique sections related to the cooperation agreement, Sections 106 and 107, both of which appear in the conference report. Section 106 (now Section 104 (d) (4)) prohibits exports of equipment, material or technology related for uranium enrichment, spent fuel reprocessing or heavy water production unless conducted in a multinational facility participating in a project approved by the International Atomic Energy Agency (IAEA) or in a facility participating in a bilateral or multilateral project to develop a proliferation-resistant fuel cycle. Section 107 (now Section 104 (d) (5)) would establish a program to monitor that U.S. technology is being used appropriately by Indian recipients. Finally, the Senate version also contained the implementing legislation for the U.S. Additional Protocol in Title II, which was retained in the conference bill. Minor differences in reporting requirements and statements of policy are compared in table I of this report.

This article provides a thematic side-by-side comparison of the provisions of the conference report with H.R. 5682 as passed by the House and by the Senate, and compares them with the Administration's initially proposed legislation, H.R. 4974/S. 2429, and the conference report. The report concludes with a list of CRS resources that provide further discussion and more detailed analysis of the issues addressed by the legislation summarized in the table.

In: India: Economic, Political and Social Issues   ISBN: 978-1-60456-509-6
Editor: Urlah B. Nissam   © 2009 Nova Science Publishers, Inc.

Chapter 1

INDIA: COUNTRY PROFILE OF CURRENT EVENTS

GEOGRAPHY

Area: 3.29 million sq. km. (1.27 million sq. mi.); about one-third the size of the U.S.
Cities: Capital--New Delhi (pop. 12.8 million, 2001 census). Other major cities--Mumbai, formerly Bombay (16.4 million); Kolkata, formerly Calcutta (13.2 million); Chennai, formerly Madras (6.4 million); Bangalore (5.7 million); Hyderabad (5.5 million); Ahmedabad (5 million); Pune (4 million).
Terrain: Varies from Himalayas to flat river valleys and deserts in the west.
Climate: Alpine to temperate to subtropical monsoon.

PEOPLE

Nationality: Noun and adjective--Indian(s).
Population (2007): 1.12 billion; urban 27.8%.
Annual growth rate: 1.3%
Density: 324/sq. km.
Ethnic groups: Indo-Aryan 72%, Dravidian 25%, others 3%. While the national census does not recognize racial or ethnic groups, it is estimated that there are more than 2,000 ethnic groups in India.
Religions: Hindu 80.5%, Muslim 13.4%, Christian 2.3%, Sikh 1.9%, other groups including Buddhist, Jain, Parsi.
Languages: Hindi, English, and 16 other official languages.
Education: Years compulsory--none. Literacy--61%.
Health: Infant mortality rate--34.61/1,000. Life expectancy--68.59 years (2007 est.).
Work force (est.): 450 million. Agriculture--60%; industry and commerce--18%; services and government--22%

GOVERNMENT

Type: Federal republic.
Independence: August 15, 1947.
Constitution: January 26, 1950.
Branches: Executive--president (chief of state), prime minister (head of government), Council of Ministers (cabinet). Legislative--bicameral parliament (Rajya Sabha or Council of States, and Lok Sabha or House of the People). Judicial --Supreme Court.
Political parties: Indian National Congress (INC), Bharatiya Janata Party (BJP), Communist Party of India-Marxist, and numerous regional and small national parties.
Political subdivisions: 28 states,* 7 union territories.
Suffrage: Universal over 18.

ECONOMY

GDP (FY 2007): $1 trillion ($1,000 billion).
Real growth rate (2006-2007 est.): 9.4%.
Per capita GDP (FY 2006-2007): $909.
Natural resources: Coal, iron ore, manganese, mica, bauxite, chromite, thorium, limestone, barite, titanium ore, diamonds, crude oil.
Agriculture: 18% of GDP. Products--wheat, rice, coarse grains, oilseeds, sugar, cotton, jute, tea
Industry: 27% of GDP. Products--textiles, jute, processed food, steel, machinery, transport equipment, cement, aluminum, fertilizers, mining, petroleum, chemicals, and computer software.
Services and transportation: 55% of GDP.
Trade: Exports (FY 2006-2007)--$127 billion; engineering goods, petroleum products, precious stones, cotton apparel and fabrics, gems and jewelry, handicrafts, tea. Software exports--$22 billion. Imports (FY 2006-2007)--$192 billion; petroleum, machinery and transport equipment, electronic goods, edible oils, fertilizers, chemicals, gold, textiles, iron and steel. Major trade partners--U.S., China, EU, Russia, Japan.

PEOPLE

Although India occupies only 2.4% of the world's land area, it supports over 15% of the world's population. Only China has a larger population. India's median age is 25, one of the youngest among large economies. About 70% live in more than 550,000 villages, and the remainder in more than 200 towns and cities. Over the thousands of years of its history, India has been invaded from the Iranian plateau, Central Asia, Arabia, Afghanistan, and the West; Indian people and culture have absorbed and modified these influences to produce a remarkable racial and cultural synthesis.

Religion, caste, and language are major determinants of social and political organization in India today. However, with more job opportunities in the private sector and better chances of upward social mobility, India has begun a quiet social transformation in this area. The government has recognized 18 official languages; Hindi, the national language, is the most widely spoken, although English is a national lingua franca. Although 81% of its people are Hindu, India also is the home of more than 138 million Muslims--one of the world's largest Muslim populations. The population also includes Christians, Sikhs, Jains, Buddhists, and Parsis.

The Hindu caste system reflects Indian occupational and socially defined hierarchies. Ancient Sanskrit sources divide society into four major categories, priests (Brahmin), warriors (Kshatriya), traders (Vaishya) and farmers/laborers (Shudra). Although these categories are understood throughout India, they describe reality only in the most general terms. They omit, for example, the tribes and those once known as "untouchables." In reality, Indian society is divided into thousands of jatis--local, endogamous groups based on occupation--and organized hierarchically according to complex ideas of purity and pollution. Discrimination based on caste is officially illegal, but remains prevalent, especially in rural areas. Nevertheless, the government has made strong efforts to minimize the importance of caste through active affirmative action and social policies. Moreover, caste has been diluted if not subsumed in the economically prosperous and heterogeneous cities, where an increasing percentage of India's population lives. In the countryside, expanding education, land reform and economic opportunity through access to information, communication, transport, and credit have lessened the harshest elements of the caste system.

HISTORY

The people of India have had a continuous civilization since 2500 B.C., when the inhabitants of the Indus River valley developed an urban culture based on commerce and sustained by agricultural trade. This civilization declined around 1500 B.C., probably due to ecological changes.

During the second millennium B.C., pastoral, Aryan-speaking tribes migrated from the northwest into the subcontinent, settled in the middle Ganges River valley, and adapted to antecedent cultures.

The political map of ancient and medieval India was made up of myriad kingdoms with fluctuating boundaries. In the 4th and 5th centuries A.D., northern India was unified under the Gupta Dynasty. During this period, known as India's Golden Age, Hindu culture and political administration reached new heights.

Islam spread across the subcontinent over a period of 700 years. In the 10th and 11th centuries, Turks and Afghans invaded India and established sultanates in Delhi. In the early 16th century, Babur, a Turkish adventurer and distant relative of Timurlane, established the Mughal Dynasty, which lasted for 200 years. South India followed an independent path, but by the 17th century large areas of South India came under the direct rule or influence of the expanding Mughal Empire. While most of Indian society in its thousands of villages remained untouched by the political struggles going on around them, Indian courtly culture evolved into a unique blend of Hindu and Muslim traditions.

The first British outpost in South Asia was established by the English East India Company in 1619 at Surat on the northwestern coast. Later in the century, the Company opened permanent trading stations at Madras (now Chennai), Bombay (now Mumbai), and Calcutta (now Kolkata), each under the protection of native rulers.

The British expanded their influence from these footholds until, by the 1850s, they controlled most of present-day India, Pakistan, Sri Lanka, and Bangladesh. In 1857, an unsuccessful rebellion in north India led by Indian soldiers seeking the restoration of the Mughal Emperor caused the British Parliament to transfer political power from the East India Company to the Crown. Great Britain began administering most of India directly, while controlling the rest through treaties with local rulers.

In the late 1800s, the first steps were taken toward self-government in British India with the appointment of Indian councilors to advise the British Viceroy and the establishment of Provincial Councils with Indian members; the British subsequently widened participation in Legislative Councils. Beginning in 1920, Indian leader Mohandas K. Gandhi transformed the Indian National Congress political party into a mass movement to campaign against British colonial rule. The party used both parliamentary and nonviolent resistance and non-cooperation to agitate for independence. During this period, however, millions of Indians served with honor and distinction in the British armed forces, including service in both World Wars and countless other overseas actions in service of the Empire.

With Indians increasingly united in their quest for independence, a war-weary Britain led by Labor Prime Minister Clement Attlee began in earnest to plan for the end of its suzerainty in India. On August 15, 1947, India became a dominion within the Commonwealth, with Jawaharlal Nehru as Prime Minister. Strategic colonial considerations, as well as political tensions between Hindus and Muslims, led the British to partition British India into two separate states: India, with a Hindu majority; and Pakistan, which consisted of two "wings," East and West Pakistan--currently Bangladesh and Pakistan--with Muslim majorities. India became a republic within the Commonwealth after promulgating its Constitution on January 26, 1950.

After independence, the Indian National Congress, the party of Mohandas K. Gandhi and Jawaharlal Nehru, ruled India under the leadership first of Nehru and then his daughter (Indira Gandhi) and grandson (Rajiv Gandhi), with the exception of brief periods in the 1970s and 1980s, during a short period in 1996, and the period from 1998-2004, when a coalition led by the Bharatiya Janata Party governed.

Prime Minister Nehru governed the nation until his death in 1964. Nehru was succeeded by Lal Bahadur Shastri, who also died in office. In 1966, power passed to Nehru's daughter, Indira Gandhi, Prime Minister from 1966 to 1977. In 1975, beset with deepening political and economic problems, Mrs. Gandhi declared a state of emergency and suspended many civil liberties. Seeking a mandate at the polls for her policies, she called for elections in 1977, only to be defeated by Morarji Desai, who headed the Janata Party, an amalgam of five opposition parties.

In 1979, Desai's Government crumbled. Charan Singh formed an interim government, which was followed by Mrs. Gandhi's return to power in January 1980. On October 31, 1984, Mrs. Gandhi was assassinated, and her son, Rajiv, was chosen by the Congress (I)--for "Indira"--Party to take her place. His Congress government was plagued with allegations of corruption resulting in an early call for national elections in 1989.

Although Rajiv Gandhi's Congress Party won more seats than any other single party in the 1989 elections, he was unable to form a government with a clear majority. The Janata Dal, a union of opposition parties, then joined with the Hindu-nationalist Bharatiya Janata Party

(BJP) on the right and the Communists on the left to form the government. This loose coalition collapsed in November 1990, and the Janata Dal, supported by the Congress (I), came to power for a short period, with Chandra Shekhar as Prime Minister. That alliance also collapsed, resulting in national elections in June 1991.

While campaigning in Tamil Nadu on behalf of Congress (I), Rajiv Gandhi was assassinated on May 27, 1991, apparently by Tamil extremists from Sri Lanka, unhappy with India's armed intervention to try to stop the civil war there. In the elections, Congress (I) won 213 parliamentary seats and returned to power at the head of a coalition, under the leadership of P.V. Narasimha Rao. This Congress-led government, which served a full 5-year term, initiated a gradual process of economic liberalization and reform, which opened the Indian economy to global trade and investment. India's domestic politics also took new shape, as the nationalist appeal of the Congress Party gave way to traditional caste, creed, regional, and ethnic alignments, leading to the founding of a plethora of small, regionally based political parties.

The final months of the Rao-led government in the spring of 1996 were marred by several major corruption scandals, which contributed to the worst electoral performance by the Congress Party in its history. The Hindu-nationalist BJP emerged from the May 1996 national elections as the single-largest party in the Lok Sabha but without a parliamentary majority. Under Prime Minister Atal Bihari Vajpayee, the subsequent BJP coalition lasted only 13 days. With all political parties wishing to avoid another round of elections, a 14-party coalition led by the Janata Dal formed a government known as the United Front, under the former Chief Minister of Karnataka, H.D. Deve Gowda. His government collapsed after less than a year, when the Congress Party withdrew its support in March 1997. Inder Kumar Gujral replaced Deve Gowda as the consensus choice for Prime Minister at the head of a 16-party United Front coalition.

In November 1997, the Congress Party again withdrew support from the United Front. In new elections in February 1998, the BJP won the largest number of seats in Parliament--182--but fell far short of a majority. On March 20, 1998, the President approved a BJP-led coalition government with Vajpayee again serving as Prime Minister. On May 11 and 13, 1998, this government conducted a series of underground nuclear tests, spurring U.S. President Clinton to impose economic sanctions on India pursuant to the 1994 Nuclear Proliferation Prevention Act.

In April 1999, the BJP-led coalition government fell apart, leading to fresh elections in September. The National Democratic Alliance--a new coalition led by the BJP--won a majority to form the government with Vajpayee as Prime Minister in October 1999. The NDA government was the first in many years to serve a full five year term, providing much-needed political stability.

The Kargil conflict in 1999 and an attack by terrorists on the Indian Parliament in December 2001 led to increased tensions with Pakistan.

Hindu nationalists supportive of the BJP agitated to build a temple on a disputed site in Ayodhya, destroying a 17th century mosque there in December 1992, and sparking widespread religious riots in which thousands, mostly Muslims, were killed. In February 2002, 57 Hindu volunteers returning from Ayodhya were burnt alive when their train caught fire. Alleging that the fire was caused by Muslim attackers, anti-Muslim rioters throughout the state of Gujarat killed over 900 people and left 100,000 homeless. This led to accusations that the BJP-led Gujarat state government had not done enough to contain the riots, or arrest and prosecute the rioters.

The ruling BJP-led coalition was defeated in a five-stage election held in April and May of 2004, and a Congress-led coalition, known as the United Progressive Alliance (UPA), took power on May 22 with Manmohan Singh as Prime Minister. The UPA's victory was attributed to dissatisfaction among poorer rural voters that the prosperity of the cities had not filtered down to them, and rejection of the BJP's Hindu nationalist agenda.

The Congress-led UPA government has continued many of the BJP's foreign policies, particularly improving relations with the U.S. Prime Minister Singh and President Bush concluded a landmark U.S.-India strategic partnership framework agreement on July 18, 2005. In March 2006, President Bush visited India to further the many initiatives that underlie the new agreement. The strategic partnership is anchored by a historic civil nuclear cooperation initiative and includes cooperation in the fields of space, high-technology commerce, health issues, democracy promotion, agriculture, and trade and investment.

GOVERNMENT

According to its Constitution, India is a "sovereign, socialist, secular, democratic republic." Like the United States, India has a federal form of government. However, the central government in India has greater power in relation to its states, and has adopted a British-style parliamentary system.

The government exercises its broad administrative powers in the name of the president, whose duties are largely ceremonial. A special electoral college elects the president and vice president indirectly for 5-year terms. Their terms are staggered, and the vice president does not automatically become president following the death or removal from office of the president.

Real national executive power is centered in the Council of Ministers (Cabinet), led by the prime minister. The president appoints the prime minister, who is designated by legislators of the political party or coalition commanding a parliamentary majority in the Lok Sabha (lower house). The president then appoints subordinate ministers on the advice of the prime minister.

India's bicameral Parliament consists of the Rajya Sabha (Council of States) and the Lok Sabha (House of the People). The Council of Ministers is responsible to the Lok Sabha.

The legislatures of the states and union territories elect 233 members to the Rajya Sabha, and the president appoints another 12. The members of the Rajya Sabha serve 6-year terms, with one-third up for election every 2 years. The Lok Sabha consists of 545 members, who serve 5-year terms; 543 are directly elected, and two are appointed.

India's independent judicial system began under the British, and its concepts and procedures resemble those of Anglo-Saxon countries. The Supreme Court consists of a chief justice and 25 other justices, all appointed by the president on the advice of the prime minister.

India has 28 states* and 7 union territories. At the state level, some legislatures are bicameral, patterned after the two houses of the national parliament. The states' chief ministers are responsible to the legislatures in the same way the prime minister is responsible to Parliament.

Each state also has a presidentially appointed governor, who may assume certain broad powers when directed by the central government. The central government exerts greater control over the union territories than over the states, although some territories have gained more power to administer their own affairs. Local governments in India have less autonomy than their counterparts in the United States. Some states are trying to revitalize the traditional village councils, or panchayats, to promote popular democratic participation at the village level, where much of the population still lives. Over half a million panchayats exist throughout India.

Principal Government Officials

President--Pratibha Patil

Vice President--Mohammed Hamid Ansari

Prime Minister--Dr. Manmohan Singh

Home Minister--Shivraj Patil

Minister of External Affairs--Pranab Mukherjee

Ambassador to the U.S.--Ronen Sen

Ambassador to the UN--Nirupam Sen

India maintains an embassy in the United States at 2107 Massachusetts Avenue NW, Washington, DC 20008 (tel. 202-939-7000, fax 202-265-4351, email indembwash@indiagov.org and consulates general in New York, Chicago, Houston, and San Francisco. The embassy's web site is http://www.indianembassy.org/.

POLITICAL CONDITIONS

Emerging as the nation's single largest party in the April/May 2004 Lok Sabha election, Congress currently leads a coalition government under Prime Minister Manmohan Singh. Party President Sonia Gandhi was re-elected by the Party National Executive in May 2005. Also a Member of Parliament, she heads the Congress Lok Sabha delegation. Congress prides itself as a secular, left of center party, with a long history of political dominance. Although its performance in national elections had steadily declined during the last 12 years, its surprise victory in 2004 was a result of recruiting strong allies into the UPA, the anti-incumbency factor among voters, and its courtship of India's many poor, rural and Muslim voters. Congress political fortunes suffered badly in the 1990s, as many traditional supporters were lost to emerging regional and caste-based parties, such as the Bahujan Samaj Party and the Samajwadi Party, but have rebounded since its May 2004 ascension to power. It currently rules either directly or in coalition with its allies in 9 states. In November 2005, the Congress regained the Chief Ministership of Jammu and Kashmir state, under a power-sharing agreement.

The Bharatiya Janata Party (BJP), led by Rajnath Singh, holds the second-largest number of seats in the Lok Sabha. Former Prime Minister Atal Bihari Vajpayee serves as Chairman of the BJP Parliamentary Party, and former Deputy Prime Minister L.K. Advani is Leader of the Opposition. The Hindu-nationalist BJP draws its political strength mainly from the "Hindi Belt" in the northern and western regions of India.

The party holds power in the states of Gujarat, Madhya Pradesh, Rajasthan, Chhattisgarh, and Orissa--in coalition with the Biju Janata Dal. Popularly viewed as the party of the northern upper caste and trading communities, the BJP made strong inroads into lower castes in recent national and state assembly elections. The party must balance the competing interests of Hindu nationalists, (who advocate construction of a temple on a disputed site in Ayodhya, and other primarily religious issues), and center-right modernizers who see the BJP as a party of economic and political reform.

Four Communist and Marxist parties are united in a bloc called the "Left Front," which controls 57 parliamentary seats. The Left Front rules the states of West Bengal and Kerala. Although it has not joined the government, Left Front support provides the crucial seats necessary for the UPA to retain power in New Delhi; without its support, the UPA government would fall. It advocates a secular and Communist ideology and opposes many aspects of economic liberalization and globalization, resulting in dissonance with Prime Minister Singh's liberal economic approach.

The next general election is scheduled for 2009.

ECONOMY

India's population is estimated at more than 1.1 billion and is growing at 1.3% a year. It has the world's 12th largest economy--and the third largest in Asia behind Japan and China--with total GDP of around $1 trillion ($1,000 billion). Services, industry, and agriculture account for 55%, 27%, and 18% of GDP respectively. Nearly two-thirds of the population depends on agriculture for its livelihood. 700 million Indians live on $2 per day or less, but there is a large and growing middle class of 325-350 million with disposable income for consumer goods.

India is continuing to move forward with market-oriented economic reforms that began in 1991. Recent reforms include liberalized foreign investment and exchange regimes, industrial decontrol, significant reductions in tariffs and other trade barriers, reform and modernization of the financial sector, significant adjustments in government monetary and fiscal policies, and safeguarding intellectual property rights.

Real GDP growth for the fiscal year ending March 31, 2007 was 9.4%, up from 9.0% growth in the previous year. Growth for the year ending March 31, 2008 is expected to be between 8.5-9.0%. Foreign portfolio and direct investment inflows have risen significantly in recent years. They have contributed to $255 billion in foreign exchange reserves by June 2007. Government receipts from privatization were about $3 billion in fiscal year 2003-2004, but the privatization program has stalled since then.

Economic growth is constrained by inadequate infrastructure, a cumbersome bureaucracy, corruption, labor market rigidities, regulatory and foreign investment controls, the "reservation" of key products for small-scale industries, and high (although declining) fiscal deficits. The outlook for further trade liberalization is mixed. India eliminated quotas on 1,420 consumer imports in 2002 and has incrementally lowered non-agricultural customs duties in recent successive budgets. However, the tax structure is complex, with compounding effects of various taxes.

The United States is India's largest trading partner. Bilateral trade in 2006 was $32 billion. Principal U.S. exports are diagnostic or lab reagents, aircraft and parts, advanced machinery, cotton, fertilizers, ferrous waste/scrap metal, and computer hardware. Major U.S. imports from India include textiles and ready-made garments, Internet-enabled services, agricultural and related products, gems and jewelry, leather products, and chemicals.

The rapidly growing software sector is boosting service exports and modernizing India's economy. Software exports crossed $28 billion in FY 2006-2007, while business process outsourcing (BPO) revenues hit $8.3 billion in 2006-2007. Personal computer penetration is 14 per 1,000 persons. The cellular/mobile market surged to 140 million subscribers by November 2006. The country has 54 million cable TV customers.

The United States is India's largest investment partner, with a 13% share. India's total inflow of U.S. direct investment is estimated at more than $9 billion through 2006. Proposals for direct foreign investment are considered by the Foreign Investment Promotion Board and generally receive government approval. Automatic approvals are available for investments involving up to 100% foreign equity, depending on the kind of industry. Foreign investment is particularly sought after in power generation, telecommunications, ports, roads, petroleum exploration/processing, and mining.

India's external debt was $155 billion in 2006-2007, up from $126 billion in 2005-2006. Foreign assistance was approximately $3 billion in 2006-2007, with the United States providing about $126 million in development assistance. The World Bank plans to double aid to India to almost $3 billion a year, with focus on infrastructure, education, health, and rural livelihoods.

DEFENSE

The supreme command of the Indian armed forces is vested in the President of India. Policies concerning India's defense, and the armed forces as a whole, are formulated and confirmed by the Cabinet.

The Indian Army numbers over 1.1 million strong and fields 34 divisions. Its primary task is to safeguard the territorial integrity of the country against external threats. The Army has been heavily committed in the recent past to counterterrorism operations in Jammu and Kashmir, as well as the in the Northeast. Its current modernization program focuses on obtaining equipment to be used in combating terror. The Army often provides aid to civil authorities and assists the government in organizing relief operations.

The Indian Navy is by far the most capable navy in the region. The Navy's primary missions are the defense of India and of India's vital sea lines of communication. India relies on the sea for 90% of its oil and natural gas and over 90% of its foreign trade. The Navy currently operates one aircraft carrier with two on order, 14 submarines, and 15 major surface combatants. It is capable of projecting power within the Indian Ocean basin and occasionally operates in the South China Sea, the Mediterranean Sea and the Arabian Gulf. Fleet introduction of the Brahmos cruise missile and the possible lease of nuclear submarines from Russia will add significantly to the Indian Navy's flexibility and striking power.

Although small, the Indian Coast Guard has been expanding rapidly in recent years. Indian Navy officers typically fill top Coast Guard positions to ensure coordination between the two services. India's Coast Guard is responsible for control of India's huge exclusive economic zone.

The Indian Air Force is becoming a 21st century force through modernization, new tactics and the acquisition of modern aircraft, such as the SU-30MKI, a new advanced jet trainer (BAE Hawk) and the indigenously produced advanced light helicopter (Dhruv). In June 2007, the Indian Government announced intentions to release a request for proposals for 126 multi-role combat aircraft for the Indian Air Force.

FOREIGN RELATIONS

India's size, population, and strategic location give it a prominent voice in international affairs, and its growing economic strength, military prowess, and scientific and technical capacity give it added weight. The end of the Cold War dramatically affected Indian foreign policy. India remains a leader of the developing world and the Non-Aligned Movement (NAM). India is now strengthening its political and commercial ties with the United States, Japan, the European Union, Iran, China, and the Association of Southeast Asian Nations. India is an active member of the South Asian Association for Regional Cooperation (SAARC).

Always an active member of the United Nations, India now seeks a permanent seat on the UN Security Council. India has a long tradition of participating in UN peacekeeping operations.

BILATERAL AND REGIONAL RELATIONS

India and Pakistan have been locked in a tense rivalry since the partition of the subcontinent upon achieving independence from Great Britain in 1947. The principal source of contention has been Kashmir, whose Hindu Maharaja at that time chose to join India, although a majority of his subjects were Muslim. India maintains that his decision and subsequent elections in Kashmir have made it an integral part of India. This dispute triggered wars between the two countries in 1947 and 1965 and provoked the Kargil conflict in 1999.

Pakistan and India fought a war in December 1971 following a political crisis in what was then East Pakistan and the flight of millions of Bengali refugees to India. The brief conflict left the situation largely unchanged in the west, where the two armies reached an impasse, but a decisive Indian victory in the east resulted in the creation of Bangladesh.

Since the 1971 war, Pakistan and India have made slow progress toward normalization of relations. In July 1972, Indian Prime Minister Indira Gandhi and Pakistani President Zulfikar Ali Bhutto met in the Indian hill station of Simla. They signed an agreement by which India would return all personnel and captured territory in the west and the two countries would "settle their differences by peaceful means through bilateral negotiations." Diplomatic and trade relations were re-established in 1976.

The 1979 Soviet invasion of Afghanistan caused new strains between India and Pakistan. Pakistan supported the Afghan resistance, while India implicitly supported the Soviet occupation. In the following eight years, India voiced increasing concern over Pakistani arms purchases, U.S. military aid to Pakistan, and Pakistan's nuclear weapons program. In an effort to curtail tensions, the two countries formed a joint commission. In December 1988, Prime Ministers Rajiv Gandhi and Benazir Bhutto concluded a pact not to attack each other's nuclear facilities and initiated agreements on cultural exchanges and civil aviation.

In 1997, high-level Indo-Pakistani talks resumed after a three-year pause. The Prime Ministers of India and Pakistan met twice, and the foreign secretaries conducted three rounds of talks. In June 1997 at Lahore, the foreign secretaries identified eight "outstanding issues" around which continuing talks would be focused. The dispute over the status of Jammu and Kashmir, an issue since partition, remains the major stumbling block in their dialogue. India maintains that the entire former princely state is an integral part of the Indian union, while Pakistan insists upon the implementation of UN resolutions calling for self-determination for the people of the state.

In September 1997, the talks broke down over the structure of how to deal with the issues of Kashmir and peace and security. Pakistan advocated that separate working groups treat each issue. India responded that the two issues be taken up along with six others on a simultaneous basis. In May 1998 India, and then Pakistan, conducted nuclear tests. Attempts to restart dialogue between the two nations were given a major boost by the February 1999 meeting of both Prime Ministers in Lahore and their signing of three agreements. These efforts were stalled by the intrusion of Pakistani-backed forces into Indian-held territory near Kargil in May 1999 (that nearly turned into full scale war), and by the military coup in Pakistan that overturned the Nawaz Sharif government in October the same year. In July 2001, Mr. Vajpayee and General Pervez Musharraf, leader of Pakistan after the coup, met in Agra, but talks ended after two days without result.

After an attack on the Indian Parliament in December 2001, India-Pakistan relations cooled further as India accused Pakistan of involvement. Tensions increased, fueled by killings in Jammu and Kashmir, peaking in a troop buildup by both sides in early 2002.

Prime Minister Vajpayee's April 18, 2003 speech in Srinagar (Kashmir) revived bilateral efforts to normalize relations. In November 2003, Prime Minister Vajpayee and President Musharraf agreed to a ceasefire, which still holds, along the Line-of-Control in Jammu and Kashmir. After a series of confidence building measures, Prime Minister Vajpayee and President Musharraf met on the sidelines of the January 2004 SAARC summit in Islamabad and agreed to commence a Composite Dialogue addressing outstanding issues between India and Pakistan, including Kashmir. The UPA government has continued the Composite Dialogue with Pakistan.

In February 2004, India and Pakistan agreed to restart the "2+6" Composite Dialogue formula, which provides for talks on Peace and Security and Jammu and Kashmir, followed by technical and Secretary-level discussions on six other bilateral disputes: Siachen Glacier, Wuller Barrage/Tulbul Navigation Project, Sir Creek estuary, Terrorism and Drug Trafficking, Economic and Commercial cooperation, and the Promotion of Friendly Exchanges in various fields. The Foreign Secretary talks resumed in November 2006, after a three-month delay following the July 11, 2006 terrorist bombings in Mumbai. The meeting generated modest progress, with the two sides agreeing to establish a joint mechanism on counter-terrorism and agreeing to a follow-on meeting in February 2007. The restart of the Composite Dialogue process is especially significant, given the almost six years that transpired since the two sides agreed to this formula in 1997-98.

Following the October 2005 earthquake in Kashmir, the two governments coordinated relief efforts and opened access points along the Line-of-Control to allow relief supplies to flow from India to Pakistan and to allow Kashmiris from both sides to visit one another.

SAARC. Certain aspects of India's relations within the subcontinent are conducted through the South Asian Association for Regional Cooperation (SAARC). Its members are Afghanistan, Bangladesh, Bhutan, India, Maldives, Nepal, Pakistan, and Sri Lanka, with the People's Republic of China, Iran, Japan, European Union, Republic of Korea, and the U.S. as observers. Established in 1985, SAARC encourages cooperation in agriculture, rural development, science and technology, culture, health, population control, narcotics, and terrorism.

SAARC has intentionally stressed these "core issues" and avoided those which could prove divisive, although political dialogue is often conducted on the margins of SAARC meetings. In 1993, India and its SAARC partners signed an agreement gradually to lower tariffs within the region. Forward movement in SAARC had slowed because of tension between India and Pakistan, and the SAARC summit scheduled for 1999 was not held until January 2002. In addition, to boost the process of normalizing India's relationship with Pakistan, the January 2004 SAARC summit in Islamabad produced an agreement to establish a South Asia Free Trade Area (SAFTA). All the member governments have ratified SAFTA, which was slated to come into force on January 1, 2006, with a series of graduated tariff cuts through 2015. As of December 2006, however, the FTA partners were still negotiating sensitive product lists, rules of origin, and technical assistance. India hosted the 2007 SAARC summit, which called for greater regional cooperation on trade, environmental, social, and counterterrorism issues.

Despite suspicions remaining from a 1962 border conflict between India and China and continuing territorial/boundary disputes, Sino-Indian relations have improved gradually since 1988. Both countries have sought to reduce tensions along the frontier, expand trade and cultural ties, and normalize relations. Their bilateral trade reached $24 billion in 2006. China is India's second-largest trading partner behind the U.S.

A series of high-level visits between the two nations has improved relations. In December 1996, Chinese President Jiang Zemin visited India on a tour of South Asia. While in New Delhi, he and the Indian Prime Minister signed a series of confidence-building measures along the disputed border, including troop reductions and weapons limitations.

Chinese Premier Wen Jiabao invited Prime Minister Vajpayee to visit China in June 2003. They recognized the common goals of both countries and made the commitment to build a "long-term constructive and cooperative partnership" to peacefully promote their mutual political and economic goals without encroaching upon their good relations with other countries. In Beijing, Prime Minister Vajpayee proposed the designation of special representatives to discuss the border dispute at the political level, a process that is still under way.

In November 2006, President Hu Jintao made an official state visit to India, further cementing Sino-Indian relations. India and China are building on growing economic ties to improve other aspects of their relationship such as counter-terrorism, energy, and trade. In another symbol of improved ties, the two countries opened the Nathu La Pass to bilateral trade in July 2006 for the first time in 40 years. Though it is the first direct land trade route in decades, trade is expected to be local and small since the pass is open only four months a year.

The collapse of the Soviet Union in 1991 and the emergence of the Commonwealth of Independent States (CIS) had major repercussions for Indian foreign policy. India's substantial trade with the region plummeted after the Soviet collapse and has yet to recover. Longstanding military supply relationships were similarly disrupted due to questions over financing. Russia nonetheless remains India's largest supplier of military systems and spare parts.

Russia and India have not renewed the 1971 Indo-Soviet Peace and Friendship Treaty and follow what both describe as a more pragmatic, less ideological relationship. The visit of Russian President Boris Yeltsin to India in January 1993 helped cement this new relationship. The pace of high-level visits has since increased, as has discussion of major defense purchases. UPA leader Sonia Gandhi and Prime Minister Singh visited Russia in July 2005. President Vladimir Putin traveled to India in January 2007 to attend an Indo-Russia Summit and was the guest of honor at India's Republic Day celebrations.

U.S.-INDIA RELATIONS

Recognizing India as a key to strategic U.S. interests, the United States has sought to strengthen its relationship with India. The two countries are the world's largest democracies, both committed to political freedom protected by representative government. India is also moving gradually toward greater economic freedom. The U.S. and India have a common interest in the free flow of commerce and resources, including through the vital sea lanes of the Indian Ocean. They also share an interest in fighting terrorism and in creating a strategically stable Asia.

There were some differences, however, including over India's nuclear weapons programs and the pace of India's economic reforms. In the past, these concerns may have dominated U.S. thinking about India, but today the U.S. views India as a growing world power with which it shares common strategic interests. A strong partnership between the two countries will continue to address differences and shape a dynamic and collaborative future.

In late September 2001, President Bush lifted sanctions imposed under the terms of the 1994 Nuclear Proliferation Prevention Act following India's nuclear tests in May 1998. The nonproliferation dialogue initiated after the 1998 nuclear tests has bridged many of the gaps in understanding between the countries. In a meeting between President Bush and Prime Minister Vajpayee in November 2001, the two leaders expressed a strong interest in transforming the U.S.-India bilateral relationship. High-level meetings and concrete cooperation between the two countries increased during 2002 and 2003. In January 2004, the U.S. and India launched the Next Steps in Strategic Partnership (NSSP), which was both a milestone in the transformation of the bilateral relationship and a blueprint for its further progress.

In July 2005, President Bush hosted Prime Minister Singh in Washington, DC. The two leaders announced the successful completion of the NSSP, as well as other agreements which further enhance cooperation in the areas of civil nuclear, civil space, and high-technology commerce. Other initiatives announced at this meeting include: an U.S.-India Economic Dialogue, Fight Against HIV/AIDS, Disaster Relief, Technology Cooperation, Democracy Initiative, an Agriculture Knowledge Initiative, a Trade Policy Forum, Energy Dialogue and

CEO Forum. President Bush made a reciprocal visit to India in March 2006, during which the progress of these initiatives were reviewed, and new initiatives were launched.

In December 2006, Congress passed the historic Henry J. Hyde United States-India Peaceful Atomic Cooperation Act, which allows direct civilian nuclear commerce with India for the first time in 30 years. U.S. policy had opposed nuclear cooperation with India because the country had developed nuclear weapons in contravention of international conventions and never signed the Nuclear Non-Proliferation Treaty. The legislation clears the way for India to buy U.S. nuclear reactors and fuel for civilian use.

In July 2007, the United States and India reached a historic milestone in their strategic partnership by completing negotiations on the bilateral agreement for peaceful nuclear cooperation, also known as the "123 agreement." This agreement will govern civil nuclear trade between the two countries and open the door for American and Indian firms to participate in each other's civil nuclear energy sector.

The U.S. and India are seeking to elevate the strategic partnership further in 2007 to include cooperation in counter-terrorism, defense cooperation, education, and joint democracy promotion.

In: India: Economic, Political and Social Issues   ISBN: 978-1-60456-509-6
Editor: Urlah B. Nissam   © 2009 Nova Science Publishers, Inc.

Chapter 2

INDIA'S QUEST FOR STRATEGIC SPACE IN THE 'NEW' INTERNATIONAL ORDER: LOCATIONS, (RE)ORIENTATIONS AND OPPORTUNITIES

Sanjay Chaturvedi

INTRODUCTION

My key argument in this paper is that India's foreign policy today is characterised by unprecedented pragmatism as well as cautious idealism. The pragmatism is rather visible in the growing realisation that, as the twenty-first century unfolds, mediated by the hegemony of trans-national liberalism, the conventional 'commonsense' understanding of the apparently fixed geographical location of India and its 'neighbourhood' (the manner in which 'regions' as well as regional groupings tend to acquire, over a period of time, a sense of territoriality and hence an image of immutability) are due for a thorough revision. As pointed out perceptively by C. Raja Mohan, 'it is not often that a country finds itself on the verge of multiple breakthroughs on foreign policy. India is at one of those rare moments' (2005: 3).

India appears far more confident than ever before to take on the challenge posed by the complex interplay between geopolitics and geoeconomics. The normative thrust of India's foreign policy relates to a critical reassessment of the country's role in global affairs, while working towards the goal of Asian (even Afro-Asian) solidarity through inter-cultural dialogue and co-operative economic diplomacy. Of late, a serious and systematic pursuit by India of its economic-energy security, at regional as well as sub-regional levels, is a good example of how normative and pragmatic considerations are being combined in innovative policy frameworks and alliance-making.

This chapter shows how 'Asia' has been framed historically and continues to be partitioned by the dominant discourse(s) on the so-called 'New' International Order. This is followed by a discussion of how Indian leadership conceptualised 'Asia' and India's geopolitical location on the continent during the Cold War. It is against such a backdrop that the analytical focus of this chapter shifts to India's quest for energy-economic security, with special reference to India's Look East policy and its engagements with 'Mid-West' and

'Central' Asia. The concluding remarks briefly reflect on various proposals and counter proposals regarding India's strategic alliances with major Asian and non-Asian powers. Finally, it is argued that what is emerging before India, and for that matter the rest of Asia, is a novel context and conceptualisation for foreign policy and diplomacy, namely 'Oceanic Asia'. Here lies both a challenge and the opportunity for those who would like to see Asia/Asians as mapmakers in their own right—with considerable autonomy in global geopolitics—rather than as passive takers of the maps of a new hegemony.

THE 'NEW' INTERNATIONAL ORDER: GEOPOLITICS VERSUS GEOECONOMICS?

Often assumed to be innocent, the geography of the world is not a product of nature, but an outcome of the histories of struggle between competing authorities over the power to organise, occupy and administer space (Mamadouoth, 1998: 246). As Neumann puts it: 'Geography, including geopolitics, is a matter of social construction' (1997: 148). Whereas the term geoeconomics, popularised by Edward Luttwak (1990), implies that 'old fashioned' geopolitics has been displaced by the new phenomenon of geoeconomics, with disposable capital becoming more important than firepower, civilian innovation more significant than military-technical advancement, and market penetration a greater mark of power than the possession of garrisons and bases.

After the end of the East-West Cold War, there have been several calls for a New International Order. However, it is forgotten at times that the earliest version of the new international order was proposed by the non-governmental South Commission, chaired by Julius Nyerere and consisting of leading Third World economists, government planners, religious leaders and others. As pointed out by Noam Chomsky: 'reviewing the miserable state of the traditional Western domains, the Commission called for a "new world order" that will respond to the "south's plea for justice, equity and justice, and democracy in the global society" though its analysis offers little basis for hope' (1994: 4). However, what emerged instead was a (re)appropriation of the phrase 'New World Order' by George Bush as a rhetorical cover for his war in the Gulf.

What is 'new' about the US-centric New World Order discourse? Where does Asia, or for that matter the Asia-Pacific region, figure in the proposed neo-liberal geopolitical version of the post-Cold War world order? While seeking an answer to these questions, it might be useful to bear in mind the following perceptive comment:

> there is a conventional picture of the new era we are entering and the promise it holds. It was formulated clearly by National Security Adviser Anthony Lake when he announced the Clinton Doctrine in September 1993: 'throughout the Cold War, we contained a global threat to market democracies: now we should seek to enlarge their reach'. The 'new world' opening before us presents immense opportunities to move forward, to 'consolidate the victory of democracy and open markets', he expanded a year later(cited in Chomsky, 1996: 94).

'ASIA' IN GLOBAL GEOPOLITICAL ORDERS: THE OLD AND THE NEW

To begin with, western imperialism defined Asia in ways to suit its own interests. Geopolitics as a discursive field helped structure a view of Asia that underlined the Continent's difference from, and inferiority to, the west, thereby legitimising a pursuit of mastering space and cultural domination (Chaturvedi, 2002). Once classical geopolitics was extended to the Cold War period, Asia was re-imagined as a 'Rimland' which had to be controlled and strategically deployed for the purposes of western containment of the Eurasian 'Heartland' power: the Soviet Union (Dodds, 2003).

The Asian space was subjected to yet another round of mapping during the 1970s, as a general economic boom spread over Asia's rimland nations. What now emerged was the notion of a larger geopolitical entity, namely, the Pacific Basin. Thus, corporate globalisation and the 'new' regionalisms can also be seen as discursive structures assimilating Asia, or certain chosen segments of it, into a new imperial order. The manner in which 'Asia Pacific' has been discursively carved out of Asia in recent times by the west demonstrates that the US strategy of preponderance now reflects the credo of economic interdependency. The underlying logic can also be used to justify US intervention virtually anywhere on the globe (Peters, 1999).

After the economic crisis of 1997, East Asia, after having been integrated into the global economy all these years, seems to have acquired a sudden and unprecedented 'uncertainty' in western geopolitical imaginations (Hitchcock, 1998). As early as 1997 some analysts (Hale, 1997: 44) predicted that the sheer pace of socio-economic transformation in this region might eventually rip apart the political framework inherited from the colonial and Cold War eras.

The post-Cold War geopolitics continues to construct Asia in ways that fit into the grand strategies of neo-conservative intellectuals of statecraft in the west. According to Weinbaum (1996-97: 1) a new strategic region called 'Three Asias'—encompassing large portions of South, West and Central Asia—is in the process of emerging. A number of issue areas of strategic importance to the United States are converging here. From the standpoint of American security and non-proliferation interests, for example, this region comprises two emergent nuclear weapon states (NWS) (India and Pakistan), one acknowledged NWS (Kazakhstan), and at least one incipient NWS (Iran). It is in this region that the American discourse concerning human rights and democratisation is filtered through western fears about the contagion of a radical, politicised brand of Islam. The western political economies remain somewhat organically linked to the energy resources as well as the markets of this region. And last, but not least, this region is held responsible for the world's second largest supply of heroin.

The emergence of landlocked Central Asia and its resource endowment in the mainstream US geopolitical thinking has an important bearing on the Indian Ocean region and India's location within it. Throughout the Cold War, Central Asia had been viewed by the western powers as a marginal concern, situated firmly within the Soviet sphere of influence, on a remote edge of the Pacific Command's main areas of responsibility, namely, China, Japan and the Korean Peninsula. The same region, stretching from the Ural Mountains to China's western border, has now become an object of the so-called 'New Great Game' due to vast reserves of oil and natural gas thought to lie under and around the Caspian Sea.

In October 1999, the US Department of Defense reassigned senior command authority over American forces in Central Asia from the Pacific Command to the Central Command. This was an important indication that a significant shift in American geopolitical thinking was underway (Klare, 2003). Since the responsibility for 'securing' the Persian Gulf region has now been reassigned to the Central Command, it implies that this area is now under the close scrutiny of those responsible for protecting the flow of energy supplies to the United States and its allies against the backdrop of intensified competition over access to critical materials (Klare, 2003). The United States also depends on the Indian Ocean for the movement of about 50 different strategic materials, including magnesium, cobalt, titanium, tin, nickel, tungsten, iron, lead, copper (Berlin, 2002: 28). The National Security Council observed in the White House's 1999 annual report on US security policy: 'the United States will continue to have a vital interest in ensuring access to foreign oil supplies'. Therefore, the report concluded, 'we must continue to be mindful of the need for regional stability and security in key producing areas to ensure our access to, and the free flow of, these resources' (quoted in Klare, 2001: 62).

No sub-region of the Indian Ocean looms as large in these geopolitical calculations as the 'Middle East', which in a recent study has also been termed the 'Eurasian Energy Heartland' (Singh, 2002: 288). The geostrategic significance of the Middle East has been further reinforced on the wider canvas of what Zbigniew Brzezinski (1997) terms 'The Eurasian Balkans' on the post-Cold War 'Grand Chess Board'. As succinctly pointed out by Francois Debrix(2003: 180): 'during the Cold War and afterwards, Eurasia plays a similar role for Brzezinski. Eurasia must be controlled by the United States because, when all is said and done, Eurasia is 'our' geographical buffer. Eurasia as a buffer allows the United States to remain unique and superior in its own sphere of influence (which, after the Cold War, seems to span the entire surface of [the] globe)' More recently, a new term, 'Greater Middle East', has entered the arena of competing geopolitical imaginings (see Harkavy, 2001: 37) of 'New' Heartlands.

The analysis so far has revealed a trend emanating from the post-Cold War global geopolitical order conceived by the one and only superpower and its allies. As perceptively pointed out by Gulshan Dietl (2004), energy security, unlike other aspects of non-traditional security, has always been very closely related to military security. More often than not, it is the hegemonic consumer-states, seeking to maintain an uninterrupted supply of energy at an affordable price, who threaten and use military force. With energy-military security nexus peaking, we are likely to witness the conflict between the multilateral quests of both state and non-state actors for energy security and the 'securitisation' of energy flows by the hegemonic power(s).

INDIA'S QUEST FOR AN ASIAN ENERGY SECURITY GRID: CHALLENGES AND OPPORTUNITIES

By the first half of the twenty-first century, India is likely to be among the top four consumers of energy, just behind the US, China and Japan, and ahead of countries like France and the UK (Dadwal, 2002; Singh, 2001). In Asia, India is ranked after China as the emerging oil and gas market (Muni and Pant, 2005; Mahalingam, 2004). Natural gas is best suited to provide India with the *clean* energy the country needs for ecologically sustainable development during the first half of the twenty-first century and beyond. At the current rate of production, India's proven reserves of natural gas are likely to last for about 25 years, and Pakistan's about 36 years (Siddiqi, 2003).

According to *The Hydro Carbon Vision 2025* document, brought out by the government of India in 1999, in absolute terms the demand for crude oil and petroleum products was expected to grow to 112 million tons in 2002, 190 million tons in 2012 and 364 million tons in 2025 (Shaw, 2005). As against this trajectory of growing demand, production has been stagnating at 33 million tons per year. Indian oil reserves might run out by 2012 even if only 30 per cent of the demand is met through domestic production (Shaw, 2005). The document underlines the urgent necessity to augment domestic production and prescribes a regime of deregulation, seeking active participation of the private sector, both Indian and foreign. It sounds a note of caution that the Indian economy will increasingly rely on oil and gas imports, and will be vulnerable to fluctuations in international energy patterns. The trend to make secure energy flows, especially in and around the Gulf, are of critical concern to India for the following reasons.

Whereas the global reach of India's sourcing to meet the growing demand for petroleum crude and products is fairly diverse (as many as 30 different countries are its suppliers), 5 countries (Nigeria, Saudi Arabia, UAE, Kuwait and Iran) account for more than 75 per cent of India's total imports (Muni and Pant, 2005: 21). Saudi Arabia, UAE, Kuwait, Qatar and Bahrain combined supply more than 50 per cent of India's needs. If the Persian Gulf is taken as the critical resource-supplying region (by also including Iran and Iraq), then this region would account for about 60 per cent of India's imports. It is to state the obvious, therefore, that India has no other option but to look in as many directions as possible and evolve a multi-pronged policy to address diverse risks on the crucial front of energy-economic security (Muni and Pant, 2005: 21).

The multi-dimensional challenge of energy security before India demands a multilateral economic diplomacy; this, in turn, questions the tilt of India's foreign policy establishment in favour of bilateralism. According to Mani Shankar Aiyar, India's Minister for Petroleum and Natural Gas: 'Unless everybody is as enlightened in his politics as he is demonstrating in his economics, we are not going to reach our goals as quickly as we need to' (Aiyar, 2005). The point made by Aiyar hints at the tension, bordering on contradiction, between geoeconomics and geopolitics in India's quest for a new strategic space. As the sections to follow demonstrate, this challenge is reflected in both India's 'Look East' and 'Look West' policies.

India's Look East Policy: Extending the Neighbourhood

As pointed out earlier, the Cold War-induced geographies of mutual suspicion and confrontation proved instrumental in undermining the prospects of international cooperation throughout Asia. Even though not directly implicated in the Cold War geostrategic containment of the 'Evil Empire', India's foreign policy establishment chose to ignore China and Myanmar, despite a very obvious geophysical proximity (Singh, 1998: 48-49; Nanda, 2003: 7). However, geographical proximity does not automatically translate itself into geopolitical propinquity. As Jawaharlal Nehru once noted astutely:

6

...India is curiously situated from the geographical view as well as many other points of view. It belongs to Southeast Asia; it also belongs to West Asia. It just depends on which way you look at it, because it happens to be the centre of all these... All international routes or routes around the world have almost inevitably to pass over India. Again when you look at it from other points of view like trade and commerce, or when you think in terms of defence, India becomes the pivotal centre of South, Southeast and Western Asia. (quoted in Nanda, 2003: 12)

What is fairly obvious in Nehru's worldview is the alleged 'Centrality' of India in Asia. We might also recall in passing that the idea of an eastern federation (Deshingkar, 1999; Tan Chung, 1998) formed the core of India's Asia policy under Nehru. Even before independence, in March 1947, India convened the Asian relations conference, 'where almost any country that was perceived as constituting India's extended neighbourhood was invited. This included Tibet and Central Asia, though their independent status was under serious dispute' (Muni and Pant, 2005: 6). India also played an important role in building the Asian Relations Organization and in convening the first and the last Afro-Asian Conference in Bandung, Indonesia. However, India's initiatives for building a cooperative Asian neighbourhood failed to materialise, largely due to intervention by the Cold War ideological geopolitics.

Nehru was quite firm in his belief that the independence of a country fundamentally consists of an independent foreign policy. Consequently, he could not hide his anger over India being 'contained' within a Cold War sub-regional grouping based on ideological and strategic parameters (namely, 'South Asia'), with the help of western allies and Pakistan. He is reported to have remarked in 1953: 'What do the Americans think they are doing? Do they think they can encircle India in Pakistan, in Nepal, in the rest of Asia somehow?' (quoted in Muni and Pant, 2005: 8). India's interaction with west-inspired, anti-communist 'Southeast Asia' during the Cold War was more noticeable in bilateral relations with individual countries than with the association as an organisation (Ghoshal, 2002).

The following excerpt, from a speech delivered by Jaswant Singh, the then External Affairs Minister of India, in Singapore, June 2000, nicely sums up the rationale behind India's Look East policy in general, and India-ASEAN relations in particular. He said:

India and ASEAN face a complex, post-Cold War environment... We search for definitions and certainties in a period that is itself struggling to find answers. The influencing factors will be the reform process in Russia; concomitant political and economic changes in China; Japan's rediscovery of a more assertive political role; the ongoing tussle between unilateralism and cooperative multilateralism in the US and the challenge and opportunity of a European economic and politico-military integration...Our participation in the ARF (ASEAN Regional Forum) reflects India's increasing engagement, both in politico-security and economic spheres contributing to the building of greater trust, confidence and stability in the region. (quoted in Mattoo, 2001: 105-106)

The attraction of engaging with the fast-growing economies of South East Asia, as well as the growing disillusionment with the slow pace of economic reforms within the country, can be described as the two key catalysts behind India's Look East policy. This also explains to some extent why, in the early and mid-1990s, when regional economic cooperation was in vogue, India, faced with the unpleasant prospects of being left out of all the regional groups emerging in Asia, decided to pursue membership of ASEAN with firm resolve (Naidu, 2004).

The reorientation of India's foreign policy was facilitated by the fact that, around the same time, ASEAN too, surfeit with capital and exportable goods and technology, was searching for new markets. Many ASEAN heads of state had pronounced their intention of making their countries members of the 'rich man's club' by 2020 (Ram, 2000: 27). Such a vision, in order to become a reality, needed a pragmatic foreign policy and pro-active engagements with China and India. ASEAN thus found it prudent to launch a 'Look West' policy of its own, primarily focusing on India (Sreekumar, 2004). The early 1990s were therefore a favorable time for India to vigorously launch and pursue a policy of intensifying, deepening and expanding overall relations with the countries of South East Asia (Ibid.).

Yet another factor that prompted India to look towards the East is the apparent failure of the South Asian Association for Regional Cooperation (SAARC), which came into existence in December 1985. The central objective was to initiate regional cooperation amidst mistrust and conflict, in the hope that the process itself would generate a dynamism of its own, facilitating confidence-building and conflict resolution. However, the hopes generated by the launch of SAARC have gradually been belied. South Asia is yet to develop genuine stakeholders in a peace constituency; the persistent tension between India and Pakistan has virtually crippled the organisation and its various attempts to initiate and sustain regional dialogues, and consultations have proved futile over the years (McPherson, 2002: 252). On the other hand, ASEAN beckons as a success story in terms of centripetal cooperative endeavours overcoming centrifugal forces of all kinds and at various levels (Sabur, 2003: 85-86).

India's reassessment of its neighbours and neighbourhood is also caused by the growing dissatisfaction of a nuclear power aspiring to permanent membership of the UN Security Council with a limited and limiting value of the 'South Asian' framework for situating security concerns. During his Singapore lecture, mentioned above, Jaswant Singh is reported to have observed:

India's parameters of security concerns clearly extended beyond confines of the convenient albeit questionable geographical definition of South Asia. South Asia was always a dubious framework for situating the Indian security paradigm. Given its size, geographical location, trade links and the EEZ [Exclusive Economic Zone] India's security environment and therefore potential concerns range from the Persian Gulf to the Straits of Malacca in the West, South and East, Central Asia in the North West, China in the North East and South East Asia (quoted in Mattoo, 2001: 105).

During much of the Cold War period, ASEAN's perception of India was based on the international systemic environment and the prevailing balance of power. At the same time, India's neglect of the region was not seen in a positive light. After the Cold War, a shift in ASEAN's perceptions of India became discernible, as the latter was invited to become a member of the ARF. India's relations with the US and China are also an enduring concern and as such are likely to influence the ways in which the region perceives India and its South Asian neighbours. The geopolitical and strategic dynamics between India and Pakistan also have a bearing on the ways in which ASEAN perceives the overall strengths and weaknesses of India as an actor with regional and global aspirations.

When all is said and done, however, the ASEAN-India dialogue relations have grown rapidly from a Sectoral Dialogue Partnership in 1992 to a Full Dialogue Partnership in 1995, and subsequently to a Summit-level interaction, with the First ASEAN-India Summit being held in November 2002. The mere fact that all of this took place in a decade seemingly reflects the confidence both ASEAN and India have developed in the dialogue partnership, which is underlined by expanding and intensifying dialogue and cooperation in many other sectors (Suryanarayan, 2002).

One important domain of this dialogue relates to the political relationship, and its related security issues. India has been an active member of the ARF since July 1996. It views the ARF as valuable in promoting stable relationships between the major powers, and as a useful complement to the bilateral alliances and dialogues which are at the heart of the region's security architecture. ASEAN and India have committed themselves to jointly contribute to the promotion of peace, stability and development in the Asia-Pacific region and the world, and respond positively to the challenges of a dynamic regional and international environment. There has been noticeable progress in trade and investment, science and technology, tourism and human resource development. The total trade between India and ASEAN increased substantially from about $US 2.5 billion in 1993-94 to the $US 6 billion mark in 1997-98. Whereas India-ASEAN trade in 2003-04 was about $US 13.25 billion (over 5 times the 1993-94 trade figure of $US 2.5 billion), India's exports to ASEAN were $US 5.8 billion while imports about $US 7.4 billion in this period (see Confederation of Indian Industry (CII): Internet Source accessed on 7 September 2005). Compared to other regional groupings, ASEAN is the fifth most important market in the world in terms of Indian exports and fourth in terms of imports.

India's economic relationship with ASEAN encompasses an active investment component. Increasingly, ASEAN businesses are undertaking FDI in India in crucial infrastructural sectors, such as roads and highways (Mattoo, 2001: 104-114). However, two-way trade and investment between ASEAN and India still remain low, although both sides are of the view that opportunities for collaboration are yet to be fully tapped.

India's Look East policy has now entered Phase-II. According to the former External Affairs Minister Yashwant Sinha:

> Phase-I was focused primarily on the ASEAN countries and on trade and investment linkages. Phase-II is characterized by an expanding definition of 'East' extending from Australia to China and East Asia with ASEAN as its core. Phase-II marks a shift in focus from exclusively economic issues to economic and security issues, including joint efforts to protect sea lanes, coordination on counter terrorism etc. On the economic side, Phase-II is also characterized by arrangements for FTAs and establishing of institutional economic linkages between the countries of the region and India. (quoted in Gupta, Chaturvedi and Joshi, 2004 211)

ASEAN has also welcomed India's willingness to develop a network of relations with ASEAN through other means of sub-regional cooperation frameworks, as this would complement the larger goal of enhancing ASEAN-India ties (Rao, 2003a). In this regard, ASEAN has encouraged India's active participation in the so-called Mekong-Ganga Cooperation (MGC). At the 33rd ASEAN Post-Ministerial Conference held in Bangkok in July 2000, the Indian delegation suggested that the entire region from India to the Mekong Basin be included in the initiative, a measure accepted by Foreign Ministers of five ASEAN countries (Thailand, Mayanmar, Laos, Cambodia and Vietnam) sharing the Mekong Basin. The key objectives of the MGC, formally launched on 10 November 2000, are to develop closer relations and better understanding among the six countries, thereby enhancing friendship, solidarity and cooperation. The two river systems have immense potential, and multi-purpose projects could benefit the respective states.

Also, ASEAN is watching with keen interest (especially in view of the centrality of China in India-ASEAN relations) the evolution of the Kunming Initiative. China organised a Track II conference for this sub-regional grouping in 1999 in Kunming itself (the capital of Yunnan Province in China's southwest[1]). Representatives of four adjoining countries (China, India, Bangladesh and Myanmar) participated. They arrived at a broad consensus on the need for regional cooperation among the four countries and their sub-regions, and the conference decided to establish a Forum for Regional Economic Cooperation. This regional move could be a challenging one in political terms, as, for the first time ever, it locks India and China into a single forum.

ASEAN has also responded quite warmly to the five-member sub-regional grouping of Bangladesh, India, Myanmar, Sri Lanka and Thailand–Economic Cooperation (BIMST-EC), which was formed in June 1997 for promoting cooperation in matters such as the exploitation of maritime resources, communications, shipbuilding, weather forecasting and combating sea piracy and terrorism, besides sustaining the trading contacts (Upreti, 2001). BIMST-EC (also known as Group-5) is 'poised to move from mere promises to actual delivery of economic benefits to the people of the region', as well as to pursue 'business opportunities' and develop 'linkages in the region' (Reddy, 2003). Each of the member states has assumed the responsibility of focusing on the identified areas of cooperation, such as transport and communications and tourism (India), energy (Myanmar), trade and investment (Bangladesh), technology (Sri Lanka) and fisheries (Thailand) (Murthy, 2000; 2002).

A recently proposed cooperative framework of a 'Bay of Bengal Community' (BOBCOM), with the inclusion of Malaysia, Singapore and Indonesia in BIMSTEC, deserves a special mention here: 'The underlying idea is not to replace SAARC or ASEAN but to have an additional organization, which will bring together India and its southern and eastern neighbors' (Surayanarayan, 2000: 60). Within such a framework, the littoral states of Southern Asia could cooperate with one another in areas such as exploitation of living and non-living maritime resources, development of maritime communications, shipbuilding, weather forecasting, prevention of pollution, combating maritime terrorism and energy security. Whether BOBCOM would be able to initiate and sustain cooperation in the above mentioned areas, and thereby eventually turn the 'extended' neighbourhood into an 'immediate' neighbourhood, remains to be seen.

A major step forward for India in its quest for energy security is the tri-nation agreement signed in Myanmar between India, Myanmar and Bangladesh on 12-13 January 2005 (*The Tribune*, Chandigarh, 15 January 2005). This gas pipeline project is based on mutual recognition of the necessity for enhanced regional cooperation in the energy and infrastructure development sector for the common benefit of the southern Asian nations. The understanding would enable commercial trans-shipment of gas from gas fields which have an estimated reserve of 5-6 Tcf located in the massive Arkan block off the coast of Myanmar. Myanmar earns approximately $US 400 million every year from neighbouring Thailand, through its annual gas sales from its Yadana and Yetagun fields in the south. Opening the

---

[1] Mineral-rich Yunnan has emerged as the industrial hub in China's South West. Yunnan also assumes a key role as China and ASEAN seriously consider the Kunming–Singapore railway line (Rao, 2003b).

market to the west (India) would significantly increase earnings from gas, which is already Myanmar's number one foreign exchange earner (Kumar, 2005).

By giving its consent to the laying of a gas transit pipeline, Bangladesh may well have taken the political and diplomatic initiative, whereby the resolution of the issues of commercial land transit to Nepal, sharing of water resources between Bangladesh, Nepal and India, and making up Bangladesh's deficit of power by importing surplus power from India and Nepal, can all be achieved. Various details are yet to be worked out through commercial agreements, while the route of the pipeline would be arrived at through mutual agreement, paying particular attention to ensuring adequate access, maximum security and optimal economic utilisation (Parthasarthy, 2001). In the opinion of some strategic affairs experts, 'for the first time India has begun to integrate its energy policy with foreign policy by consciously promoting oil diplomacy geared towards seizing energy-related opportunities overseas. What it is not doing is to blend its energy policy with defence policy' (Chellaney, 2005).

The US-led war on 'global terrorism' has posed a series of difficult questions for India. As a civilisational polity, complete with the world's second-largest Muslim population, India simply cannot afford to internalise the 'clash of civilisations' thesis first propounded by Samuel P. Huntington (1993). India cannot turn a blind eye to the fact that internal divisive forces, dictated and driven by parochial religious and communal considerations, are already adversely affecting India's relations with its neighbouring countries, especially the Muslim countries. As pointed out by J.N. Dixit:

> the geo-strategic fact is that from Egypt and Turkey in the north and to the Philippines in the south-east, and to the countries of the Gulf in between, India's neighborhood contains a large number of Muslim societies. To look at these societies through the prism of narrow communalism would be detrimental to India's national interests (2003: 516).

Nor can India afford to accept at face value the neo-conservative discourse of 'Rogue States', or, for that matter, let it come in the way of its economic diplomacy.

According to A.N. Ram (2003), a distinguished Indian diplomat who had played a key role in drafting India's 'Look East' policy, India's bilateral relations with the ASEAN countries have yet to evolve into a meaningful partnership in which both sides have a vital stake. After the Asian financial crisis, ASEAN trade with, and investments in, India have stagnated. ASEAN also appears somewhat disillusioned with 'India's daunting procedures, requirements and an unresponsive bureaucracy' (Ram, 2003).

The long-term success of India's Look East policy also calls for institutional reforms at various levels. For example, there appears to be a problem with the decision making structure in India's Ministry of External Affairs (MEA), with regard to a newly-'discovered' Southeast Asia. India-ASEAN relations are being approached and analysed at three different levels within the MEA. Whereas Dialogue Partnership issues are being dealt with by the Economic Division, ARF-related activities are handled under the Disarmament Division. Other bilateral aspects are said to be the responsibility of the South Division. Consequently, it becomes an enormously difficult task for these divisions to take unanimous decisions, and then implement them. In the absence of any formal mechanism being available (except the central cabinet in New Delhi), the coordination among various ministries and departments (External Affairs, Commerce and Industry, Defence, Human Resource Development) also leaves much to be desired (Naidu, 2003).

INDIA LOOKS WEST: THE NEW GREAT GAME?

The kind of enthusiastic attention that India's Look East policy continues to receive has at times overshadowed a series of Indian initiatives *vis-à-vis* Afghanistan and Central Asia. Described by some analysts as a *de facto* Look West policy (Muni and Raja Mohan, 2004), the challenge before these initiatives has acquired a new level of complexity due to the events of 11 September and the subsequent launch of the American war on terrorism. While hoping that 11 September has facilitated a better understanding of India's concerns against terrorism in the United States and international community, India, with its very large Muslim population, has been cautious with regard to the 'western' discourses on terrorism in general, and the 'clash of civilisations' thesis in particular.

It is precisely in the context of 'globalisation from above' that the long-standing image (and, indeed, the reality) of many segments of Central Asia as suppliers of natural resources and markets is currently being reinforced (Bayarkhuu, 2004). Central Asia is being re-imagined as a geo-economic space awaiting development. While the intellectuals of statecraft are trying to figure out the 'new' Central Asia in all kinds of geo-economic ('Scramble for Resources'), geostrategic ('New Great Game') and 'civilisational' ('Clash of Civilisations') equations, the five landlocked republics of Kazakhstan, Turkmenistan, Uzbekistan, Tajikistan and Kyrgyzstan are coping simultaneously with an array of formidable tasks, including state-building, seeking and consolidating political legitimacy, national integration and nation-building, and accommodating pressures for political participation and social-economic justice (Dawisha and Parrott, 1997). These states are also handicapped by the lack of experience in self-government and international cooperation, communication networks, trained indigenous administrative and technical elites, and also beset by ethno-linguistic tensions both within and across the geographical region (Sievers, 2003).

The emergence of landlocked Central Asia in the international strategic context, and the discovery of substantial quantities of strategic minerals (as mentioned earlier), has discursively transformed the centrality of Central Asia in terms of resource geopolitics. India, amongst the first countries to establish diplomatic ties with these republics,[2] would not only like to see these states retain their moderate religious outlook and moorings, but also acquire and sustain a meaningful political and economic presence in the region. India and the five Central Asian republics are now well-connected by air, and greater connectivity by land and sea is being actively sought through the trilateral agreement, and the North-South corridor (Dadwal, 2002). The geopolitical and economic objectives of India in Central Asia are graphically captured in the following lines of a speech given by Yashwant Sinha in Tashkent:

> Our co-operation with Central Asia includes cultural, economic, defence and security considerations. For us Central Asia is our *'immediate and strategic neighborhood'*...Indian companies are interested in setting up refineries and new pipelines...I am convinced that Central Asia, with its oil, gas, gold, silver and other mineral wealth and water resources, can become a new silk road of prosperity once again. But we need peace and stability for full economic progress. Unfortunately both India and Central Asia have become victims of terror for a long time...for us in the region, the concern is even greater because the epicenter of

---

[2] After Tajikistan opened its mission in Delhi in October 2003, all Central Asian countries are currently represented in India.

terror lies in our common neighborhood...If our neighborhood is peaceful and stable, if the only interference from outside is one of economic inputs, then Central Asia can once again be a bridge between the East and West...We are civilizational partners, we want our ancient links to have contemporary colour (reproduced in Gupta, Chaturvedi and Joshi, 2004: 228-229).

The references above to defence and security considerations have also reinforced certain apparent speculations that India has been trying to develop its military bases in the region, including a military base in Tajikistan. Against the backdrop of what appears to be a scramble for setting up military bases in Central Asia, on the one hand, and, on the other hand, growing security and defence interaction between India and Central Asian countries, both India and Tajikistan have denied that it is a 'base for India' (Raja Mohan, 2003a). Be that as it may, many analysts would argue that 'the competition with Pakistan for influence in Afghanistan and Central Asia is a reality', but, at the same time, 'while making all possible efforts to skirt around Pakistan, New Delhi must also look at the prospects for neutralizing or co-opting Islamabad in its search for access and expanded presence in Afghanistan and Central Asia' (Muni and Raja Mohan, 2004: 327).

LOOKING AHEAD: TOWARDS NEW 'STRATEGIC' ALLIANCES?

At the beginning of the twenty-first century, foreign policy establishments all over the world are in the process of re-orienting themselves, seeking new roles and alliances to meet the challenge of a globalising international geopolitical economy. India, as this chapter has shown, is no exception to a trend that is likely to become more pronounced in the decades ahead. Such a trend has also opened up the prospects of India entering into certain 'strategic' alliances with major powers within, and outside, Asia.

India and the USA as Natural Allies?

One frequently heard viewpoint on the India-US 'strategic' partnership, especially in the wake of the visit to India in March 2005 by US Secretary of State Condoleezza Rice, is that what is opening before India is a 'window of opportunity' (Subrahmanyam, 2005), provided the policymakers to shun the proclivity of running from one extreme to another. While on one hand it has been argued that,

> an uncritical alliance with the United States could significantly affect India's credibility as an independent power; the search, on the other hand, for a countervailing alliance to the United States could send India on a fool's errand. With particular reference to Asia, following the US lead and direction in the east could shrink India's strategic space in relation to China and parts of the ASEAN, and in the northwest, it may constrain India's cooperation with Russia, Iran and a number of other Islamic countries and Persian Gulf countries (Muni and Raja Mohan, 2004: 318).

What made the headlines in the Indian media coverage of the visit of the US Secretary of State was the news that Dr Rice had made it very clear to India that the Bush administration is rather uncomfortable at the prospect of a $US 4 billion gas pipeline bridging the economies of Iran and India. Moreover, she is reported to have proposed that the US would be happy to provide superior technologies and even nuclear power, one of the most expensive energy alternatives, to India (Barman, 2005). In case India opts to 'jump on the bandwagon' with the United States by abandoning the Iran-Pakistan-India pipeline project, it might not be possible for India to escape altogether the geopolitical trappings of the US-sponsored 'New International Order', as outlined earlier. However, the message conveyed so far to the United States is that India not only enjoys cordial relations with Iran, but also that the proposed pipeline via Pakistan is a part of India's brave new geopolitical imagination of an Asia-centric design of an energy security grid (a grander scheme of pan-Asian corridors and pipelines criss-crossing from Myanmar, Bangladesh in the east, and Turkmenistan and Central Asia in the northwest) that could eventually feed into China's vast industrial belts in the south and south-west.

One thought-provoking comment on India-US relations from the standpoint of a new non-alignment has come from Pratap Bhanu Mehta (2005), who argues that the time has come to go beyond the Cold War connotation of the term 'non-alignment'. According to him, 'it is precisely in the current moment that the core aspirations of "non-alignment" need to be reiterated to give India's foreign policy a new cogency. While there is every reason for India to pursue an intense economic and political dialogue with the US, India has to be wary that this dialogue does not, slowly and unwittingly, lock India into the embrace of the US' (Mehta, 2005). According to him, India should not give up on the normative dimension of what is apparently a pragmatic imperative (that it is in its interests to cultivate and nurture such relationships with Iran as it deems fit). After all, 'America's opposition to the pipeline from Iran is not cogent politics or economics: it is simply an assertion of hegemony' (Mehta, 2005).

Geopolitics of 'Asian' Alliances?

Ever since former Russian Prime Minister Yevgeny Primakov proposed a new Big Three Alliance (consisting of Russia, China and India) to counterbalance an increasingly hyperactive US (Bhattacharya, 2004), a great many Indians have reacted enthusiastically to the concept, including the former Indian Prime Minister, Atal Behari Vajpayee. According to V.P. Dutt (1999), it needs to be clarified at the very outset that the proposal for an India-China-Russia alliance carries no military, or even 'strategic' (in the correct sense of the word) overtones, although the word 'strategic' has been loosely applied in recent times. According to Dutt, what Primakov meant was far removed from the concept of a military alliance, in which none of the countries involved was interested. He was building a case for closer dialogue and interaction between the three countries on important issues in the international arena, so that one or two countries did not become hegemonic. Furthermore, he was also pleading for greater geopolitical space for all the three major powers of Asia. The idea proceeded from the assumption that US dominance in the world order would be total, unless there were some countervailing pressures that could be applied to moderate this dominance.

In Moscow's view, such pressure could only be generated through a more coordinated interaction between China, Russia and India (Dutt, 1999).

It has been argued by another perceptive analyst, that, while this surely is a possibility worth examining, a number of factors and forces are likely to work both for and against the idea of an Asian *Directoires* of these three great powers (Sahni, 2004). The first set of factors relates to economic growth rates, competitiveness and cooperation. Varun Sahni raises a series of issues, which, in his view, have a direct bearing on the prospects for such a coalition:

> Three questions, in particular, are germane in this context: Is China going to remain the only rising power, or would the Russian decline eventually be reversed, or would India start catching up? Would Russia and India be forced to 'balance against' a rising China? Would greater economic interaction and the inevitable competition that will follow, lead to instability, or would it lead to the discovery of a larger set of mutual interests? (Sahni, 2004: 258-59).

Some of the other geopolitical issues that might further complicate the formation of a Big Three Alliance include unresolved border conflicts. The differentials, in terms of demographic growth, might also cause unregulated population movements, both within and across sovereign borders. Finally, there is the crucial question of socio-economic cleavages and regional imbalances in these large states, which potentially undermines the cohesive and territorial integrity of these states. Whereas, according to Dutt:

> [when] all [is] said and done, the logic of the world situation should push them [China, India and Russia] towards greater cooperation. The Chinese themselves have been talking a great deal about a multi-polar world and warning against one superpower hegemony. If they mean what they say, and are serious about it, then they must also contribute to the evolving of greater multiplicity in the world. What could be more effective in promoting multi-polarity than more intensive Indian-Chinese-Russian consultations and cooperation in international relations? (Dutt, 1999).

According to Varun Sahni (2004: 260-261), neither opposing axes and balance of power,[3] nor the *Directoire* of Great Powers are likely to ensure a sustainable security architecture for Asia. These arrangements, according to him, are not going to serve India's best interests in Asia. Instead, he would prefer to see the construction of a regional security arrangement in Asia, as an alternate means of containing China, maintaining stability in Asia and minimising the role of the US on the Asian continent—some kind of 'Asian Helsinki process with "baskets" of issues, 'some pertaining to inter-state relations, others to matters *within* sovereign boundaries' (Sahni, 2004: 260-261).

It would be worthwhile, it could be argued, to add the issue of 'energy security' to this basket as a matter of priority. Economic/energy interdependencies among the Asian nations could provide one of the critical foundations for supporting and sustaining a cooperative security architecture which is truly Asian, although not necessarily inward-looking. It could be added that such a cooperation need not (in fact, *cannot*) be continent-centric. In such a

---

[3] Washington-New Delhi-Jakarta-Hanoi-Tokyo axis to contain China or, alternately, Tehran-New Delhi-Kuala Lumpur-Beijing axis aimed against the West.

scheme of things, the continental pipelines and the sea-lanes of communication would complement rather than negate each other.

CONCLUSION

A 'new' mapping of India and its neighbourhood is under way; this process might bring about not only a shift in India's image of itself *vis-à-vis* the rest of the world, but also represent a critical rethinking of the conventional categorisation and compartmentalisation of the global geopolitical space. There are also positive indications that India's foreign policy now is far more willing to engage seriously with maritime issues. The much overdue process of decolonising the geographical imaginations inherited from the Cold War can neither be arrested nor reversed. A series of internal/domestic, regional and global forces are at work behind a seriously felt political urge among India's political elite to reorient India in terms of hitherto ignored directions.

A systematic analysis of an issue-area which straddles national boundaries, such as energy security, reveals beyond doubt that boundaries between various segments of partitioned Asia (for example, between 'Asia-Pacific' and the rest of Asia, on the one hand, and between the Indian Ocean and the Pacific Ocean on the other) are, in fact, already blurred and porous. The Indian Ocean region, washing the shores of the Southeast Asian countries, is fast emerging as the fulcrum of the twenty-first century global geopolitics (Rumley and Chaturvedi, 2004; Berlin, 2004; Chaturvedi, 2003). As discussed at length by Sam Bateman (2004: 13), the Indian Ocean represents some peculiarly complex problems for maritime security management, including the matter of how to ensure freedom of navigation. Despite their common stake in the freedom of navigation, and for that matter ocean management generally, earlier attempts at building cooperation in the Indian Ocean region have not been resounding successes, and the level of existing cooperation is not as high as elsewhere in the world. India has considerable capability and experience to share with the countries of Oceanic Asia in peacekeeping, anti-piracy and search and rescue operations. Useful partnerships can also be forged to meet the challenge of the transport of illegal arms, drugs and fissile material through the Indian Ocean.

What is slowly, but surely, emerging as the new context of India's foreign policy is a pattern of dynamic strategic spaces that defy fixed boundaries, something that could be termed 'Oceanic Asia'. This notion is based on the assumption that there is a steadily growing mismatch between traditional categorisations/visualisations of Asia, and the transformations induced or facilitated by various facets of globalisation. It is by acknowledging such a fact that the countries of Asia will be in a position to bring the historical mobility of Asia out of the shadows, and exploit emerging opportunities for cooperative endeavours.

REFERENCES

Aiyar, Mani Shankar (2005) 'Excerpts from the Address by Mani Shankar Aiyar, Honorable Minister for Petroleum and Natural Gas on 16th of March at the Observer Research Foundation'. *ORF Energy News Monitor*, 1(38): 3-4.

Barman, A. (2005) 'Pipe Dream: Rice Attempts to Derail India's Oil Diplomacy'. *The Times of India*, New Delhi, 2 April.

Bateman, S. (2004) 'Freedom of Navigation and Indian Ocean Security: A Geopolitical Analysis'. In D. Rumley and S. Chaturvedi (eds), *Geopolitical Orientations, Regionalism and Security in the Indian Ocean*, New Delhi: South Asian Publishers.

Bayarkhuu, D. (2004) 'Geopolitics of the New Central Asia'. *World Affairs: The Journal of International Issues*, 8(1): 58-83.

Berlin, D. (2002) 'Indian Ocean Redux: Arms, Bases and Re-Emergence of Strategic Rivalry'. *Journal of Indian Ocean Studies*, 10(1): 26-45.

Berlin, D.L. (2004) 'The "Great Base Race" in the Indian Ocean Littoral: Conflict Prevention or Stimulation'. *Contemporary South Asia*, 13(3): 239-255.

Bhattacharya, A. (2004) 'The Fallacy in the Russian-India-China Triangle'. *Strategic Analysis*, 28(2): 358-363.

Bracken, P. (1999) *Fire in the East: The Rise of Asian Military Power and the Second Nuclear Age*, New York: HarperCollins.

Brzezinski, Z. (1997) *The Grand Chessboard: American Primacy and Its Geostrategic Imperatives*, New York: Basic Books.

Chaturvedi, S. (2002) 'Can there be Asian Geopolitics?' In Ranabir Samaddar (ed.), *Interpreting Space, Territory and the State: New Readings in International Relations*, Hyderabad: Orient Longman.

——— (2003) 'Re-Visioning the Indian Ocean Rim: An Indian Perspective'. *What Next? Key Issues for Corporate Decision Makers*, Fremantle: Future Directions International, December: 4-5.

Chellaney, B. (2005) 'Great Game on Energy'. *The Economic Times*, New Delhi, 18 March.

Chomsky, N. (1994) *World Orders, Old and New*, London: Pluto Press.

——— (1996) *Powers and Prospects: Reflections on Human Nature and the Social Order*, New Delhi: Madhyam Books

Confederation of Indian Industry (CII) (1992) "Enhancing India-ASEAN Trade", http://www.ciionline.org/common/92/default.asp?Page=ASEAN%20Countries.htm

Dawisha, K. and B. Parrott (1997) *Conflict, Cleavage, and Change in Central Asia and the Caucasus*, Cambridge: Cambridge University Press.

Dadwal, S.R. (2002) *Rethinking Energy Security in India*, New Delhi: Knowledge World.

Debrix, F. (2003) 'Tabloid Realism and the Revival of American Security Culture'. *Geopolitics*, 8(3): 151-190.

Deshingkar, G. (1999) 'The Construction of Asia in India'. *Asian Studies Review*, 23(2): 173-188.

Devare, S.T. (2002) 'ASEAN-India: On the Threshold of a New Era in Partnership'. *The Hindu*, Delhi, 12 November.

Dietl, G. (2004) 'New Threats to Oil and Gas in West Asia: Issue in India's Security'. *Strategic Analysis*, 28(3): 373-389.

Dixit, J.N. (2003) *India's Foreign Policy: 1947-2003*, New Delhi: Picus Books.

Dodds, K. (2003) 'Cold War Geopolitics'. In J. Agnew, K. Mitchell and G. Toal (eds), *A Companion to Political Geography*, Oxford: Blackwell: 204-218.

Dutt, V.P. (1999) 'India, China, Russia Syndrome'. *The Tribune*, Chandigarh, 17 April.

Ghoshal, B. (2002) 'India's Relations with ASEAN: The Historical Setting'. *World Focus*, September: 3-6.

Gupta, A., M. Chaturvedi and A. Joshi (2004) *Security and Diplomacy: Essential Documents*, New Delhi: Manas Publications (published in collaboration with National Security Council Secretariat).

Hale, D. (1997) 'Is Asia's High Growth Era Over'. *The National Interest*, 47: 44-57.

Harkavy, R. (2001) 'Strategic Geography and the Greater Middle East'. *Naval War College Review*, 54(4): 37-53.

Huntington, S. (1993) 'The Clash of Civilizations'. *Foreign Affairs*, 72: 22-49.

Hitchcock, D.I. (1998) 'Internal Problems in East Asia'. *The Washington Quarterly*, 21(2): 121-134.

Katzenstein, P.J. and T. Shiraishi (eds) (1997) *Network Power: Japan and Asia*, Ithaca: Cornell University Press.

Klare, M. (2001) *Resource Wars: The New Landscape of Global Conflict*, New York: Metropolitan/Owl Book.

——— (2003) 'New Geopolitics'. *Monthly Review*, 55(33).

Kumar, A. (2005) 'India-Myanmar Gas Pipeline Through Bangladesh: Pipe Dream?' 7 September, http://www.saag.org//%5Cpapers13%5Cpaper1216.html

Lieven, A. (2002) 'The Secret Policemen's Ball: The United States, Russia and the International Order after 11 September'. *International Affairs*, 78(2): 245-59.

Ludden, D. (2003) 'Maps in the Mind and the Mobility of Asia'. *Journal of Asian Studies*, 62(4). AAS Presidential Address: www.aasianst.org/catalog/jas.htm

Luttwak, E.N. (1990) 'From Geopolitics to Geo-economics, Logic of Conflict, Grammar of Commerce'. *The National Interest*, 20: 17-24.

Mahalingam, S. (2004) 'Energy and Security in a Changing World'. *Strategic Analysis*, 28(2): 249-271.

Mamadouoth, V.D. (1998) 'Geopolitics in the Nineties: One Flag, Many Meanings'. *Geojournal*, 46: 237-256.

Mattoo, A. and F. Grare (eds) (2003) *Beyond the Rhetoric: The Economics of India's Look East Policy*, New Delhi: Manohar: 115-128.

Mattoo, A. (2001) 'ASEAN in India's Foreign Policy'. In A. Mattoo and F. Grare (eds) *India and ASEAN: The Politics of India's Look East Policy*, New Delhi: Manohar: 91-118.

McMpherson, K. (2002) 'SAARC and the Indian Ocean'. *South Asian Survey*, 9(2): 251-261.

Mehta, Pratap B. (2005) 'A New Non-Alignment? India Must Talk to the US Without Getting Locked into Its Embrace'. *The Indian Express*, Chandigarh, 23 March.

Muni, S.D. and G. Pant (2005) *India's Energy Security: Prospects for Cooperation with Extended Neighborhood*, New Delhi: Rupa and Company.

Muni, S.D. and C. Raja Mohan (2004) 'Emerging Asia: India's Options'. *International Studies*, 41(3): 313-334.

Murthy, P. (2000) 'BIMST-EC: Making Positive Moves'. *Strategic Analysis*, 24(4): 833-836.

——— (2002) 'India ASEAN Relations Towards a Dynamic Partnership'. *Indian Ocean Digest*, 17(2): 53-57.

Nanda, P. (2003) *Rediscovering Asia: Evolution of India's Look-East Policy*. New Delhi: Lancer.

Naidu, G.V.C. (2003) 'India and Southeast Asia: An Analysis of the Look East Policy'. Paper Presented at the conference on *India-ASEAN: Post Summit Perspectives,* held by the Centre for the Indian Ocean Studies, Osmania University, Hyderabad, 3-5 July.

——— (2004) 'Whither the Look East Policy: India and Southeast Asia'. *Strategic Analysis*, 28(2): 331-346.

Neumann, I.B. (1997) 'The Geopolitics of Delineating "Russia" and "Europe": The Creation of the "Other" in European and Russian Tradition'. In O. Tunander, P. Baev and V.I. Einagel (eds), *Geopolitics in Post-Wall Europe: Security, Territory and Identity*, London: Sage, 147-173.

Nehru, Jawaharlal (1941) *The Unity of India: Collected Writings, 1937-40*, London: Lindsay Drummond.

Palmer, N.D. (1991) *The New Regionalism in Asia and the Pacific*, Lexington: Heath.

Parthasarthy, G. (2001) 'Some Policy Options for India'. In J. Singh (ed.), *Oil and Gas in India's Security*, New Delhi: Knowledge World: 107-115.

Peters, S. (1999) 'The "West" Against the "Rest": Geopolitics After the End of the Cold War'. *Geopolitics*, 4(3): 29-46.

Raja Mohan, C. (2003a) 'India's Pamir Knot'. *The Hindu*, New Delhi, 10 November.

——— (2003b) *Crossing the Rubicon: The Shaping of India's New Foreign Policy*, New Delhi: Viking.

——— (2005) 'India's Diplomatic Spring'. *The Indian Express,* Chandigarh, 22 March.

Ram, A.N. (2000) 'Historical Perspectives'. *Seminar* (New Delhi), 487 March: 25-31.

Ram, A. N. (2003) 'India's Look East Policy—A Perspective'. Paper Presented at the conference on *India-ASEAN: Post Summit Perspectives*, organised by the Centre of the Indian Ocean Studies, Osmania University, Hyderabad from 3-5 July.

Rao, P.V. (2003a) 'India and Regional Co-operation: Multiple Strategies in an Elusive Region'. In P.V. Rao (ed.), *India and Indian Ocean: In the Twilight of Millennium*, New Delhi: South Asian Publishers: 122-151.

——— (2003b) 'Regional Cooperation in ASEAN: Sino-Indian Strategies'. Paper presented at the conference on *India-ASEAN: Post Summit Perspectives,* organised by the Centre of Indian Ocean Studies, Osmania University, Hyderabad, 3-5 July.

Ravenhill, J. (1995) 'Competing Logic of Regionalism in the Asia-Pacific'. *Journal of European Integration*, 28(2-3): 179-199.

Reddy, Y.Y. (2003) 'Mekong-Ganga Cooperation: A Milestone in India Southeast Asia Partnership'. Paper presented at the conference on *India-ASEAN: Post Summit Perspectives,* organised by the Center of Indian Ocean Studies, Osmania University, Hyderabad, 3-5 July.

Rumley, D. (1999) 'Geopolitical Change and the Asia-Pacific: The Future of New Regionalism'. *Geopolitics*, 4(1): 83-97.

Rumley, D. and S. Chaturvedi (eds) (2004) *Geopolitical Orientations, Regionalism and Security in the Indian Ocean*, New Delhi: South Asian Publishers.

Sabur, A.K.M.A. (2003) 'Management of Intra-Group Conflicts in SAARC: The Relevance of ASEAN Experiences'. *South Asian Survey*, 10(1): 85-99.

Sahni, V. (2004) 'From Security in Asia to Asian Security'. *International Studies*, 41(3): 245-262.

Shaw, D. (2005) *Securing India's Energy Needs: The Regional Dimension*, The Centre for Strategic and International Studies, www.csis.org/saprog/0505_shaw.pdf.\

Sievers, E.W. (2003) *The Post-Soviet Decline of Central Asia: Sustainable Development and Comprehensive Capital*, London and New York: Routledge Curzon.

Siddiqi, T.A. (2003) *Enhancing Clear Energy Supply for Development, A Natural Gas Pipeline for India and Pakistan*, Honolulu, Global Environment and Energy, BALUSA for Peace Inc.

Singh, C.P. (1998) Towards a New Equilibrium: India, the Asia-Pacific and Global Geopolitical Change'. In D. Rumley, T. Chiba, A. Takagi and Y. Fukushima (eds), *Global Geopolitical Change and the Asia-Pacific: A Regional Perspective*, Aldershot: Ashgate: 260-282.

Singh, J. (2001) *Oil and Gas in India's Security*, New Delhi: Knowledge World.

Singh, K.R. (2002) 'Geo-Strategy of Commercial Energy'. *International Studies*, 39(3): 259-288.

Sreekumar, S.S. (2004) 'India and ASEAN: Geopolitical Concerns'. *World Affairs: The Journal of International Issues*, 8(1): 100-106.

Subrahmanyam, K. (2005) 'The American Offer: India Should Make Use of the Opportunity'. *The Tribune* (Chandigarh), 31 March: 10.

Suryanarayan,V. (2000) 'Prospects for a Bay of Bengal Community'. *Seminar* (New Delhi), 487 March: 58-61.

————— (2002) 'Plea for a New Regional Organization'. *South Asian Survey*, 9(2): 263-273.

Tan Chung, A. (1998) 'Nehru's dreams of an Eastern Federation'. In S. Mansingh (ed.), *Nehru's Foreign Policy, Fifty Years On*, New Delhi: Publication Info.

Upreti, B.C. (2001) 'Sub-Regional Cooperation in the Indian Ocean: Emerging Trends and Prospects in the Specific Context of BIMST-EC'. In P.V. Rao (ed.), *Regional Cooperation in Indian Ocean: Trends and Perspectives*, New Delhi: South Asian Publishers: 232-245.

Weinbaum, M.G. (1996-97) 'The Three Asias: Security, Economic, and Cultural Linkages Across Central, West, and South Asia'. *Swords and Ploughshares*, 10: 1-2.

In: India: Economic, Political and Social Issues
Editor: Urlah B. Nissam

ISBN: 978-1-60456-509-6
© 2009 Nova Science Publishers, Inc.

Chapter 3

POLICIES AND MECHANISMS FOR TECHNOLOGY TRANSFER TO SMES IN A GLOBALIZING ECONOMY – INDIAN PERSPECTIVE

S. P. Agarwal and *Ashwani Gupta*

ABSTRACT

Globalization has thrown many challenges as well as opened several opportunities for the SMEs. Today, SMEs need to network more intensely with the academic and R&D institutions and among themselves for their very survival. Since contribution of SMEs to economic and industrial development, worldwide is substantial, a pro-SME policy becomes necessary. Growing performance of high technology users in sectors such as auto-components and pharmaceuticals in India underlines the importance of technology transfer to SMEs. SMEs in India number more than 11 million, employ more than 28 million people, contribute to around 40% of industrial production and 35% of exports. SME sector in India is undergoing reforms to enable the units to take on the increased competition in the globalizing economy.

The Government of India has many schemes and programmes that support acquisition, management, development and commercialization of technology by the SMEs. Specialized agencies and mechanisms have been established that transfer the technology from laboratories to industry and facilitate their commercialization. The FDI policy is being further liberalized that is conducive to foreign investment and technology inflow in the country. Many venture capital mechanisms that support technology transfer exist in the country. Among the infrastructure facilities for technology transfer, a number of Science and Technology Entrepreneurship parks (STEPs) and Technology Business Incubators (TBIs) have been set-up in the vicinity of institutions and industry clusters. Policies and infrastructure facilities for technology transfer to SMEs should be aimed at enhancing their competitiveness in the globalized economy. Besides this, the policies and mechanisms should be innovative that encourage the SMEs to participate aggressively in

---

* S.P. Agarwal is a Professor and Head (Centre for International Trade in Technology) at Indian Institute of foreign Trade, New Delhi and Ashwani Gupta is a Director in Department of Scientific and Industrial Research, Government of India.

the technology transfer process. Easier access to foreign technologies, internationalization, and encouragement to generate intellectual property and promote innovation clusters, start ups etc. are needed, besides innovative financing including venture capital.

1. PREAMBLE

SMEs constitute a significant percentage to GDP, industrial production and exports in most countries and therefore, any policy formulation or infrastructure planning need to necessarily focus on SMEs. In the emerging world trade rules, the technology transfer process and its modes are fast changing. SMEs in several countries, particularly in developing countries lack a proper technology perspective and are not aware of new technology transfer mechanisms. A comparative picture of SMEs in the developing and the developed or advanced developing countries can be seen in Table 1.[2] SMEs can be broadly categorized into two classes, viz. SMEs in the traditional or the brick and mortar sectors such as food, textiles, metal working etc. and SMEs in the knowledge based sectors viz. electronics, pharmaceuticals, bio-technology, renewable energy etc. The technology transfer mechanisms to these two classes of SMEs need to be different, e.g. SMEs in the traditional sector require access to proven technologies or incremental innovation in existing technologies but SMEs in the knowledge based sectors need to shop globally for cutting edge technology or develop the technology they require through own R&D efforts. Also, SMEs in the manufacturing and the services sectors require different treatment.

Yet another class of SMEs belongs to start ups and innovative or internationalised SMEs which are based more on research entrepreneurship or academic intellectual property. This paper dwells upon the impact of globalization on SMEs, need for technology transfer policy to SMEs in India, policies, programmes, schemes and infrastructure facilities established by the Government and associated agencies and financial institutions to facilitate technology transfer to SMEs. The paper concludes by emphasizing that SMEs need to integrate with global supply chains, adopt a technology strategy that is well integrated with business strategy and need to establish intense linkages with R&D laboratories in the emerging world trade policy environment. Further, the paper recommends that FDI should be encouraged to allow foreign technology in-flows and policies and infrastructure facilities for technology transfer to SMEs should be aimed at enhancing their competitiveness in the globalized economy.[9]

2. GLOBALIZATION AND ITS IMPACT ON SMES

Globalization has not only affected the competitiveness of SMEs but has threatened their very survival as well as provided business opportunities. It has forced them to re-think their manufacturing and marketing strategies. Small and large sized companies have realized that to compete globally they need to work more closely with each other than before.

Table 1. Technology related characterstics of SMEs in developing and developed countries

Features	Developing Countries	Developed/Advanced Developing Countries
Objectives of SMEs	Employment, local development	National Competitiveness and internationalization
Thrust Sectors for SMEs	Low tech and resource based	High tech and innovations
Policies, incentives and mechanisms	Weak	Strong
NIS and SIS	Almost non-existent, synonymous with S&T	Advancing
National Competitiveness	Low	High
R&D	Weak	Strong
Private R&D	Very low	High
Innovativeness	Very low	High
IPR culture	Very low	High
Use of technology in SMEs	Low technology	High or innovations
Linkages with R&D and academics	Weak	Strong
Skill levels	Low	High
S&T manpower, training and education system	Weak	Strong
Clusters, incubators, S&T parks, etc.	General, employment	Innovative, specialized, Technology development encouraged
Technology acquisition, transfer, information etc. incentives	Weak	Strong
Technology Commercialisation, 'start ups'	Weak	Stronger
Standardisation and quality control	Weak	Strong
Technology Financing	Very Weak	Innovative methods
FDI policies, venture capital, loans, grants, fiscal incentives, tax concessions, investment companies, angel investors	Not technology oriented, inefficient, FDI not encouraged	Tech. oriented, efficient FDI encouraged
Internationalisation, networking, Associations, preparedness for WTO	Very weak	Important and strong
ICT applications in SMEs	Weak	Widely used
Technology management, knowledge management and networking	Very weak, practically non existent	Gaining
Public-private partnership	Very weak	Stronger
Technopreneurship	Weak	Stronger
Government Procurement	No specific incentives	Preferred, and incentives
Protection and reservations	Practiced	Competition encouraged
Political and societal commitment, including stable policy regime	Weak	Strong

Source: Agarwal, S.P.; Report on Strategy for Enhancing Competitiveness of SMEs based on Technology Capacity Building; UN ESCAP, Bangkok, November, 2005.

·prises can provide the benefits of knowledge, research, marketing, branding and
es even financing. Small enterprises can be the low cost engines of production and
~~~ ⅇ jobs. This could be a perfect combination.

Globalization has in effect thrown many challenges as well as opened several
opportunities for the SMEs. The challenges include:

a *Internationalization of domestic markets*: With many foreign companies establishing
joint ventures and wholly owned subsidiaries in India and setting up manufacturing
facilities the domestic market is flooded with large number of products manufactured
by these outfits poses competition for the products manufactured by domestic
companies.

b *Availability of Imported products at cheaper price than local products*: Landed price
of imported products have become cheaper than the price of products manufactured
domestically due to revision of tariffs and duty structure, as demanded by WTO. As a
result of this, many companies have been forced to shut down their manufacturing
operations and take up trading instead.

c *Brakes on Reverse Engineering*: Due to alignment of IPR laws with the TRIPs
agreement of WTO, product patent regime has been introduced in the country,
bringing down the shutters on process patent regime and seriously hitting the
fortunes of companies who were thriving on the basis of reverse engineering or new
process development.

d *New trade barriers imposed by Agreements of WTO*: The Technical Barriers to Trade
(TBT) notifications issued by many countries have resulted in rejection of many
export consignments, affecting the exports of companies. Sanitary and Phyto-
Sanitary measures stipulated in the SPS agreement has forced companies to look at
the sanitary and hygienic conditions in their factories and make investments to
improve the same. General Agreement on Trade in Services (GATS) has affected the
movement of professionals.

The opportunities that globalization has unfolded include:

a *Increased flow of foreign investment and technology*: The globalization process has
attracted more and more foreign companies to bring in investments and technology
into the country and establish joint ventures. This has provided an opportunity to the
local SMEs to build up their capabilities and capacities.

b *Outsourcing or Re-location of pieces of Supply Chain*: The globalization process has
opened up many opportunities for design outsourcing and contract manufacturing for
the local SMEs.

c *Access to foreign Markets*: The globalization process has enabled the local SMEs to
look beyond the national boundaries and access foreign markets for their products
and services.

d *Mergers and acquisitions*: The globalization process has promoted mergers and
acquisitions among companies resulting in enhancement of economies of scale,
quality, delivery schedules etc. of the local SMEs.

e   *New areas of business*: The globalization process has resulted in opening up new areas of businesses for local SMEs such as business process outsourcing, medical transcriptions, clinical research trials, design & engineering etc. It has also encouraged some of the SMEs to look at emerging technologies such as biotechnology, nanotechnology etc.

f   *Internationalisation* : SMEs would need to internationalise to grow sustainably in foreign markets and network with relevant agencies. Some of the forward looking and dynamic SMEs have seen these opportunities and integrated themselves with the global supply chains.

Globalization has also given rise to a number of multi-lateral and bi-lateral agreements such as the Preferential Trade Agreements (PTAs) or Free Trade Agreements (FTAs) between nations which also present opportunities as well as threats.

PTAs and FTAs - Opportunity or Threat

The Preferential Trade Agreements (PTAs) or Free Trade Agreements (FTAs) between nations have been as old as history of nations. Under these agreements two or more contracting countries agree to reduce the Customs Duties on a few or on the entire tariff lines for trade among themselves for the goods manufactured in these countries. The reduction could be incremental (5% or 10% or 50% etc.) covered under Preferential Trade Agreement or there could be complete elimination of import duties usually termed as Free Trade Agreement. With coming into being of Multilateral institutions- where substantially large number of countries agree to bring down their duties simultaneously, such as under WTO, it was expected that PTAs/ FTAs would loose their sheen. However, the number of PTAs/ FTAs have skyrocketed since the birth of WTO due to several reasons. The EU, NAFTA, ASEAN and SAPTA are the examples of such PTAs/FTAs. Whether PTAs/FTAs are more beneficial than the multilateral systems as WTO, is a hotly debated issue globally.

There is a general perception that international agreements concern those who are in international trade either importing or exporting. This is far from truth. The PTAs/ FTAs affect all kind of businesses and their impact is seen on: (a) on the competitiveness of domestic industry; and (b) on the accessibility of markets. Take for example one country is good in manufacturing steel and the other is good at manufacturing machine. If one requires steel at competitive prices to manufacture machine and the other requires machine at competitive prices, it makes economic sense that one lower import duty on steel and the other on machines. It increases competitive strength of both nations. However, the country that requires steel, keeps the import duty on steel at same level but reduces the import duty on machine, it will lead to reverse tariff escalation. More duty on steel and less duty on machine. It would make the country un-competitive and it would be more economical to import machine in that country than to manufacture locally. Therefore, PTAs and FTAs present both, the opportunity and threat.

Indian SMEs can hold their own in the global marketplace by supplementing each other strengths. They should also strive for greater knowledge through networking and sharing success stories.

3. THE NEED FOR A PRO-SME POLICY AND TECHNOLOGY TRANSFER TO SMES

It has been observed that a thriving SME sector is a characteristic of flourishing economies. SMEs are the powerhouses of industries. Worldwide, they account for up to 99.7% of all enterprises. Since the SMEs contribute substantially to the economic and industrial development in most countries,[1] it becomes necessary to put in place a policy mechanism that will facilitate their growth. The proponents of a pro-SME policy give the following justification:

(a) *Social Benefits:* SMEs enhance competition and entrepreneurship and thus the economy benefits by way of greater efficiency, innovation and productivity. So direct government support of SMEs can help countries reap social benefits.

(b) *Economic Growth & Development:* Proponents often claim that SMEs are generally more productive than large firms but are impeded in their development by failures of financial markets and other institutions. Thus, pending financial and institutional improvements, direct government support of SMEs can boost economic growth and development.

(c) *Poverty Reduction:* Some argue that the growth of SMEs boosts employment more than the growth of large firms because SMEs are more labour intensive. So subsidizing SMEs may help reduce poverty.

It is becoming amply clear that only those SMEs which are competitive would be able to survive in the globalized economy. Now what does competitiveness imply? Being competitive means having the ability to produce high quality goods and services at market determined prices or even at prices lower than that and supplying them as per committed delivery schedules. It also means supplying products with innovative features that conform to international standards, supplying products that are rugged, user-friendly as well as having a customer appeal. Many of these competitiveness parameters hinge upon application of modern state-of-the-art technology. For example, use of advanced process technology usually result in better product quality and durability, technology usually helps in reducing cost by effecting savings in material, energy or through replacement of conventional materials with cheaper alternative materials and technology can make a product rugged such as scratch proof, unbreakable etc. Therefore, technology transfer to SMEs must be facilitated to enable them to become competitive and contribute effectively in country's economic and industrial development. Also, SMEs must build capacities to attract technology from outside and then absorb and adapt it for newer applications. The growing performance of high technology users in sectors like auto components and pharmaceuticals only underlines the need for technology transfer to SMEs in India.

4. SMEs in India

SMEs in India today include small-scale industries, small-scale enterprises, tiny enterprises and SSSBE (Small Scale Service Business Enterprises) and medium-size enterprises. The focus is mainly on the manufacturing sectors such as textile, auto ancillary and engineering industries. The definition used by the Indian authorities is based on the level of investment in plant, machinery or other fixed assets whether held on an ownership, lease or hire purchase basis. Currently this limit is Rs. 10 million. In order to enhance the competitiveness of the small scale sector, in the changing scenario of economic liberalization and globalization, the investment limit in respect of certain hi-tech and export oriented items was enhanced to Rs.50 million to enable them to undertake technological upgradation. Till last year, the number of items, which had investment ceiling of Rs.50 million in plant and machinery was 71. The SSI ministry's efforts to raise the investment limit for 69 more products in the small and medium enterprises (SME) sector from Rs 10 million to Rs 50 million is likely to come into force shortly. Items included in the list for which investment limit is going to be raised vary from the auto component to food processing and pharmaceuticals sector. Once this comes through, the total number of products in the SME sector with an investment limit of Rs 50 million will go up to 140. [1,5]

The following are the figures that reflect the significance of Indian SMEs to the national economy:

- Estimated number of enterprises: 11.86 million
- Estimated employment: 28.29 million
- 91% of total industrial units
- 39.42% of total industrial production
- 34% of total exports
- 6.81% of GDP
- Growth rate of about 8% per year over last 10 year, vis-a-vis about 5% for whole industrial sector
- Wide range (over 7500) of products manufactured - from traditional to hi-tech
- Over 21,400 ISO-9000/14001 certified units

Reforms in the SME sector in India have kept pace with those for other aspects of the economy, with results there for everyone to see. As a result of policy reforms, the Indian SME sector is in a better position to take on competition from the globalized world than ever before. This can be attributed to not only policy changes, but also to a new found confidence amongst entrepreneurs who are taking a more global view of their businesses just like SMEs from many other countries including Italy, South Korea, Taiwan and China, to name a few.

Some of the recent and proposed policy reforms for the SME sector in India are the following:

- New legislation [Small and Medium Enterprises Development (SMED) Bill, 2005] just introduced in the Parliament

- Substantial enhancement in investment limits proposed for small enterprises (SEs) and medium enterprises (MEs) sought to be defined formally
- Enhancing existing limit (24%) of equity investment in incorporated SEs by large enterprises (including higher limits of FDI)
- Accelerating development of clusters
- SME Fund of US$ 2.27 billion operationalised
- New Scheme of Credit-cum-Performance Rating of SEs launched; establishment of dedicated Credit Rating Agency
- "Scheme of Fund for Regeneration of Traditional Industries" ["SFURTI"]
- Guarantee coverage under Credit Guarantee Fund for SEs expanded substantially
- New Promotional Package for SEs (including Tiny Enterprises)
- Accelerating initiatives on technology incubation and hand holding services
- New legislation on Limited Liability Partnerships

SMED 2005 Bill

The bill clarifies what it defines as small and medium enterprises.

a   in the case of the enterprises engaged in the manufacture or production of goods pertaining to any industry specified in the First Schedule to the Industries (Development and Regulation) Act, 1951 as –

b   a small enterprise, where the investment in plant and machinery does not exceed Rs. 50 million; or

c   a medium enterprise, where the investment in plant and machinery is more than Rs. 50 million but does not exceed Rs. 100 million;

d   in the case of the enterprises engaged in providing or rendering of services in relation to any industry specified in the First Schedule to the Industries (Development and Regulation) Act, 1951, as –

e   a small enterprise, where the investment in equipment does not exceed Rs. 20 million; or

f   a medium enterprise, where the investment in equipment is more than Rs. 20 million but does not exceed Rs. 50 million.

5. POLICIES AND PROGRAMMES FOR TECHNOLOGY TRANSFER TO SMEs IN INDIA

India's S&T Policy 2003 states –

A strong base of science and engineering research provides a crucial foundation for a vibrant programme of technology development. Priority will be placed on the development of technologies which address the basic needs of the population; make Indian industries - small, medium or large - globally competitive; make the country economically strong; and address the security concerns of the nation. Special emphasis will be placed on equity in development, so that the benefits of technological growth reach the majority of the population, particularly the disadvantaged sections, leading to an improved quality of life for every citizen of the country. These aspects require technology foresight, which involves not only forecasting and assessment of technologies but also their social, economic and environmental consequences.

Thus, emphasis is on development and transfer of innovative technologies and making Indian industry, in particular SMEs globally competitive. While the corporate sector is more or less well equipped to meet its technology demands, it is the SME sector that needs hand holding for technology development and transfer. Government has formulated a number of schemes that facilitate this. Some of them are described below: [4,7]

5.1. Technology Development and Demonstration Programme (Erstwhile PATSER)

The *Technology Development and Demonstration Programme (TDDP)* of DSIR aims at catalyzing and supporting activities relating to technology absorption, adaptation and demonstration including capital goods development by involving industry and R&D organizations.

Under the programme, innovative technologies are up-scaled from the *'proof of concept stage'* to *'pilot plant/pre-commercial stage'* by the *industry*. The projects involve research, design, development and engineering and are executed by industry, overseen by experts from university/laboratory.

DSIR has supported over 165 projects so far since inception of the scheme in 1992, when it was called PATSER. More than 100 projects have been completed and 45 projects have gone into commercial production, which are paying lump sum premia/royalty. So far, more than Rs.50 million royalty/premia have been received. About 20 patents have been filed based on projects supported under the scheme. The scheme has synergized around 85 private sector companies (mainly SSI), 30 public sector companies and 25 R&D laboratories. It is estimated that more than 30% of budget earmarked for Technology Development and Demonstration Programme benefits the SME sector. Some of the successfully completed projects, involving SMEs are: Development of Hand Held Optical Test Equipment (M/s. Aishwarya Telecom), Efficient Solvent Extraction Plant (M/s. Mecpro Heavy Engineering), Laser Lamps (M/s. Litex Electricals), Integrated Pilot Demonstration Plant for Spice Processing (MATA Foundation), Liposomal Amphoterecin (M/s. Lifecare Innovations), Micro Balancer (M/s. Atcom Technologies), Air Circuit Breaker (M/s. JSL Indus Ltd.), Complete Automatic Solution for Hydrography (M/s. Pan India Electronech), Digested Organic Supplement (M/s. T.Stanes & Co.) etc.

5.2. Technopreneur Promotion Programme(TePP)

Ministry of Science & Technology, Government of India launched a novel programme known as "Technopreneur Promotion Programme (TePP)" in 1998-99 to tap the vast innovative potential of Indian citizens. The programme aims to support individual innovators, from informal knowledge system as well as from formal knowledge system so as to enable them to become technology-based entrepreneurs (technopreneurs). TePP provides financial support to individual innovators to convert an original idea/invention/know-how into a working prototype/process. Under the programme, any Indian citizen, viz. artisan, technician, engineer, architect, doctor, scientist, housewife, student, farmer etc. having innovative idea could aspire to become technology based entrepreneur (technopreneur). The proposal can be made, either by an individual on his own or jointly with sponsoring/collaborating organization involved in technology development and promotion. The proposals from the owner of 'start-ups' are also considered for TePP support, if the annual turnover of the company doesn't exceed Rs. 3.0 million.

During last six years of its operation, the programme has been able to fulfill the dreams of many innovative Indian citizens in their pursuit of becoming technopreneurs. Since its inception, the Government of India under TePP programme has given financial support to over 115 projects. Out of these, around 50 projects have been completed and around 25 projects have been commercialized. The scheme has resulted in grant of domestic patents to more than 10 innovators and US patent to 3 innovators, besides commercialization of the processes/gadgets. Some of the successfully completed/commercialized projects under TePP are tiltable bullock cart, innovative cotton stripper machine (US patented), small 10 H.P. tractor, small sprayer (5 ltr. capacity), design cutting machine, solid bio-mass fired furnace, alkali lignin from dry pine needles, diagonal inverter for operation microscope, protein dialysis device(US patented), on-line time domain moisture measurement, neem oil for non-healing wounds, novel process for manufacturing heterocyclic chemicals, bus heating system, DC MCBs, etc.

5.3. International Technology Transfer Programme of DSIR

The programme promotes and supports the technology transfer process among Indian and foreign enterprises. This is done through activities such as participation in international technology exhibitions and fairs, interaction between industrial delegations of various countries in buyer-seller meets, international awareness-cum-training programmes etc. Some examples of technology transfer by Indian SMEs, catalyzed by the programme include motor control technology to USA and Europe, dairy processing plants to Africa and Middle East, carbon dioxide plant to Iran, soaps and detergent plant to Madagascar, form-fill and seal machinery to Ghana and product & industrial design consultancy to South Africa.

5.4. Technology Development Board (TDB)

To accelerate the development and commercialization of indigenous technology or adapting imported technology for wider domestic application in a dynamic economic environment, the Government of India enabled the placing of the proceeds of an existent cess on the import of technology into a fund called the Fund for Technology Development and Application. To administer the fund, the Technology Development Board (TDB) was set up by Government of India on 1st September, 1996 and the operation of fund was assigned to

Department of Science & Technology, Government of India. The Board provides financial assistance in the form of equity, soft loans or grants. TDB's participation in a project generally does not exceed 50% of the project cost. The projects funded by the Board include sectors such as medicine and health, engineering, chemicals, agriculture and transport. Till 31st March, 2005, the TDB had handled 141 projects valued at a total cost of Rs. 20,438.9 million. Of the TDB's commitment of Rs. 6,629.4 million towards these projects, it has already released Rs.5,264.1 million. Of these projects, at least one third relate to the SME sector. TDB also gives an annual award to an SME for successful commercialization of technology.

5.5. Pharmaceuticals Research and Development Support Fund (PRDSF)

The Department of Science and Technology (DST) launched a Drug Development Programme during 1994-95 for promoting collaborative R&D in drugs & pharmaceuticals sector involving industries and institutions. 50 Projects have been supported under the Programme involving 22 institutions and R&D establishments and 23 industries, a significant percentage of which are SMEs. These projects were about development of new chemical entities, new vaccines, assay systems, drug delivery systems and herbal drugs. These projects have resulted in filing of 4 product patents and 12 process patents. The Programme has also led to setting up of eight National Facilities for R&D.

The Government established a 'Pharmaceuticals Research and Development Support Fund' (PRDSF) with an allocation of Rs. 1500 million (US $ 35 million) for the year 2005-06. The programme supports Pharma R&D projects by extending soft loan @ 3% interest.

5.6. New Millennium India Technology Leadership Initiative (NMITLI)

Government of India has recognized the power of innovation and had launched a new initiative during 2000 to enable Indian industry to attain a global leadership position in a few selected niche areas by leveraging innovation-centric scientific and technological developments in different disciplines. The programme is backed by the national determination to turn sound technology ideas into realities by symbiotically promoting and fostering private-public partnership in a Team India spirit. Only companies that are registered in India and having more than 50% shareholding by Indians or Non-Resident Indians can participate. The R&D centre of the applicant company must be recognized by the DSIR (or recognition must be obtained within 12 months). The financial support is provided as a grant to public institutions and as a loan with an interest rate of 3% to private sector companies.

In a very short span, NMITLI has crafted more than 37 path setting technology projects involving over 65 industry partners, a significant percentage of which are SMEs and 175 public funded R&D institutions with an outlay of Rs. 2500 million. These projects are setting new global technological paradigms in the areas such as nano material catalysis, industrial chemicals, gene-based new targets for advanced drug delivery systems, bio-technology, bio-informatics, low cost office computers, improved liquid crystal devices and so on. The scheme is being implemented by Council of Scientific & Industrial Research (CSIR).

5.7. Small Business Innovation Research Initiative (SBIRI)

Biotechnology industries are at the forefront of another technological revolution and are definitely going to prove as the industry of the new millennium. Biotechnology research has vast potential for commercialization in the areas of agriculture, human and animal health, environment, diagnostics, immuno-biologicals and various industrial products like antibiotics, industrial enzymes, vitamins etc. The global biotechnology has been undergoing dynamic changes in terms of perspective and priorities. Innovation is needed for development of new products and processes. The Small Business Innovation Research Initiative (SBIRI) is a new scheme launched by the Department of Bio-technology to boost public-private-partnership effort in the country. The distinctive feature of SBIRI is that it supports the high-risk pre-proof-of-concept research and late stage development in small and medium companies lead by innovators with science backgrounds which is unique in nature to support private industries and to get them involved in development of such products and processes which have high societal relevance.

Funding norms for Phase – I are: if the actual project cost is upto Rs. 2.5 million, 80% of the project cost will be available as a government grant; If the actual project cost is between Rs. 2.5 million and Rs. 10 million, 50% of the project cost will be available as government grant subject to a minimum of Rs. 2 million and maximum of Rs. 5 million; If the project cost is beyond Rs. 10 million, in addition to the Govt. grant of Rs. 5 million, the unit will be eligible for interest free loan upto 50% of the amount (subject to a limit of Rs. 5 million as loan) by which the total project cost exceeds Rs. 10 million.

Funding norms for Phase – II are: soft loan upto Rs. 100 million for a project as per its requirement. Soft loan upto Rs. 10 million will carry a simple interest of 1% while the interest rate will be 2% (simple interest) on the amount of loan beyond Rs. 10 million. The role of public R&D institution at this stage too is critical, as many of the projects would continue to require technical support from the public funded R&D institutions. The partner in the public institution at this stage will get the R&D support as grant.

Besides support for innovative technology development as available through the above programmes, the government has also adopted a FDI policy that facilitates technology transfer and commercialization.

5.8. Foreign Direct Investment (FDI) and Foreign Technology Transfer

Although foreign direct investment is allowed on the automatic route in most sectors, under a liberalized policy regime there exists a limit on foreign direct investment in SMEs. According to the rules in force, a small scale unit cannot have more that 24% equity in its paid up capital from any industrial undertaking, either foreign or domestic. Cumulative FDI inflows in the country till September, 2005 were US$ 35.52 billion with around US$ 4 billion annually in the last 4-5 years. The total number of foreign collaborations approved during August 1991 to August 2004 were 26,117 out of which foreign technical collaborations (that involve foreign technology transfer) were 7,635. The percentage share of foreign technical collaborations in total number of foreign collaborations has been dropped in the recent years indicating that technology transfer is taking place along with equity participation.

Sector wise share in FDI approvals since January 1991 to March 1004 is as follows:

Telecom	20%
Power	15%
Oil Refinery	12%
Electrical Equipment	10%
Transportation	8%
Others	35%

Seeing this trend, the Government has communicated its consent to the enhancement of equity investment limit in SMEs from 24% to 49%. This should ease the investment choking that many SMEs felt and would attract technology to India. Foreign collaboration approvals involving SMEs in India are generally with equity investments up to Rs. 10 million. Based on this, the cumulative value of foreign equity approvals in SMEs is just around 2% of the total amount of foreign equity approvals into the country. This is illustrated in Table 2. However, there is a scope to increase this to 10% and appropriate policy mechanisms need to be put in place to achieve this.[8]. Tables 3 to 6 gives details of FDI approvals during 2001-2004.

Table 2. Percentage share of cumulative value of foreign equity approvals of value up to rs. 10 million in total foreign equity approvals

S.No.	Sector	Total Value of Foreign Equity Apprd in Rs. million (a)	Cum. Value of Foreign Equity Approval of value upto Rs. 10 million (b)	B (b) as a % of (a)	Total no. of approvals (c)	No. of Approval of Value upto Rs. 10 million (d)	((d) as a % of (c)
1.	Alternate Renewable Energy	377.3	–	–	4	–	–
2.	Chemical	6795.1	103.239	1.51	137	43	31.3
3.	Electrical & Electronics	21430.6	191.352	0.89	186	83	44.6
4.	Industrial Machinery	332.8	89.144	26.7	38	20	52.6
5.	Mechanical Engineering	3676.1	67.687	1.84	103	34	33.0
6.	Machine Tools	102.0	13.61	13.3	13	6	46.1
7.	Metallurgical	1928.5	62.721	3.25	47	26	55.3
8.	Textile	1843.4	150.171	8.14	28	15	53.5
9.	Transportation	16291.3	40.439	0.24	83	17	20.4

Table 2. (Continued)

S.No.	Sector	Total Value of Foreign Equity Apprd in Rs. million (a)	Cum. Value of Foreign Equity Approval of value upto Rs. 10 million (b)	B (b) as a % of (a)	Total no. of approvals (c)	No. of Approval of Value upto Rs. 10 million (d)	((d) as a % of (c)
10.	Consultancy and other services	34347.6	1110.312	3.23	944	616	65.2
11.	Miscellaneous	20703.1	373.343	1.80	305	159	52.1
	Total	107827.8	2101.128	1.94	1888	1019	53.9

Source: Foreign Collaborations : DSIR, 2002.

Table 3. FDI Approvals with investment up to Rs. 10 m

Year	No. of total FDI approvals A	No. of approvals involving investment upto Rs. 10 m B	$B \times 100$ A
2001	1982	905	45
2002	1966	911	46
2003	1533	884	47
2004	1500	1054	63

Table 4. FDI investment with investment of Rs. 10 m to 50 m

Year	No. of total FDI approvals	No. of approvals with investments between Rs. 10 m to 50 m	$B \times 100$ A
2001	1982	300	16
2002	1966	225	11
2003	1533	247	16
2004	1500	180	12

Table 5. FDI cases with investments less than Rs. 10 mn

Year	Total amount of Approvals Rs. in mn A	Amount approved Rs. in mn B	$B \times 100$ A
2001	2,68,746.71	1872.95	0.69
2002	1,11,397.83	1554.46	1.39
2003	60,421.94	1405.75	2.32
2004	1,05,915.00	1014.00	1.00

Table 6. FDI Approvals in the range Rs. 10mn to Rs. 50mn

Year	Total amount of Approvals Rs. in mn A	Amount of approved Rs. in mn B	B x 100 A
2001	2,68,746.71	6287.18	2.33
2002	1,11,397.83	5308.68	4.76
2003	60,421.94	3708.50	6.13
2004	1,05,915.00	2676.00	4.00

Source: Agarwal S.P., FDI in SMEs in India; International Conference for Development and Revitalisation of SMEs in China, DMU, China, 14th July 2005 (for Table no. 3, 4, 5, and 6)

6. INFRASTRUCTURAL FACILITIES FOR TECHNOLOGY TRANSFER TO SMES IN INDIA

The government has set up an impressive S&T infrastructure in the country that is engaged in technology development and transfer. Some of the components of this infrastructure are described below:

6.1. National R&D Laboratories

There are 12 major scientific agencies in the country, viz. Defence Research Development Organisation (DRDO) with over 50 laboratories; Department of Space (DOS) with around 8 laboratories, Indian Council of Agricultural Research (ICAR) with over 70 laboratories, Department of Atomic Energy (DAE) with around 15 laboratories, Department of Scientific & Industrial Research including Council of Scientific & Industrial Research (CSIR) with 39 laboratories, Ministry of Environment & Forests, Department of Science and Technology (DST) with around 20 scientific institutions, Department of Biotechnology (DBT) with around 6 laboratories, Indian Council of Medical Research (ICMR) with over 25 laboratories, Department of Ocean Development (DOD), Department of Information Technology and Ministry of Non-conventional Energy Sources (MNES). In addition to the R&D laboratories and establishments, there exists a vast network of universities, technical institutions and colleges in the country. There are around 250 universities/deemed universities, including 11 institutions of national importance and around 12,000 colleges.

With R&D being viewed as a business worldwide, it becomes imperative that new ideas and technologies identified in the R&D laboratories are carried forward by technological innovation and piloted into commercial production. Many of the national laboratories have set up their own business development groups for technology transfer to industry, including SMEs. In a most recent example, the Regional Research Laboratory, Thiruvananthapuram, a CSIR laboratory has transferred a pioneering technology for processing fresh spices and botanicals to a company in the south Indian town of Kochi, viz. M/s. Synthite Industrial Chemicals.

There is a lot of potential in India's science and technology institutions for technology transfer to industry. Institutions like the CSIR and the Indian Institute of Science, Bangalore are promoting technopreneurship and they are seeking assistance and tie-ups with Harvard scientists and MIT's Technology Licensing Office in fine tuning their process of licensing technology innovations. MIT's experience in issuing 102 technology licenses based on which 20 companies have been founded can prove to be invaluable to Indian institutions. CSIR has handpicked 40 scientists to become technopreneurs. These scientists are working in areas such as path breaking cancer research, development of a cheap ocular implant, development of a low cost compound used in perfumery and development of a special plant variety that can yield anti-malarials with exciting commercial possibilities.[6]

Besides this, certain specialized agencies have been also set up by the government to facilitate technology transfer and commercialization to industry. One such agency is National Research Development Corporation (NRDC), a public sector enterprise, which is described below.

6.2. NRDC Transforming Innovative Research into Profitable Technology

NRDC is India's premier service enterprise whose business is to be the identifier, the carrier and the pilot of technology transfer. For over forty years, NRDC has played a key role in speeding the commercial applications of research and in effecting the transfer of technology from effecting the transfer of technology from laboratory to enterprise. NRDC guides and assists the entrepreneur in executing his technological business plans. NRDC's extensive network of national and international contacts in scientific bodies, technology transfer agencies, industrial and engineering concerns, and venture-capital providers, has enabled it to act as an effective catalyst translating innovative research into marketable industrial products, processes and services. NRDC works in close conjunction with over 200 national R & D laboratories and has licensed over 2000 technologies for commercial exploitation, of which nearly 1000 are in production with a current annual turnover of about Rs 12,000 million (Rs. 12 billion). Technologies licensed by NRDC cover areas such as chemicals, drugs and pharmaceuticals, food, agro-processing, bio-technology, metallurgy, electronics, instrumentation, building materials, manufacturing techniques and utility processes including pollution control. NRDC is the one-stop provider of comprehensive business services, devoted to satisfying the demanding customer of competitive technology. To this end, NRDC nurtures new ideas and inventions by providing finance and rewards; ensuring intellectual property protection; efficiently effecting transfer of know-how from laboratories to industry; providing access to new technologies from India and abroad; exporting Indian technological expertise and offering an array of technology consultancy services.

6.3. Small Industry Development Organization (SIDO)

Small Industry Development Organization headed by the Development Commissioner of Small Scale Industries, is an apex body for formulating, coordinating, implementing and monitoring policies and programmes for the promotion and development of the small scale industries in the country. It provides a comprehensive range of facilities and services to small scale units through a network of 30 Small Industries Service Institutes (SISIs), 28 Branch SISIs, 7 Field Testing Stations, 4 Regional Testing Centres, 2 Small Entrepreneur Promotion and Training Institutes (SEPTI) and 1 Hand Tool Design Development and Training Centre. For the benefit of Small Scale Industries seeking information about the latest technologies available all over the world, Technology Resource Centres (TRCs) have been set up in all 30 SISIs. These TRCs are acting as an agency for identifying appropriate technology, help in acquiring skills for use of technology, as well as facilitate absorption of technology. The TRC work as a facilitator and enable the small industries to access different web sites for the latest information and help the industry to adopt viable advanced technology suitable to local conditions. There are also a few specialized institutions, like The Central Institute of Tool Design, Hyderabad, The Central Tool Room & Training Centres at Bhubaneswar and Kolkata, Central Tool Room at Ludhiana, 3 Indo-German Tool Rooms at Indore, Aurangabad and Ahmedabad and Indo-Danish Tool Room at Jamshedpur, Institute for Design of Electrical Measuring Instruments (IDEMI), Mumbai, Electronics Service & Training Centre, Ramnagar (Uttaranchal), 2 Central Footwear Training Institutes at Agra and Chennai, 2 Process-cum-Product Development Centres at Agra & Meerut and Fragrance and Flavour Development Centre, Kannauj and Centre for Development of Glass Industry, Ferozabad which provide training and technical services in their respective specified fields.

The Govt. of India gives away National Awards for Research and Development Efforts in the Small Scale Industries to promote the concept of in-house research and development efforts and to strengthen technical soundness and spirit of innovation amongst the units, in the larger interest of overall qualitative development of the Small Scale Industries.

6.4. Small Industry Cluster Development Programme

The Office of the Development Commissioner of Small Scale Industries had launched a scheme on Technology Upgradation and Management Programme called UPTECH in 1998 for cluster of industries, where there is commonality in the method of production, quality control and testing, energy conservation, pollution control etc. among the units (of the cluster). The scheme focused on technology development of the cluster. In view of globalization of economy, small scale sector faces a stiff competition not only on quality and price front but other fronts, like marketing, export, raw material procurement etc. and a collective approach by the SSI units to mitigate the common problems of the cluster have been considered to be effective for cluster development. The scheme has, therefore, been renamed as Small Industry Cluster Development Programme (SICDP) so that it can focus on all the aspects viz marketing, export, study visit, skill upgradation, etc. for development of the cluster in addition to technology as a holistic approach is more appropriate for cluster development. Seventy eight clusters have so far been taken for development under SICDP.

6.5. Infrastructural Facilities of National Small Industries Corporation (NSIC)

NSIC - Technical Service Centres/Extension Service Centres

NSIC - Technical Services Centres / Extension Centres provide valuable technology and common facility support to SSIs. This support is in the form of conventional & hi-tech machining facilities, specialized testing facilities and other quality upgradation services. Services in the area of energy/ environment audit, consultancy for ISO 9000 and preparation of project exports for SSIs are also provided. NSIC-TSCs at New Delhi, Howrah, Rajkot, Chennai and Hyderabad enjoy the status of 'In House R&D Centres' of Department of Scientific and Industrial Research (Ministry of Science & Technology). In order to cater to the needs of SSIs to face the challenges arising due to recent economic & policy changes like lifting of quantity restrictions & globalization, the Technical Centres have taken the challenge head on and started several hi – tech training programmes in the area of CAD/CAM, hydraulic and pneumatic controls etc.

Software Technology Parks

Recognizing the importance of information technology in the globalize economy, NSIC has established two Software Technology Parks (STP) – one at New Delhi in 1995 and second at Chennai in 2001. These two parks are established under the Software Technology Parks of India (STPI) Scheme of Ministry of Information Technology. The STPs provide infrastructural facilities and create conducive business environment for the software exporters. NSIC has created requisite infrastructure in terms of fully built up working space, high speed data communication facilities, business centres, round the clock power backup and other logistics support to the small scale software exporters. In addition to the infrastructural facilities, NSIC also provides value addition services in terms of making the project reports, liaisoning with the authorities of the project, facilitating custom bonding formalities etc. The software enterprises can start the business operations with minimum lead-time. Since, the developed infrastructure is readily available, they also save capital expenditure on creation of such facilities. In NSIC-STP at Okhla, 28 software export units have utilized the facilities since its inception in 1995. Around 10 enterprises grew big and vacated the space. At present, there are 14 units operating in the STP. Chennai STP houses 12 software export units.

Technology Transfer Centre

Technology Transfer Centre at Okhla, Delhi disseminates technological information relevant to the needs of SSIs, facilitates enterprise to enterprise relationships, assists in upgradation of technology and encourages industry – institutional linkages.

6.6. Science and Technology Entrepreneurs Parks (STEPs)

The Science & Technology Entrepreneurs Park (STEP) programme was initiated by Department of Science and Technology (DST) to provide a re-orientation in the approach to innovation and entrepreneurship involving education, training, research, finance, management and the government. A STEP creates the necessary climate for innovation, information exchange, sharing of experience and facilities and opening new avenues for students, teachers, researchers and industrial managers to grow in a trans-disciplinary culture, each understanding and depending on the other's inputs for starting a successful economic venture. STEPs are hardware intensive with emphasis on common facilities, services and relevant equipments.

The major objectives of STEP are to forge linkages among academic and R&D institutions on one hand and the industry on the other and also promote innovative enterprise through S&T persons.

Objectives

- To forge a close linkage between universities, academic and R&D institutions on the one hand and industry on the other.
- To promote entrepreneurship among Science and Technology persons, many of whom were otherwise seeking jobs soon after their graduation.
- To provide R&D support to the small-scale industry mostly through interaction with research institutions.
- To promote innovation based enterprises.

The DST has so far catalysed 15 STEPs in different parts of the country which have promoted nearly 788 units generating annual turnover of around Rs. 130 crores and employment for 5000 persons. More than 100 new products and technologies have been developed by the STEPs / STEP promoted entrepreneurs. In addition, over 11000 persons have been trained through various skill development programmes conducted by STEPs.

6.7. Technology Business Incubators (TBIs)

The need for instruments such as TBI has been recognised the world over for initiating technology led and knowledge driven enterprises. Studies also show that such mechanisms help not only in the growth of technology based new enterprises but also in improving their survival rate substantially (from 30 per cent to over 70 per cent). TBIs also facilitate speedy commercialisation of research outputs. The essential feature of a TBI is that the tenant companies leave the incubator space in 2-3 years.

TBIs are promoted to achieve the following objectives:

- Creation of technology based new enterprises,
- Creating value added jobs & services,
- Facilitating transfer of technology,
- Fostering the entrepreneurial spirit,
- Speedy commercialisation of R&D output,
- Specialised services to existing SMEs.

A scheme on establishment of TBI in and around academic/R&D institutions was initiated by the Department of Science and Technology (DST) during 2000-2001. Under this scheme, grant-in-aid is provided by the Department both on capital and recurring account for a stipulated period. Presently, TBIs are being implemented at 12 locations in the country.

Besides DST, country's leading technological institutes are also adopting the concept of business incubation. IIT Delhi's technology business incubation unit has incubated and spun-off 7-8 technology based firms as commercial enterprises in areas such as IP phones, GIS-based tools, Bluetooth enabled energy meters and sunscreen creams. Another centre at IIT Mumbai, Society for Innovation and Entrepreneurship is facilitating the conversion of research activity into entrepreneurial ventures. Incubates at the centre have set up start-ups dealing with creative ideas portal, wireless gateways and connectivity bridges. IISc's venture with TCS – Advanced Product Design and Prototyping has developed helmets for Indian Air Force pilots and low cost refrigeration unit for motels. IIT Madras has developed "corDECT" - wireless in local loop (WLL) technology and many other telecom related technologies that have led to establishment of 14 start-ups.

6.8. National Automotive Testing and R&D Infrastructure Project (NATRIP)

NATRIP is the largest and one of the most significant initiatives in Automotive sector so far. It represents a unique joining of hands between the Government of India, a number of State Governments and Indian Automotive Industry to create a state of the art Testing, Validation and R&D infrastructure in the country. The Project aims at creating core global competencies in Automotive sector in India and facilitate seamless integration of Indian Automotive industry with the world as also to position the country prominently on the global automotive map.

NATRIP envisages an investment of Rs. 17.18 Billion (about USD 380 million) in setting up, inter alia, independent automotive testing centres within the three automotive hubs in the country, at Manesar in Northern India, Chennai in Southern India and Pune & Ahmednagar in Western India. A world class Proving Ground will be built at Indore in Central India, on 4098 acres of land as a part of the core NATRIP facilities. NATRIP also envisages the setting up of comprehensive Testing and Validation facilities including Field Tracks for Agricultural Tractors, Trailers, Construction Equipments and various other off-road vehicles at Rae Bareilly in Northern India. This centre will house India's first state of the art Road Accident Data Analysis facility. Two specialised Driving Training Centres will be set up at Silchar in North Eastern India (for specialised Hill Area Driving) and Rae Bareilly in Northern India (for specialised Vehicles and Cargo). A model Inspection and Maintenance (I&M) Centre for vehicles will also form part of NATRIP facilities at Silchar.

With the launch of NATRIP, India is set to provide a major fillip to its fast growing Automotive industry and harness India's major strengths in the realm of Automotive Engineering, Information Technology and Electronics by achieving a high degree of convergence. The infrastructure under NATRIP will offer wide spectrum of services for Product Development and Validation, not only to the domestic industry, but also to global Automotive fraternity. The objective is to help India's emergence amongst the strongest hubs for product development in Global automotive landscape.

NATRIP, as a key initiative of the Ministry of Heavy Industries & Public Enterprises, aims to usher India into the group of countries with fully developed automotive industry. Indian Automotive Industry, with a turnover of USD 37 Billion (2005) is growing annually at a rate of 18-20%. It contributes around 17% of national kitty of indirect taxes and provides direct and indirect employment to more than 13 million people (2004). Rapidly increasing mobility needs of more than a billion Indians, coupled with growing demand for quality Automotive products from India in the International markets are driving scales, investments and innovations in Indian Automotive environment. Indian exports have touched USD 3.5 Billion and are growing annually at a rate of 35-40%. However, this growth represents only a fraction of the potential of the Indian Automotive industry. A robust Automotive Testing Infrastructure has been identified as the key driver for tapping this potential. NATRIP is India's response to this felt need.

The investment of Rs. 1718 crore will be funded jointly by the Government and the Industry, over a period of 6 years. The first phase of NATRIP (first 3 years) will focus on building Infrastructure and capabilities for Testing and Validation to meet emerging requirements in line with National Automotive Safety and Emission roadmaps. In the subsequent phase (next 3 years), key 'Centers of Excellence' will be set up to develop national capabilities in frontier automotive technologies. Some of these 'Centers of Excellence' will aim at achieving high degree of convergence of India's strengths in areas like Information Technology, Electronics, Alternative Energy sources, etc.

6.9. Financing Mechanisms for SMEs

The Government has set up a Rs. 1,00,000 million fund for the small scale industry. SIDBI is responsible for operationalizing the fund. The fund is made available to the SSI sector for their technology upgradation and infrastructural needs at 2 % points below the prime lending rate (PLR).

Venture Funds are recognised globally as the most suitable form of providing risk capital for the growth of innovative and high technology businesses. Innovative SME units are expected to play a catalytic role in the post liberalised economic environment in the country. Keeping in view the level of dispensation of venture finance to the SME thus far, Small Industries Development Bank of India has launched SME GROWTH FUND, a new venture capital fund with a large corpus of Rs. 5,000 million, dedicated to the SME sector. The 8-year life Fund is being established with an objective to meet the long-term risk capital requirement of innovative and technology oriented units in this sector. The new Fund with its size of Rs. 5,000 million is a significant milestone. It is a unique initiative sponsored by SIDBI jointly with major public sector banks. The Fund shall invest in domestic SME units having superior growth potential, rapid scalability, a strong committed team and enjoying unique and sustainable long term competitive advantage. The fund will identify unlisted SME entities in various growing sectors such as life sciences, retailing, light engineering, food processing, information technology, infrastructure related to services such as health care, logistics and distributions, etc.

ICICI Venture has become the country's first homegrown private equity investor to touch the $ 1 billion mark in terms of total funds under management. Between 1988 to 2003, ICICI Venture raised $ 600 million across eight funds. In 2004, it launched the $ 240 million India

Advantage Fund and its latest fund is the $200 million India Advantage III. ICICI Venture focuses on Indian companies that want to move up the ladder. It recently concluded a non-equity R&D financing deal with Dr Reddy's Laboratories. ICICI also has Technology Support and Services Programme (TSSP) which has programmes for promotion of collaborative R&D projects like Sponsored Research & Development (SPREAD) programme and Technology Institutions (TI) programme.

Credit Linked Capital Subsidy Scheme (CLCSS)

The Credit linked Capital Subsidy Scheme extends credit to SMEs for technology upgradation. The scheme provides 15 % capital subsidy on the loan in specified products / sub-sectors. The ceiling on the loan amount is Rs. 10 million. SIDBI and NABARD are the nodal agencies for the scheme. In another scheme, cost of acquiring ISO 9000/14001 certification is reimbursed to the eligible SME.

Technology Upgradation Fund Scheme for Textile Industries (TUFS)

TUFS has been launched with a view to sustaining as well as improving the competitiveness and overall long term viability of the textile sector. The scheme intends to provide timely and adequate capital at internationally comparable rates of interest in order to upgrade the textile industry's technology level.

7. CONCLUSIONS AND RECOMMENDATIONS

(i) SMEs will have to integrate with global supply chains. They will have to identify their core areas of strength and concentrate solely on them. For business components falling outside their core areas, they must establish forward and backward linkages to stay competitive.

(ii) Small and medium enterprises will have to adopt a technology strategy which is well integrated with the business strategy to stay competitive in the globalized economy. The technology strategy for the short term could be to access technology from R&D institutions/another company in India or abroad or to do a patent search and license a patented technology for immediate production. The technology strategy for the long term could be to enter into a strategic joint venture with a competitor holding key technology for mutual gains or to develop technology for product innovation, diversification etc. R&D expenditures needs to be increased, and mind set to be more forward looking, with risk taking capacity.

(iii) Though a number of policy measures and infrastructure facilities for technology transfer have been put in place by the Indian Government and its associate agencies, apparently only a small percentage of the 11 million odd SMEs in the country are able to take advantage of them. In order to increase the percentage of beneficiaries, there should be a wide spread publicity of the available technology transfer policies and schemes and the norms for availing the benefits of technology transfer schemes should be further simplified.

(iv) articipation of SMEs in international exhibitions, business delegations and buyer-seller meets must be facilitated to assist them in accessing foreign technology for their production requirements.

(v) FDI limit of 24% equity participation in SMEs need to be liberalized to enable them to attract foreign technology.

(vi) Technology transfer should aim at enhancing the competitiveness of SMEs and they need to be convinced about the benefits of technology transfer. It must be demonstrated to the units that technology will reduce their inventory by a certain percentage, it will reduce their cycle time significantly, it will improve their productivity and quality and also reduce costs.

(vii) Though technology transfer mechanisms exist, technologies do not get transferred at times because they are not packaged properly. Usually, the technologies that are available with the laboratories are not completely ripe for commercialization or the imported technology needs modifications, prior to its implementation. Thus, there is a need to set up specialized agencies that acquire technologies from labs and foreign suppliers, add value to them and then offer a complete technology package to the SMEs. Technology data bases, indigenous and foreign may be set up. The government may encourage access to foreign technologies and participation in trade fairs etc. abroad.

(viii) Innovative mechanisms need to be put in place to promote technology transfer from institutions and R&D establishments. Innovative mechanisms for financing technology transfer need to be evolved. For example, government may consider sharing a certain percentage of cost involved in technology transfer from public funded institutions to industry. Government may also oversee and support commercialization of the technology transferred to industry. Subsequent to successful commercialization, the government may recover its cost to be ploughed back into other similar ventures.

(ix) Banks need to adopt a higher risk taking attitude to fund technology development and commercialization projects of SMEs.

(x) The SMEs will have to establish intense linkages with R&D institutions to bring about adaptations in acquired technology and carry out technology upgradation in the long term to keep pace with rapid technological obsolescence in the globalized economy.

(xi) Innovative SMEs must not loose sight of patenting the value additions that hey bring about in acquired technology and build a patent portfolio in the long run. This would enhance their long term competitiveness and also, build their brand image.Also, patent information may be useful in developing new products and processes.

(xii) Skill upgradation is important for encouraging technology transfer and getting access to foreign technologies or foreign partnerships. Therefore, training etc. needs to be encouraged.

(xiii) There is no clear cut policy for technology transfer to SMEs though embedded technologies are encouraged. New mechanisms such as encouragement to generate intellectual property in academic institutions and innovative start-ups, innovative and intellectual clusters, etc. would accelerate technology transfers in new and emerging areas.

REFERENCES

[1]   Background Paper of CII-Min of SSI "India Global Summit on MSMEs"; 25-26 November, 2005, New Delhi

[2]   S.P. Agarwal; Report on Strategy Development for Enhancing Competitiveness of SMEs based on Technology Capacity Building for UN-ESCAP; November, 2005

[3]   Ashwani Gupta and P.K. Dutta; Paper on "Indian Innovation System – Perspectives and Challenges" in Asia-Pacific Forum on National Innovation Systems (NIS) For High-Level Policy Makers: April 28-29, 2005, New Delhi

[4]   India's S&T Policy 2003

[5]   Annual Report 2004-05 of Ministry of Small Scale Industries

[6]   National Newspaper Dailies:
      – *The Economic Times*
      – *The Financial Express*
      – *Business Standard*
      – *The Hindu Business Line*

[7]   Websites:
      – www.dst.gov.in
      – www.dsir.gov.in
      – www.dbtindia.nic.in
      – www.nrdcindia.com
      – www.sidbi.com
      – www.nsic.com

[8]   Agarwal S.P., FDI in SMEs in India; International Conference for Development and Revitalisation of SMEs in China, DMU, China, 14th July 2005

[9]   Agarwal, S.P., Ashwani Gupta, and G.P. Gandhi; Technology Transfer Trends. The Indian Experience; Asia Pacific Tech. Monitor, APCTT, May – June 2004, 36-41.

In: India: Economic, Political and Social Issues
Editor: Urlah B. Nissam

ISBN: 978-1-60456-509-6
© 2009 Nova Science Publishers, Inc.

Chapter 4

INDIA TRADE BARRIERS AND TRADE SUMMARY

TRADE SUMMARY

The U.S. goods trade deficit with India was $11.7 billion in 2006, an increase of $920 million from $10.8 billion in 2005. U.S. goods exports in 2006 were $10.1 billion, up 26.3 percent from the previous year. Corresponding U.S. imports from India were $21.8 billion, up 16.1 percent. India is currently the 21st largest export market for U.S. goods.

U.S. exports of private commercial services (i.e., excluding military and government) to India were $5.2 billion in 2005 (latest data available), and U.S. imports were $5.0 billion. Sales of services in India by majority U.S.-owned affiliates were $2.2 billion in 2004 (latest data available), while sales of services in the United States by majority India-owned firms were $1.8 billion.

The stock of U.S. foreign direct investment (FDI) in India in 2005 was $8.5 billion (latest data available), up from $7.7 billion in 2004. U.S. FDI in India is concentrated largely in the information, manufacturing and banking sectors.

IMPORT POLICIES

India's tariffs remain high. U.S. producers encounter tariff and non-tariff barriers that impede their exports, despite the government of India's (GOI) economic reform program initiated in 1991. While U.S. exports continued to grow in 2006 – continuing a positive growth trend since 2001 – substantial expansion in bilateral trade will depend on continued and significant additional Indian liberalization.

The GOI has made substantial progress in restructuring tariffs applied to non-agricultural goods. In February 2007, the GOI's 2007-2008 budget proposes to reduce the peak applied duty on most nonagricultural products from 12.5 percent to 10 percent. Despite tariff cuts on these goods, India's maximum (peak) tariff applied to non-agricultural goods has increased substantially over the years. The government applies high tariffs to petrochemicals, automobiles, motorcycles and finished steel products. Also, the U.S. textile industry continues to have concerns about non-transparent applications of tariffs and taxes. India's agricultural tariffs – which are among the highest in the world – remain untouched.

India's simple average applied tariff rate was 27 percent in 2005, including excise taxes. The GOI in February 2007 announced cuts deeper than that level in the basic custom duty on many raw materials and intermediates. For example, polyester fibers, yarn and other raw materials was lowered from 10 percent to 7.5 percent. The GOI also adjusted downward tariffs on chemicals and plastics from 12.5 percent to
7.5 percent.

The GOI assesses a 1 percent customs handling fee on all imports in addition to the applied customs duty. The GOI's 2007-2008 budget proposes to levy an additional education "cess" of 1 percent on top of the 2 percent education fund assessment already levied on all sales, both imported and domestic. The education "cess" is a surcharge applied to nearly all direct and indirect taxes to help finance education. The GOI includes tariffs in calculating the value upon which to assess additional charges, except where specifically exempted. Finally, various states apply local duties within their jurisdictions in many cases. The cumulative effect of these various additional charges renders the effective applied duties substantially higher on retail prices of imported goods.

The United States has actively sought market-opening opportunities in India, both bilaterally and multilaterally in the Doha Development Round. The U.S. Trade Representative (USTR) and India's Minister of Commerce chair the United States-India Trade Policy Forum (TPF) meeting, which was constituted during Prime Minister Sing's visit to Washington in 2005. As part of the United States-India Economic Dialogue, the TPF meets regularly through its five focus groups – agriculture, innovation and creativity (including Intellectual Property Rights), investment, services, and tariff and non-tariff barriers – to discuss the full range of bilateral trade and investment issues.

In the World Trade Organization (WTO), India has bound tariffs in 2006 on 73.8 percent of its tariff lines, an increase from the 68 percent of lines bound in 2005. However, the majority of these bindings exceed India's applied rates of duty. In agriculture, India's WTO bound tariffs range from 100 percent to 300 percent, also higher than the applied rates in many product areas.

For example, India's applied – and WTO bound – base tariff on imports of spirits is 150 percent *ad valorem*. Since 2001, India has applied "additional duties" on imports of wines and spirits, which are assessed on top of the basic customs duty and vary depending on the per-case CIF value of the imported products. In March 2006, India's Finance Ministry established a 4 percent *ad valorem* "extra additional duty" on all imports, including wines and spirits, with a few exceptions. The extra additional duty is applied on top of the basic customs duty and additional duty. The application of the additional and extra additional duties on top of the base tariff yields effective tariff rates on imported spirits that range from 225 percent to 550 percent *ad valorem*. The applied tariff on wines is 100 percent *ad valorem* (the bound rate is 150 percent) and, along with additional and extra additional duties, yield effective tariff rates of 150 percent to 264 percent *ad valorem*. In December 2006, the United States requested to join the European Communities' WTO dispute settlement consultations on India's additional and extra additional duties on wines and spirits. India rejected that request. On March 6, 2007, the United States requested WTO dispute settlement consultations with India over the additional and extra additional duties.

The Indian government publishes tariffs and additional tax rates that apply to imports, but there is no single official publication that includes all information on tariffs, fees and tax rates on imports. The system lacks transparency. Importers must consult separate tariff and excise tax schedules, as well as any applicable additional public notifications and notices, to determine current tariff and tax rates. The rate at which the customs duty is imposed on the goods depends on the classification of the goods determined under the Customs Tariff. The Customs Tariff is generally aligned with the Harmonized System of Nomenclature (HSN). The rate at which the excise duty is imposed on the goods also depends on the classification of the goods under the Excise Tariff, which is primarily based on the HSN. Each Indian state also levies taxes on interstate commerce, which creates additional confusion.

Import Licensing

Importers of vehicles of any type face restrictive and trade-distorting import practices. For example, the GOI requires special licenses for importing motorcycles. These licenses are virtually impossible to obtain. Import licenses for motorcycles are granted only to foreign nationals: (1) permanently residing in India; (2) working in India for foreign firms that hold greater than 30 percent equity; or (3) working at embassies located in India. Certain domestic importers are eligible to import motorcycles without a license but only if these imports are offset by exports attributable to the same importer.

India also maintains a negative import list. The negative list is currently divided into three categories: (1) banned or prohibited items (e.g., tallow, fat, and oils of animal origin); (2) restricted items which require a non-automatic import license (e.g., livestock products, certain chemicals); and (3) "canalized" items (e.g., petroleum products, some pharmaceuticals, and bulk grains) importable only by government trading monopolies subject to cabinet approval regarding timing and quantity.

India has liberalized many restrictions on the importation of capital goods. The government allows imports of second-hand capital goods by the end-users without requiring an import license, provided the goods have a residual life of five years. Refurbished computer spare parts can only be imported if an Indian Chartered Engineer certifies that the equipment retains at least 80 percent of its residual life, while refurbished computer parts from domestic sources are not subject to this requirement.

India requires foreign exporters of unshredded scrap metal to register with the Director General of Foreign Trade (DGFT) in the Indian Department of Commerce to enable such products to enter the Indian market. The registration process has been hampered by inefficiency and a lack of transparency. The United States continues to urge the DGFT to implement a transparent registration system.

Fertilizer Subsidy Regime

The Indian government subsidizes di-ammonium phosphate (DAP) fertilizer. Under the current system, the GOI sets a maximum retail price that can be charged to farmers for DAP. This price is not adequate to cover the cost of producing or importing DAP. The excess costs for domestic producers and importers are subsidized and at different levels that favor domestic DAP over imports. From July 2004 through June 2005, base rate subsidies were equalized but final subsidy amounts continued to disadvantage imports. The disadvantage has limited regular commercial import transactions. In addition to this disadvantage, the current system fixes the subsidy on a retroactive basis and in a non-transparent manner, which in turn acts as a further deterrent for importers. The United States continues to press India to end its costly, trade-distorting treatment of DAP.

Customs Procedures

The GOI appears to apply discretionary customs valuation criteria to import transactions. Valuation procedures allow Customs to reject the declared transaction value of an import when a sale is deemed to involve a reduction from the ordinary competitive price. U.S. exporters have reported that India's customs valuation methodologies do not reflect actual transaction values and effectively increase tariff rates. The United States is working through the WTO Committee on Customs Valuation to obtain further information from India on its valuation methods and will continue to examine the customs valuation procedures for consistency with India's obligations under the WTO Customs Valuation Agreement.

Indian Customs requires extensive documentation, which inhibits the free flow of trade and leads to frequent processing delays. In large part this red tape is a consequence of India's complex tariff structure and multiple exemptions, which may vary according to product, user, or specific Indian export promotion program.

In line with its unofficial policy of revising edible oil reference prices once every 15 days, the Indian government announced reduced tariff values for palm and soybean oils in January 2006. India continues to maintain a reference price system for soybean oil to address alleged under-invoicing. The reference price is the basis upon which India assesses its 45 percent customs duty. When the GOI reference price for soybean oil rises above the transaction price, the effective rate of duty may also increase above India's 45 percent WTO-bound tariff. Although the reviews are done periodically, India has not formally defined this procedure, making it non-transparent and unpredictable. Exports of U.S. crude soybean oil to India are negligible after reaching a peak of $25 million in 2002. The U.S. Government continues to raise this issue with India, but has not received a response from the Indian government that clarifies its policy and the reference price scheme's relationship to India's WTO commitments.

Certain customs procedures impede importation of automotive products. Motor vehicles may be imported through only three specific ports and only from the country of manufacture. Declared transaction values of automotive products may be rejected, insofar as legitimate reductions in the wholesale price of such products are ignored.

Indian Customs has taken the position that certain types of automatic teller machines (ATMs) do not qualify as ATMs and, therefore, are not entitled to duty-free treatment under the WTO Information Technology Agreement.

In 2005, India proposed a Draft Integrated Food Law. U.S. industry remains concerned that, if enacted, the proposed law would provide inadequate due process because it: (1) imposes the burden of proof on the food producer when food products are "seized" by a food inspector; and (2) provides limited procedural options to permit food manufacturers to appeal inspector decisions.

STANDARDS, TESTING, LABELING AND CERTIFICATION

The GOI has identified over 100 specific commodities (including food preservatives and additives, milk powder, infant milk foods, certain types of cement, household and similar electrical appliances, gas cylinders, tires, and multi-purpose dry cell batteries) that the Bureau of Indian Standards (BIS) must certify before the products are allowed to enter the country. A system now exists by which foreign companies can receive automatic certification for products made outside India, provided BIS has first inspected and licensed the production facility (at the manufacturer's expense). Licensing fees include the cost of the initial inspector's visit and tests, an annual fee of approximately $2,000 and a marking fee that ranges from 0.2 percent to 1 percent of the value of certified goods imported into or produced in India.

In 2004, Indian Customs began to require registration or an exemption certificate for imported boric acid. The Ministry of Agriculture's Central Insecticides Board and Registration Committee has not published adequate information on the criteria and procedures for obtaining this documentation. Imports of boric acid are, therefore, effectively blocked. Indian government rulemaking has been *ad hoc* and confusing. India may be the only country that requires registration of boric acid intended for non-insecticide use. U.S. industry is required to register, although 90 percent of all boric acid imports into India are for non-insecticide uses (such as glassmaking) and should qualify for an exemption. India's boric acid producers are not subject to the same requirements. The U.S. Government has raised this issue with the GOI on numerous occasions, but India has taken little action to address the concerns except to web-post general contact information indicating which ministries are responsible for issuing no-objection certificates to import non-insecticidal boric acid, based on the end use of the product.

The U.S. Government is increasingly concerned over India's failure to notify certain technical regulations to the WTO. India's procedures for establishing vehicle emissions standards, for example, are vague and non-transparent. The emissions standards seem to favor small displacement motorcycles that are primarily manufactured by Indian producers. Even the latest low-emission technology used by U.S. manufacturers of large motorcycles – which are not manufactured in India – fails to meet India's prohibitive requirements. The U.S. Embassy and private industry have sought to convince the GOI that very stringent emissions standards for large motorcycles already widely in use in many countries (e.g., the United States or European Union), address India's environmental concerns.

In bilateral and multilateral forums, the U.S. Government has discussed with, and raised concerns about, the Indian government's use and implementation of technical regulations, standards and conformity procedures. For example, the United States raised concerns about India's implementation in 2006 of new regulatory requirements for medical devices. While welcoming regulations that improve product safety and effectiveness, U.S. companies report that the "guidelines" are causing confusion, and they would benefit from greater clarity and consistency with international standards and practice.

The GOI is considering making mandatory a new certification system for tires. Industry alleges that this would require, among other things, foreign tire manufacturers to retest their tires in India, subject them to higher licensing fees than domestic manufacturers, and emboss the logo of the BIS along with an approval number to gain access to the Indian market. Tire industries in the United States, the European Community, and Japan have raised concerns about this new measure unnecessarily restricting trade by requiring redundant testing, labeling and conformity assessment, which significantly increases costs to tire manufacturers. The U.S. Government conveyed industry's concerns bilaterally to India's Ministry of Commerce and BIS. Additionally, the United States raised the issue before the WTO Technical Barriers to Trade Committee, along with the European Community and Korea.

The state of Maharashtra's Food and Drug Administration (FDA) has tried to restrict sales of dietary supplements in tablet or capsule form to pharmacies by reclassifying such products from foods to drugs. An interim stay order issued by the Maharashtra High Court has prevented implementation of the Maharashtra FDA's measure. India also enacted the Food and Safety Standards law that U.S. companies' hope will clarify the legal status of dietary supplements. It is still unclear which ministry will be responsible for implementing the law.

In September 2005, as part of the U.S.-India Commercial Dialogue, officials of the U.S. Government and the Indian government initiated a Standards Dialogue Working Group to seek transparency and understanding of how standards impact upon our bilateral commerce. Three sessions of the dialogue were held in 2005, and several more meetings were held in 2006. More Commercial Dialogue sessions are anticipated in 2007.

Sanitary and Phytosanitary (SPS) Measures

The U.S. Government has raised concerns with the GOI regarding India's failure to notify certain SPS measures to the WTO. Bilateral technical level discussions within the Trade Policy Forum's Agriculture Focus Group are ongoing and have resulted in long-term agreements to allow continued entry for key U.S. export commodities such as almonds. The U.S. Government continues to impress upon India the need to base its SPS measures on science, including those affecting almonds, apples, bovine genetics, dairy products, pulses, poultry, pet food, specific pathogen free eggs, forest products, and food derived from biotechnology.

The U.S. Government calls for establishing food standards on the basis of risk analysis and strongly recommends that the results of a risk assessment must be taken into consideration in risk management decisions. The U.S. objects to India's use of undefined principles, which can result in an unscientific application of risk management. The end result can potentially block trade in food and agricultural products.

GOI implementation of the "Plant Quarantine (Regulation of Import into India) Order, 2003" and its amendments, prior to notifying them to the WTO SPS Committee, threatens U.S. exports of U.S. pulses, fresh fruits and vegetables, among others. Through substantial effort, the U.S. Department of Agriculture has maintained market access for these products, but such access is continually under threat from opaque and unscientific regulations.

The Indian government has implemented several sanitary restrictions that do not appear to be based on Office of International Epizootics (OIE) and CODEX recommendations. The OIE and CODEX are the international standard setting bodies for animal health issues and food products, respectively, recognized in the WTO Sanitary and Phytosanitary Agreement. Such restrictions have unduly restricted Indian imports of poultry and poultry products, pet food, bovine genetics, and dairy products.

In the absence of a transparent policy framework for assessing the safety of biotechnology commodities and foods, the GOI decision-making process is slow, non-transparent and arbitrary. Meanwhile, Indian researchers themselves are engaged in the domestic development of agricultural products derived from biotechnology such as mustard seed, potatoes, tomatoes, cabbage, cauliflower, chilies, groundnuts, and rice. They, too, have expressed frustrations regarding the approval process. The GOI reports that it is currently reviewing its policy for evaluating the safety of foods made using biotechnology.

On August 24, 2006, the government enacted an integrated food law, which is called the "Food Safety and Standards Act, 2006." This new legislation attempts to consolidate the existing multitude of laws and regulations governing the food and food-processing sectors. It also establishes a Food Safety and Standards Authority (FSSA). The FSSA will be responsible for establishing food safety standards for packaged and processed foods and regulating India's manufacturing storage, distribution, sale, and import sectors. Reportedly, under the FSSA's authority, all existing regulations, including PFA Rules (1955), EPA Rules (1989), and Plant Quarantine (2003), would be repealed with a view toward adopting international norms and food regulatory systems. At this time, it is unclear which Ministry will house the FSSA.

GOVERNMENT PROCUREMENT

India is not a signatory to the WTO Agreement on Government Procurement. Indian government procurement practices and procedures are non-transparent. Foreign firms rarely win Indian government contracts due to the preference afforded to Indian state-owned enterprises in the award of government contracts and the prevalence of such enterprises. The Purchase Preference Policy (PPP) applied by government enterprises and government departments gives preference to any state-owned enterprise that makes an offer that is within 10 percent of the lowest bid. The GOI renewed this policy for three years, until March 31, 2008, with some modifications.

EXPORT SUBSIDIES

The tax exemption for profits from export earnings was phased out over a five-year period that ended in March 2005. Tax holidays continue for Export Oriented Units and exporters in Special Economic Zones. In addition to these programs, India continues to maintain several duty drawback programs that appear to allow for drawback in excess of duties levied on imported inputs. India also provides pre-shipment and post-shipment export financing to exporters at a preferential rate. India also provides incentives to its textile industry through several programs, such as the Technology Upgradation Fund Scheme (TUFS) and the Scheme for Integrated Textile Parks (SITP). India has not submitted a notification to the WTO Committee on Subsidies and Countervailing Measures since 2001.

Intellectual Property Rights (IPR) Protection

India amended its patent laws effective January 1, 2005. Large-scale copyright piracy, especially in the software, optical media, and publishing industries, continues to be a major problem. The United States retained India on the "Priority Watch List" as part of the 2006 Special 301 review. These issues are discussed in the Trade Policy Forum's Innovation and Creativity Focus Group.

Patents

The amended patent law extends product patent protection to pharmaceuticals and agricultural chemicals. While a positive step, these changes do not address several important weaknesses in India's patent law. For example, the new law does not clarify some ambiguities regarding the scope of patentable inventions. There is also a large backlog in pending patent applications, resulting in long waiting periods for patent approval. The GOI is currently reviewing legislation and implementing regulations to address these deficiencies.

Additionally, the U.S. Government is aware of growing concerns by some pharmaceutical companies that the application of the new pre-grant opposition rules and post-grant challenge opportunity impede timely grant of patent applications for new compounds and protection once granted. The law also contains ambiguities concerning the enforcement of patents issued from mailbox applications.

Indian law does not provide for adequate protection against unfair commercial use of test or other data that companies submit in order to obtain government marketing approval for their pharmaceutical or agricultural chemical products. The GOI currently is preparing a report that will make a recommendation on adopting data protection legislation for submission to Parliament in 2007. Without specific protection against unfair commercial use of clinical test data, companies in India are able to copy certain pharmaceutical products and seek immediate government approval for marketing based on the original developer's data. Recognizing the role that effective data protection plays in fostering innovation and investment, a small but growing domestic Indian constituency, comprised of Indian pharmaceutical companies, technology firms, and educational and research institutions, favors changes to improve protection of data.

Copyrights

India's copyright laws need updating and enforcement is weak. The GOI has proposed amendments that would update the copyright laws to address issues related to the Internet and digital works. However, the proposed amendments have some deficiencies. For example, the law does not appear to provide adequate legal protection and effective legal remedies against circumvention of effective technological protection measures. The GOI is not a party to either the 1996 WIPO Copyright Treaty (WCT) or the WIPO Performances and Phonograms Treaty (WPPT).

Piracy of copyrighted materials (primarily software, films, popular fiction works and certain textbooks) remains a problem for both U.S. and Indian producers. Costs to the U.S. industry amounted to nearly $440 million in 2005. Pirated semiconductors are often sold in violation of copyright and semiconductor mask laws. India has not adopted an optical disc law to deal with optical media piracy, although inter-ministerial consultations to examine whether optical disk legislation is necessary are now underway. Classification of copyright and trademark infringements as "cognizable offenses" has expanded police search and seizure authority. The law provides for minimum criminal penalties, including mandatory minimum jail terms, though these penalties are not often implemented effectively.

The establishment of a Copyright Enforcement Advisory Council with responsibility for policy development and coordination, as well as the initiation of a program for training police officers and prosecutors concerned with enforcement of copyright laws, has not been vigorously pursued. Due to backlogs in the court system and documentary and other procedural requirements, few cases recently have been prosecuted. U.S. and Indian industries report that piracy levels in all sectors remain high.

Cable television piracy continues to be a significant problem, with estimates of tens of thousands of cable operators who operate without a license in India. Copyrighted U.S. product also is transmitted without authorization by licensed cable operators often using pirated videocassettes, video compact discs (VCDs), or DVDs as source materials. This has had a significant detrimental effect on all motion picture market segments in India – theatrical, home video, and television. For instance, pirated videos are available in major cities before their local theatrical release. While noting pockets of positive movement, the United States continues to press for adequate and effective copyright protection.

Enforcement

India's criminal justice system does not effectively support the protection of intellectual property. India's criminal IPR enforcement regime, including border protection against counterfeit and pirated goods, remains weak. There have been few reported convictions for copyright infringements resulting from raids, including raids against repeat offenders. Adjudication of cases is extremely slow. Police action against pirates of motion pictures has improved since 2004. Obstruction of raids, leaks of confidential information, delays in criminal case preparation, and the lack of adequately trained officials have further hampered the criminal enforcement process.

Amendments to the Code of Civil Procedure are being considered that would require civil cases to be completed within one year. These amendments may provide more expeditious disposition of the civil cases in Indian courts.

SERVICES BARRIERS

Indian government entities have a strong ownership presence in some major services industries such as banking and insurance. Nevertheless, private firms play a preponderant or exclusive role in a number of rapidly growing parts of the services sector, including the information technology sector, advertising, the professions, car rental, and a wide range of business consulting services. There is a growing public awareness of India's potential as a major services exporter and increasing demand for a more open services market. While India has submitted an initial offer to provide further services liberalization in the WTO Doha Round, the offer does not remove existing limitations in such key sectors as distribution, telecommunications, financial services and the professions. The United States will continue to press India bilaterally in the Trade Policy Forum's Services Focus Group and at the WTO to open its services markets.

Insurance

The Insurance Regulatory and Development Authority (IRDA) law opened India's insurance market to private participation with a limit on foreign equity of 26 percent of paid-up capital. In addition, all partners must divest ownership stakes to a maximum of 26 percent within ten years of the joint venture's formation. In July 2004, the GOI announced its intention to amend the IRDA law to increase that cap to 49 percent. However, opposition from Leftist parties has thus far prevented the GOI from allowing greater foreign participation in the insurance sector.

Banking

Foreign banks may operate in India through one of three channels: a direct branch, a wholly-owned subsidiary, or through a stake in a private Indian bank. However, no foreign bank may purchase more than 5 percent of an Indian private bank without approval of the Reserve Bank of India (RBI), and no non-bank, foreign or domestic, may purchase more than 10 percent of such banks without RBI approval. All foreign stakes, taken together, cannot exceed 74 percent of the capital of an Indian private bank. Although India has opened up to privately-held banks, most Indian banks are government-owned, and entry of foreign banks remains highly regulated. State-owned banks hold roughly 80 percent of the assets of the banking system, although private banks are growing rapidly.

The RBI has granted operating approval to 31 new foreign banks or bank branches since issuing new guidelines in 1993. As of January 2007, there were 29 foreign banks with 255 branch offices operating in India. Under India's branch authorization policy, foreign banks are required to bring in an assigned capital of $25 million at the time of the opening of their first branch and also are required to submit their internal branch expansion plans on an annual basis. Five U.S. banks now have a total of 16 branches in India. They operate under restrictive conditions including directed lending and asset allocation requirements. Their ability to expand organically is severely limited by non-transparent quotas on branch office expansion and the granting of licenses by the RBI. Under its WTO commitments, India pledges to grant 12 new foreign branch office licenses annually, but according to Indian government sources, the GOI issued 20 licenses in 2006. In contrast, domestic private Indian banks received 100 branch office licenses in 2006. Foreign banks are allowed to establish wholly-owned subsidiaries but must divest their ownership stakes down to 26 percent by 2009, making this option largely unattractive. As a result, there are no wholly-owned subsidiaries of foreign banks in India.

Foreign ownership of the banking system is capped by law at 15 percent. Aggregate foreign direct investment (FDI), foreign institutional investment (FII) or portfolio investment and investments by nonresident Indians is capped at 49 percent (up to 74 percent with permission of a bank's Board). Ownership by foreign individuals is capped at 10 percent. In addition, voting rights in a local bank are capped at 10 percent for all aggregate foreign investors.

Audiovisual and Communications Services

The Indian government has removed most barriers to the import of motion pictures, although U.S. companies have experienced difficulty in importing film/video publicity materials and are unable to license movie-related merchandise due to royalty remittance restrictions.

Entertainment taxes on motion pictures are estimated on a countrywide basis by U.S. industry at 35 percent to 40 percent of the admission price. Such taxes vary by state, from 15 percent to over 100 percent. Some states charge zero or lower tax rates on films in the local language than on films in other languages.

In March 2004, in the face of considerable distributor and consumer resistance, as well as confusion surrounding pricing issues and other rules, the GOI suspended implementation of the Conditional Access System (CAS) for cable television. However, CAS was implemented, in accordance with a Delhi High Court Order, on January 1, 2007. The CAS requires television subscribers to install set-top-box decoders to view premium channels. By providing tighter regulation of the cable industry as a whole, CAS is expected to help reduce the problem of pirated broadcasts.

The government of India FDI of up to 49 percent in Indian cable networks and companies that uplink from India. Total foreign investment in "direct-to-home" (DTH) broadcasting has been restricted to 49 percent, with an FDI ceiling of 20 percent on investments by broadcasting companies and cable companies. At present, news channels are permitted to have up to 26 percent foreign equity investment. They must also ensure that a dominant Indian partner holds at least 51 percent equity. Operational control of the editorial content must be in Indian hands. The Indian government has also announced restrictive minimum capitalization requirements. In addition, all pay television content providers are required to make their content available to all cable and satellite television system operators; and content providers must give 30 day public notification before terminating their signals to non-paying system operators.

In November 2005, the Ministry of Information and Broadcasting announced its "Policy Guidelines for Downlinking of Television Channels" – ostensibly to guard against harmful content – that include major new restrictions on foreign pay-television channels doing business in India. These channels are received through cable television systems that reach 62 million Indian households, mainly in urban areas, and also through direct-to-home satellite services now coming online. These regulations, if left unchanged, will deter future investment by non-Indian broadcasters by imposing new, onerous bureaucratic processes, fees, and litigation expenses; extracting new taxation; threatening revenues from, and protection of, purchased rights for broadcasting programs; and restricting India-directed content, news, and advertising.

Accounting

Only graduates of an Indian university can qualify as professional accountants in India. Foreign accounting firms can practice in India if their home country provides reciprocity to Indian firms. Internationally recognized firm names may not be used, unless they are comprised of the names of proprietors or partners or a name already in use in India. This limitation applies to all but the two U.S. accounting firms that were established prior to the imposition of this rule. The Institute of Chartered Accountants of India (ICAI) continues to ban the use of logos of accounting firms. Only firms established as a partnership may provide financial auditing services. Foreign accountants may not be equity partners in an Indian accounting firm.

Construction, Architecture and Engineering

Many construction projects are offered only on a non-convertible rupee payment basis. Only government projects financed by international development agencies permit payments in foreign currency. Foreign construction firms are not awarded government contracts unless local firms are unable to perform the work. Foreign firms may only participate through joint ventures with Indian firms.

Legal Services

India requires that anyone wishing to practice law must enroll as a member of the Bar Council, and if that person happens to be a foreign national, then he must belong to a country that allows Indian nationals reciprocal rights to practice in their country. FDI is not permitted in this sector, and international law firms are also not authorized to open offices in India. Foreign services providers may be engaged as employees or consultants in local law firms, but they cannot sign legal documents, represent clients, or be appointed as partners. India has not made any offers for opening up the legal services sector at the WTO. In 2006, the U.S. Government and the Indian government announced the formation, under the Trade Policy Forum, of a bilateral Legal Services Working Group to promote greater cooperation between U.S. and Indian lawyers and to address market access issues.

Telecommunications

India has taken positive steps towards liberalizing, and introducing private investment and competition in, its telecommunications services market. Concerns remain regarding India's weak multilateral commitments in basic and value-added telecommunications services and the apparent bias of telecommunications policy towards government-owned services providers. Despite many pro-competitive recommendations the telecommunications regulator proposes after a process of public consultations, the Department of Telecommunications (DOT) often delays adoption of those recommendations or rejects them without adequate explanation.

India's national telecommunications policy allows private participation in the provision of all types of telecommunications services. In November 2005, foreign equity limits were raised from 49 percent to 74 percent for National and International Long Distance (NLD/ILD) services. However, inter-ministerial differences related to the implementing regulations have prevented companies from taking advantage of the market opening. Thus, while companies may obtain a license for NLD and/or ILD services, the absence of implementing regulations causes a great deal of uncertainty in the market. The GOI has proposed new requirements on how international networks are managed in India, which U.S. operators believe seriously impede their ability to do business. In the face of widespread complaints, the GOI agreed to delay implementation of these rules for a third time (until early 2007) while it finds a solution to address industry concerns. The U.S. Government is currently confirming reports that the GOI has taken steps to mitigate industry concerns.

Competitive carriers have expressed concerns about the neutrality and fairness of government policy. The GOI retains a significant ownership stake and interest in the financial health of three telecommunications firms, all of which formerly enjoyed monopoly status in their areas of operation. The government holds a 26 percent interest in the international carrier, VSNL; a 56 percent interest in MTNL, which primarily serves the Delhi and Mumbai metropolitan areas; and a 100 percent interest in BSNL, which provides domestic services throughout the rest of India.

U.S. telecommunications companies have complained about the restrictive polices adopted by incumbent Indian international service provider VSNL on international submarine cable access and landing stations in India. U.S. companies have requested that the Indian government intervene to ensure that VSNL makes available submarine cable capacity to other suppliers and provides access to, and use of, cable landing stations on a reasonable and non-discriminatory basis. In December 2005, the Telecommunications Regulatory Authority of India (TRAI) issued recommendations in its "Measure to Promote Competition in International Private Leased Circuits in India," which were adopted by the Department of Telecommunications (DOT) in late 2006. USTR is encouraged that the DOT finally adopted the recommendations, but quick implementation by TRAI will be important to ensure that U.S. carriers enjoy equal access to essential facilities in India. If adopted, these recommendations would potentially resolve many of the U.S. telecommunications companies' problems in this market.

India's Access Deficit Charge ("ADC") regime disproportionately impacts consumers making international calls to India. India's telecommunications regulator, TRAI, implemented the ADC in 2003 in relation with its Telecommunications Interconnection Usage Charge ("IUC") Regulation. However, the ADC is not an "interconnection charge," but rather, a supplemental collection to subsidize socially desirable services and a component of India's overall universal service regime.

There have been longstanding concerns with the ADC, and in particular with the high ADC applied to inbound international long distance traffic, which is currently twice the level of the ADC for outbound international calls. The ADC paid on domestic calling in India is a mere fraction of these amounts.

Although modifications in the ADC rules in February 2006 brought significant reductions in the ADC rates for international calls, India continues to place an unreasonable and discriminatory ADC burden on foreign international service providers and their customers making calls to India. India has stated that the ADC will be cut in proportion to a glide path which allows for the ADC to enter a sunset regime in 2008. The U.S. Government will continue to monitor this issue.

Though Voice over Internet Protocol (VoIP) services were legalized in India in 2002, one U.S. trade association reports that certain restrictions imposed by TRAI on the connection of the services to a PSTN, as well as non-industry standard quality of service requirements developed by TRAI have hampered the ability of companies to expand the provision of this service in India.

U.S. satellite operators have long complained about the closed and protected satellite services market in India. For many services, specific preferences are granted to those using Indian satellites over those seeking to use a foreign satellite system, even though current Indian regulations do not preclude the use of foreign satellites. In practice, for most services, including domestic VSAT services, domestic television distribution and Direct-to-Home (DTH) television services, foreign satellite capacity must be provided through the Indian Space and Research Organization (ISRO). That is, the foreign operator must sell its capacity to ISRO, a direct competitor of the foreign operator, who then resells it to the customer. This middleman scenario raises a number of concerns: first, it creates additional costs for the consumer that pays a markup added by ISRO (the amount of which varies); second, it allows ISRO to negotiate the terms under which the foreign satellite capacity will be provided, with the goal (explicitly stated at times) of moving the service to one of ISRO's satellites once capacity is available; and third, the market grows at the rate determined by ISRO. Finally, U.S. satellite operators have said that the policy and practice involved in selling satellite services in India is opaque and confusing.

In 2004, TRAI recommended that India adopt an "open skies" policy and allow competition in the satellite services market. Prior to that date, India had already instituted a partial open skies policy with respect to international VSAT connections to the U.S. Internet Backbone for Indian ISPs. However, to date, the further liberalization proposed by the TRAI recommendations has not been adopted by the government of India, and likely faced resistance from ISRO for protectionist reasons.

Distribution Services

The retail sector in India is largely closed to foreign investment. In January 2006 the GOI began allowing foreign direct investment in single-brand retail stores, subject to a foreign equity cap of 51 percent. Foreign direct investment in multi-brand retail outlets is not permitted. With regard to directly selling, current Indian law does not sufficiently differentiate between legitimate direct selling operations and pyramid schemes.

Postal and Express Delivery

In 2006, India's Department of Post made public a draft of the India Post Office (Amendment) Bill 2006. The draft bill updates the 1898 Post Office Act but also includes provisions with potentially harmful effects for the operations of private express delivery companies. The key issues of concern to U.S. industry are: (1) the draft bill includes a provision requiring all registered service providers to contribute to financing the regulator's universal service obligation; (2) the postal monopoly would be expanded by providing the Indian Postal Department the exclusive right to carry all "letters" up to 300 grams; (3) the bill would require registration of companies carrying anything categorized as a "postal article," effectively placing the express industry under the authority of the postal regulator, rather than an independent body; and (4) the bill would impose limits on foreign investment and might force foreign-owned express companies to divest their existing operations in India. The U.S. Government continues to encourage the GOI to strike these problematic provisions from any final postal reform legislation as currently drafted.

Education

A Group of Ministers recommended to the Indian Cabinet in November 2006 that it introduce legislation in parliament that would allow foreign universities to establish campuses in India.

INVESTMENT BARRIERS

Equity Restrictions

Most sectors of the Indian economy are now at least partially open to foreign investment, with certain exceptions. The Indian government continues to prohibit or severely restrict FDI in certain politically sensitive sectors, such as agriculture, retail trading, railways, and real estate. At the same time, the GOI has liberalized other aspects of foreign investment and eliminated various government approvals. Automatic FDI approval in many industries, including bulk manufacturing activities, is now allowed while some sectors still require government approval.

The Indian government's stringent and non-transparent regulations and procedures governing local shareholding inhibit inward investment and increase risk to new entrants. Foreign purchaser attempts to acquire 100 percent ownership of a locally traded company, permissible in principle, faces regulatory hurdles that render 100 percent ownership unobtainable under current practice. Price control regulations have undermined incentives for foreign investors to increase their equity holdings in India. Some companies report forced renegotiation of contracts in the power sector to accommodate government changes at the state and central levels. Press Note 18, promulgated in 1998 by the Ministry of Industry, poses major impediments to investment in India by requiring prior approval of the Indian party to a joint venture before the foreign partner can pursue other investment opportunities in

India. This provision was widely abused, holding foreign partners hostage, even for failed joint ventures. In January 2005, the GOI partially lifted Press Note 18 by eliminating its application to all new joint ventures and relaxing the hold local firms have on the future business plans of foreign partners for existing joint ventures.

Investment Disputes

There has been significant progress toward resolving several payment disputes that American power sector investors have with the State of Tamil Nadu. The GOI, which has limited jurisdiction over commercial disputes involving matters under state jurisdiction, has been helpful in convincing Tamil Nadu to settle these commercial disputes. The United States continues to urge the GOI that in order to create an attractive and reliable investment climate, India and its political subdivisions need to provide a secure legal and regulatory framework for the private sector, as well as institutionalized dispute resolution mechanisms to expedite resolution of commercial issues.

ANTICOMPETITIVE PRACTICES

India suffers from a slow bureaucracy and regulatory bodies that reportedly apply monopoly and fair trade regulations selectively. With little or no fear of government action and with a clogged court system where cases linger for years, Indian firms face few if any disincentives to engage in anticompetitive business practices.

OTHER BARRIERS

India has an unwritten policy that favors counter trade (a form of trade in which imports and exports are linked in individual transactions). The Indian Minerals and Metals Trading Corporation is the major counter trade body, although the State Trading Corporation also handles a small amount of counter trade. Private companies also are encouraged to use counter trade. Global tenders usually include a clause stating that, all other factors being equal, preference will be given to companies willing to agree to counter trade. The exact nature of offsetting exports is unspecified, as is the export destination. The Indian government does try, nonetheless, to eliminate the use of re-exports in counter-trade.

India's medicines policy is of concern to U.S. pharmaceutical companies. While the scope of the rigid government-controlled pricing system has been reduced, final steps to eliminate it have stalled.

Some politicians and GOI officials continue to call for expanding price controls as the preferred means to confront inflationary trends. The GOI is currently reviewing proposed legislation that would significantly expand price controls over medicines. Indian states fail to apply consistently certain national laws and regulations. This creates uncertainty for U.S. companies exporting to, and investing in, India. U.S. companies affected by such inconsistency include: cable television content providers of programming subject to conditional access system rules and distilled spirits producers who face non-uniform state-level taxes despite the national government's directive to harmonize such taxes. In addition, less than universal adoption of a state-level value added tax by all Indian states and conflicting regulations continue to hamper the free flow of goods within India.

India has continued to apply aggressively its antidumping law. During the past year for which WTO statistics are available, India initiated 36 (highest among all WTO Members) antidumping cases and imposed 14 (fourth highest among all WTO Members) antidumping measures. India's new investigations focused largely on plastics and textiles, and only one of these initiations involved U.S. exports. India's implementation of its antidumping regime has raised concerns in key areas such as transparency, due process and notification.

The United States will continue to seek clarification and address concerns both bilaterally and multilaterally. In September 2004, the United States participated in a technical exchange with Indian antidumping administrators to obtain a better understanding of India's trade remedies laws and their compliance with India's WTO obligations. The United States and India have agreed within the context of the U.S.-India Commercial Dialogue to continue these discussions on trade remedy issues and are in the process of scheduling another technical exchange.

In: India: Economic, Political and Social Issues
Editor: Urlah B. Nissam
ISBN: 978-1-60456-509-6
© 2009 Nova Science Publishers, Inc.

Chapter 5

MATERNITY AND IDENTITY AMONG ETHNICALLY INDIAN IMMIGRANT WOMEN IN MELBOURNE, AUSTRALIA

Natasha Maharaj

INTRODUCTION

As I shared the news of my own pregnancy, my research participants, now my friends, immediately gave me advice on ways to abate my morning sickness, on what to eat and what not to eat, and on how much rest I should be getting during the first few 'fragile' months. My colleagues and fellow students, many mothers themselves, reacted quite differently. While they shared in my excitement, they did not automatically deliver the pregnancy care instructions that my Indian friends relayed to me with authority and importance. Such support is expected in Indian culture, even if unsolicited. It is given without hesitation by all mothers to any mother to be. This striking difference reminded me of one of my greatest needs, and one of my clearest observations of my participants: the strength of female familial support networks.

The distinction between Australians and Indians appears stereotypical: Australians minding their own business and Indians minding everyone else's. It highlights the incongruence of world views and cultural attitudes, emphasising ethnic or cultural differences and identity (Dasgupta, 1998). This incongruence can cause difficulties in acculturating, as immigrants negotiate the values and norms of the host society and adapt to new ways of life. My own desire to have family around to guide and nurture me through pregnancy and early motherhood mimics those of the women in my study, for whom the familiarity of culture and tradition brings comfort and reassurance, while also providing the support and care that is paramount at this time. Women, traditionally the keepers of culture, continue Indian customs relating to mother and infant care upon immigration, designating senior women in the family most significant in the transfer of culture (Mani, 1992; Tummala-Narra, 2004).

The reproduction of customs and rituals by the women's female familial support network allows for a reiteration of identity for immigrants, as they are constantly reminded of their culture through the various traditions surrounding pregnancy, birth and early motherhood. This solidifies their role and place in the family as 'mother', and in the host society as 'Indian'. The Indian community, a minority distinguishable from the Anglo-Australian majority, has the opportunity to articulate its ethnic and cultural identity through this process of mothering (Dasgupta, 1998). Mothers and mothers-in-law play important roles in their daughters' and daughters'-in-law mothering, in the retention of cultural knowledge, and in the reaffirmation of identity. Daughters will be expected to do the same eventually for the following generation, as Dasgupta (1998) illustrates for daughters of Indian immigrants in the United States, who maintain ethnic or cultural identity by retaining certain values and behaviours.

In this chapter, I outline my research among the Indian diaspora in Australia. I describe the traditions of the homeland surrounding care of the infant and the mother and amongst the study population in Melbourne. Two case studies illustrate both ends of the spectrum of mother and infant care and the negotiation of this within a cross-cultural context, demonstrating the diversity that exists intraculturally. I conclude by discussing how early motherhood is a vehicle for the reiteration of cultural knowledge and identity among ethnically Indian immigrants, and how this has implications for health and social care.

The research on which I draw is an urban ethnography of early motherhood, immigration and identity. It was conducted in various areas of metropolitan Melbourne with immigrant women who identified as ethnically Indian. The participants were born in India, Fiji, Britain and South Africa. Women were expecting a child, gave birth and weaned during the course of this study. All were from middle-class backgrounds; the majority had a tertiary qualification and about half were in paid employment. The study was conducted with 12 case studies, through participant observation and in-depth interviews with women and their families, in their homes, over a period of one year. All women were recruited from Indian obstetricians during the provision of antenatal care, and all gave birth in either public or private hospitals.

I am also ethnically Indian, an immigrant and new mother. Born in South Africa, my family immigrated to New Zealand when I was 13; I migrated to Australia at the age of 26 to pursue my doctorate. My positioning in this work is therefore not only as a researcher, but an active member of the diaspora, and hence, literally participant-observer (Dasgupta, 1998). The perspectives I present are personal as well as researched; I am an 'insider' endeavouring to take a critical look at my own position in society and the 'instrument' through which the subjective experiences and understandings of my participants are interpreted and analysed.

THE HISTORY OF INDIAN IMMIGRATION IN AUSTRALIA

Indian immigration to Australia began in the early nineteenth century. This chiefly comprised indentured labourers ('coolies'); the first party of 41, mainly from northeast India, arrived in New South Wales in 1837. Although this trade appeared to come to an abrupt end in 1839 with the enacting of legislation in India prohibiting coolie emigration, small shipments of labourers continued in the 1840s and 1850s (Rajendra, 1994). In the late 19th century, Queensland and South Australia attempted to reintroduce coolie emigration, but were unsuccessful due to continued restrictions by the Indian Government. Some still arrived under some form of unofficial or disguised indenture system, mainly from Punjab. The Punjabis living in Gordon Vale, Queensland and Woolgoolga on the north coast of New South Wales, form the largest groups of pioneer Indians in Australia (Rajendra, 1994).

In the late 1890s, the introduction of legislation excluding Asians, Africans and Pacific Islanders from Australia prevented the immigration of large numbers of Indians. The Immigration Restriction Act of 1901 prohibited further Indian immigration to Australia, although Indians already in Australia were allowed to bring their wives and minor children as permanent residents. Immigration was liberalized to some degree in 1948 when Indians were declared British subjects. However, they could not apply for residential status until 1966 with the beginning of the abandonment of the White Australia Policy. This and the implementation of a points system in Australia's immigration policy led to an increase of highly educated Asian immigrants in Australia (Ip, 1993), including Indians from India and the diaspora.

In 2001, there were 95 452 Indian-born people in Australia. Of those living in Melbourne and identifying as ethnically Indian, 21 318 were born in India, 4 792 were born in Fiji, 622 were born in England and 601 in South Africa (ABS, 2001). India is Victoria's second largest source of new immigrants and the largest group of Indian-born residents in Australia live in Victoria. Most Indians in Victoria live in the Melbourne metropolitan areas of Monash, Greater Dandenong and Casey and are from white-collar professional backgrounds (ABS, 2001).

The majority of Indian immigrants to Australia find that their professional qualifications are not recognized, despite the fact that it is these qualifications that have allowed them entry to this country (Ip, 1993). Immigrants from the medical, teaching and accountancy professions suffer the most in this regard. Many are forced to seek employment in other fields whilst others go on to set up their own businesses working long hours in small retail and service-oriented enterprises. Such enterprises are crucial in providing these immigrants with a source of income and rehabilitating professionally qualified people from the trauma of downward social mobility (Ip, 1993).

Although Indians are fluent in English, the majority speak an Indian language at home, such as Hindi and Tamil, and have strong religious affiliations as Hindus, Muslims or Christians, drawing on this as a source of values and ideals. Cultural identity is very important, and Indian immigrants express concern about the lack of knowledge of their culture in Australia among other Australians (Bilimoria et al., 1988).

CARE OF INFANT AND MOTHER

Motherhood takes its meanings from the family and the wider community. Motherhood is considered compulsory for a married woman, serves an important role in the fashioning of the familial hierarchy in Indian society, and is negotiated by older women in the family (Reissman, 1998). For Indian women, early motherhood is bound with cultural expectations that perpetuate the transfer of culture by elder familial women to the next generation of women (Mani, 1992). Caring for an infant is an opportunity for mothers and mothers-in-law to pass on cultural knowledge and their own personal experience whilst providing support for women during an important transitional time. This support reaffirms traditional understandings of health and well-being and encourages its practice.

Variations in prescriptions for the care of infant and mother observed among the study group reflect historical and developmental trends in Indian communities, both homeland and diasporic, as well as the experience of integrating into Australian society, involving some cultural reinvention and reconstruction.

Supernatural Belief

The presence of the supernatural influences the care of mother and baby in India. Both are supposed to be keep out of the dark, not go outside the house, and not be alone during the first several months, as they are susceptible to possession by spirits who prey on their vulnerability (Nielson et al., 1997). Lights are left on at night and the baby kept in view at all times, sleeping with the mother (Assanand et al., 1990).

Immigrant women from this study generally explain the various superstitions surrounding motherhood with reference to what they see as the original logic behind them. Many stated that they, as educated, modern women, do not necessarily accept the supernatural elements of such beliefs. Not leaving the baby unattended for example, may be explained as vigilance to prevent Sudden Infant Death Syndrome (SIDS), while leaving the light on at night is explained as enabling the mother to monitor the baby and to wake and feed him or her at night.

Rest Period

In India, the new mother usually returns to her natal home temporarily, before giving birth. Here, surrounded and pampered by family, she rests and recuperates for approximately 40 days after birth, before heading back to her marital home (Assanand et al., 1990). During this time, her family feeds her many rich foods as well as dishes made with *Ayurvedic* medicines that help her heal and regain strength.

With immigration to Australia, visiting family, such as parents or in-laws, allow the women bed rest and recuperation, taking on household chores and preparing special foods for the new mother. Some women find it difficult to be confined to bed in their own homes, waited on by aged parents, and insist on resuming their normal household duties. Husbands often assist with these chores, indicative of the fact that they are young, educated men and women whose gender relations differ from those of earlier generations.

Traditional Medicine

Traditionally, *Ayurvedic* medicines, including spices such as cummin, pepper, cloves, cardamon and asophetida are added in extra quantities to food specially prepared for the new mother to help heal her body after delivery. *Ayurvedic* tonics also relieve back pain, restore appetite, improve digestion and assist other post-partum complaints (Reissland and Burghart, 1988). A drink of boiled milk and spices such as tumeric, ginger, garlic, celery seed, onion seed and Indian linseed is supposed to initiate the production of breastmilk (Morse, 1982).

These spices are traditionally ground together at home. The new mother may also have herbal baths to help her regain vitality after the birth.

For most women in this study, *Ayurvedic* medicines are taken as spices in food, administered as tablets or syrup, and added to baths. Some women have these preparations brought from India to Australia by visiting family members. The medicines may also be purchased here from Indian grocers. Elder female family members with knowledge of which spices to include and the quantities required prepare the medicines. It is an important duty for these family members to pass on this knowledge of post-natal care, consistent with their role as senior women.

Food Promotion and Prohibition

In India food items are believed to be either 'hot' or 'cold', and a balance between 'hot' and 'cold' is necessary for the body's well-being. Foods that are classified as 'hot' and 'cold' are not done so on the basis of temperature or pungency, but on the perceived effects on the person who consumes them. There is much variation in the perception of vegetables as 'hot' and 'cold' among and within communities (Nag, 1994). Generally, animal food such as eggs, fish and meat are seen as 'hot', while milk, yoghurt and buttermilk are commonly perceived as 'cold'. Most fruits are seen as 'cold', however, papaya, jackfruit and pineapple are seen as 'hot'. Postpartum women should avoid cold foods to prevent 'catching a cold' and getting sick. Lactating mothers are encouraged to eat a spiced wheat dish with dried fruit and nuts to bring on their milk, and to drink plenty of milk to sustain its production (Reissland and Burghart, 1988).

For the immigrant women, foods that are discouraged include lentils, potatoes and fruits such as pineapples and mangoes, as well as "too much" chilli, as these are seen to cause gas or wind for the baby when the mother breastfeeds. Foods encouraged include red meats, fish, green vegetables and traditional breads cooked with extra ghee or clarified butter. This was without mention of the hot-cold system of classification, however. Most women tend to adhere to these prescriptions to some degree due to the encouragement of visiting mothers or mothers-in-law. Employed women, however, prefer to return to their pre-pregnancy weight as quickly as possible and go back to work, and try to refrain from eating fattening additions to food such as ghee.

Traditional Massage and Breastfeeding

Massage and breastfeeding are considered the two most important practices of motherhood in India (Reissland and Burghart, 1987). From birth, the mother and baby are massaged daily; the mother for several weeks, and the baby, generally until toddlerhood, by a traditional midwife (*dhai*), the mother, female relatives or a housemaid. In the case of the post-parturient woman, the massage to the stomach is intended to coax the uterus to contract back to its usual size and to expel its lining quickly. For the baby, massage is supposed to straighten the body from the cramped postures of the womb. The womb is said to soften skin and bones due to its damp conditions (Reissland and Burghart, 1987) and massage is said to strengthen these. Stretching movements follow, which are similar to yogic exercises and are meant to make the body more flexible. Massages with oil are also thought to help the baby put on weight, because oil is seen as a fatty substance, and is supposed to add to the fatty tissue in the body when absorbed by the skin (Reissland and Burghart, 1987). Mustard, sesame, coconut or olive oil is used.

The women in this study do not have the luxury of a traditional midwife or housemaid to massage them and are generally reluctant to have their mother or mother-in-law do so. Modesty plays a part in this, as they feel uncomfortable baring themselves to an elder family member, especially an in-law. They may either opt for a few massages with a professional masseur after they have returned home from the hospital and feel ready to go out of the house, or refrain from this practice altogether. The baby is usually massaged by the visiting mother or mother-in-law, and later the new mother continues the practice. The chosen oils, however, are generally the commercial baby oils available from supermarkets.

CASE STUDIES

Motherhood varies in meaning, including for women in this study. Some women are more 'traditional' or 'Indian' in their knowledge, attitudes and practices, as Sharmila's case illustrates, whilst others exhibit more 'modern' or 'Australian' traits, as in Patricia's case (all names are pseudonyms). Despite this, motherhood is still shaped by cultural expectations and attitudes. This includes the dominant role of senior women in the family who reiterate custom and tradition, making mothering an important process in reaffirming 'Indian' culture and identity.

Sharmila's Story

When I first met Sharmila, she had been in Australia for about eight months and was six months pregnant. She migrated from northern India in late 2003, to be reunited with her husband, Anil, who had already been living in Melbourne for six months. Two and a half years earlier, they had met each other at work, fell in love, and married. They came to Australia for a better quality of life, and to Melbourne specifically because they knew other people from India who had immigrated to this city. Unfortunately, neither Sharmila nor Anil was able to gain employment in their fields of Information Technology (IT), despite Anil later attaining a Masters degree in IT from an Australian university.

I visited them about a week after Sharmila and their baby, Anjini, returned home, on the day of their visit from the maternal and child health nurse. They said they thought 'she was okay', but were perturbed by her telling them that they should not sleep with the baby in their bed. They were thrilled by the arrival of their daughter; they felt she had really changed their lives in a positive way and had brought unanticipated joy and fulfilment. They shared the news with their family in India over the phone, and Anil made arrangements for the naming of their daughter:

Yes, we have to give the exact time of birth to the pundit so they look at the astrological chart, what name is going to suit, what time is suitable for the naming ceremony. We called our Dad this morning to go to the pundit, 'this is the exact time, so get the things done', so he is going to get it done.

They also observed the custom of deflecting the evil eye from the newborn baby by applying kohl to the baby's eyelids and forehead during the naming ceremony, held at home the second week after the birth. Anil reports:

The *kajal* that we get from the market [in India], we don't use that. It is self prepared at the home. We get some wood and wrap some cotton and it is held over the coals, the wood burns and gets some charcoal. Mother, mother-in-law or new born baby's mother's mother can put that...yes, that is to save the baby from evil eyes. Like you don't know who is evil, who is good or who's bad. [We put it] on the left side of the forehead.

Sharmila's mother-in-law, Aarti, came from India to assist them. She looked after Sharmila, cooked for the couple, and showed them how to take care of their baby. They both felt indebted to her, as they did not think that they would have been able to cope as well without her. They said that they felt afraid and unsure every time the baby coughed or sneezed, and would have been constantly running to the doctor had it not been for Aarti's assurances. The baby had some indigestion and reflux, which worried them:

...Sometimes she cries too much, she's upset, she don't sleep, she don't take feed, I'm upset and I went to doctor, but my mother-in-law she comes to know immediately what's wrong with her, that is what she is like, she is experienced. This is my first time, [mothering] it will come easily, but I come to know much from my mother-in-law in this period in time. Even, I don't know how to put on the nappies, how to give bath to baby, she helped me a lot with everything. Without her it would have been difficult because she knows much, much, much more than us (Sharmila).

Aarti prepared and served Sharmila special food and *Ayurvedic* remedies to aid her breastmilk production and healing after the birth; this was seen as an integral part of post-natal care, an essential role of an elder woman in the family:

The food that helps the most to get the milk out of the mother is like liquid food like milk, mother can drink a lot of milk...*Pinjeeri*, it is basically like flour, pure ghee, 16 different types of *Ayurvedic* medicines and almonds. So we heat that up till it gets brown. That is very helpful for pains in the back bone because it has 16 different types of *Ayurvedic* medicines. In our local language we say it binds you back...it is sweet, we will give you with some tea, because normally we take it with some milk because that gives warmth to your body from the inside (Sharmila).

Sharmila was not supposed to eat certain foods after delivery and while she was breastfeeding. She could not observe the food restrictions during her stay at the hospital, and this caused distress as both Sharmila and Anil felt they had no control over this:

She should not be eating too much spicy (food) because according to the old ladies, they say whatever you eat, even if you drink orange juice, if you breastfeed the baby, it can affect her throat. If you eat something bitter, your milk is going to be bitter. If you are going to eat spicy, the baby is going to have spicy milk. One day at the hospital, early morning, in the breakfast, there was tomatoes in the sandwich, she had a bit of a sore throat, Sharmila, same as the child, baby had a sore throat for two days. They are both fine when they are home, because now she [his mother] is cooking very light food…she said we shouldn't be giving green chillies or red chillies to the mother because it can cause digestion problems in the child as well as some problems with the urine, because you can have a burning feeling when you pass urine or go to the toilet (Anil).

According to convention, a new mother should not do housework for approximately 42 days after the delivery, and Aarti waited on Sharmila during this period to allow her to rest and recuperate while they also observed certain supernatural beliefs:

After delivery no, for at least 11 days, you can't leave her alone, even if she is here, somebody has to be here…it is in our tradition, when a girl gives birth to a baby, she is reborn. The girls itself is reborn and she is so delicate and fragile that you can't leave her alone. She can't go out at night because she is vulnerable to evil things. Evil things can harm her very easily at this stage, because they just look for a body. That's why my Mum is here all the time…after a woman has given birth, they have different kind of meal, especially those which give them strength. Like they have raw egg in milk, and ghee, heavy fatty stuff, that gives you strength. At least for forty days, you have to be on this diet (Anil).

Aarti cared for Anjini, as was her duty as the elder female in the house, and slept with her at times to let Sharmila have a restful night's sleep. Aarti also massaged Sharmila and the baby:

Baby and mother both need massage, baby need some oil massage when the sun is out. You can put the baby in the sun. For the mother, the best oil is mustard oil. For the baby I put Johnson's baby oil or olive oil (Aarti).

These customs and traditions are passed on from generation to generation by older women, the keepers of cultural knowledge, to younger ones in the family. Anil commented that these norms and values are both part of everyday life and an important part of their cultural identity:

Either your grandma will be talking about those things, your neighbour will be talking about those things, you are travelling in a bus and two ladies are talking about the same things, you get all of these things from your society… few of them we are aware because they are normal talks at home, these are not extraordinary that we are hearing for the first time.

Sharmila had to start weaning her baby from one month of age in order to go back to work two months after the delivery; Aarti fed the baby formula during the day when she was at work. Sharmila and Anil were not keen for Anjini to be put into childcare as they wanted her to be cared for by people who loved her. They decided that it would be best for Aarti to take Anjini back home to India with her to be looked after by the family. Sharmila ceased breastfeeding at four months when she sent Anjini to India with her mother-in-law. Sharmila talked of their decision to send their daughter to India:

Because I have seen her, she is not going well. She is good with my mother-in-law because from the time she was born, she is with her, and she takes care of her more than me, because most of the day she is with her. And over there [in India] she is comfortable and lucky. And even I consult my health care and doctor, they all say she is better, good. Because she had a problem at the time of the birth, acidity and heartburn, it is all gone there...it is too hard, but it is okay, this is more happy thing like she is okay there and she is doing well there, everything is suited there, atmosphere, climate and everything goes right.

Their daughter was welcomed very warmly in India. The important rituals and ceremonies were all attended to: she had her hair shaved off and was prayed for at various temples. This was very important to Sharmila and Anil as they had these things done for them when they were children. Sharmila says:

We have to give the charity, on behalf of my daughter, we have to give the money to the temple, to the pundit and all...So if we don't go and do that, we feel guilty inside you know, that is why we did everything.

Aarti returned Anjini to Sharmila and Anil at eight months of age. She will stay with her parents until she has to go to high school, when Sharmila and Anil plan for her to return to India for her secondary school education. Sharmila talked about this prospect:

Until four years [of age] she is going to stay with us, but after that we will see, she studies here for primary school and then go back to India because I don't think the culture over here for youngsters is good. Primary school, maybe she is here, let's see what is going to happen.

With no family residing permanently in Australia, they said that they worried about sending Anjini to childcare and school, fearing she might learn what they called 'wrong values', rather than the morals and ideals of their own culture. Anil talked about this:

I feel when she is going to stay with my parents, her ethical values are going to grow, her social values are going to grow. Somebody is always going to be with her. The problem here, what I feel, we can't spend time with our children, most of the time they are in day care centres, and most of them they feel alone and if we are working, and we need rest, even then they don't have time...for me, children are like blank paper, whatever you write, they just grab.

Sharmila and Anil celebrated their daughter's first birthday at an Indian restaurant with friends. They said they were happy and felt adapted to Australia, although they would always consider themselves 'Indians'; they were just unsure about how long their daughter would stay here due to their desire to ensure that she understood her 'Indian' identity. Anil spoke of this:

Yeah, now used to it. It is okay for us because we are now grown up and we know what we have to do. There is no other choice, we are here, and we have to adopt this life and this culture. But for our baby there is more options, they can stay in India or whatever they want. Because we are there, we know what is good and what is bad for them. For us we have to stay here because we are here, what jobs come.

In the meantime, they said they would make regular trips to India so that Anjini could know her culture and family there. They already had plans to visit India towards the end of the year and were very much looking forward to this.

Patricia's Story

When I first met Patricia in mid 2004, she was in her last trimester of pregnancy with her second child. She had an older daughter, Poppy, about 18 months of age. Patricia immigrated here with her family when she was four years old as they had family here already. Patricia was born in England; her parents had immigrated from southern India for a better quality of life. Patricia used to be a flight attendant but did not return to work after her first daughter was born. Andrew, of Sri Lankan heritage, is a builder and runs his own business from home; she helps him with the bookwork. When I met her, they had been married for four years, and had known each other for just over two years before they married. They have a large extended family in Melbourne, and many Indian and Sri Lankan friends.

Their first child had slept with Patricia and Andrew in their bed from the time she was born, even at the hospital. They had intended for her to do so before she was born but were also afraid of her getting used to sleeping with them. She was therefore placed in a bassinet the first night at home, but after staying up worrying about every noise she made, Andrew decided to bring her into their bed and they have loved it being that way ever since; in fact both Patricia and Andrew said they slept better that way.

Patricia said that she had a lot of help at home with Poppy from both her husband and her parents; her father came over four days a week when her mother was working, and she dropped Poppy off at her parent's place when they were both at home on the other three days, so she could get some shopping done and work at home for their business. Her husband helps when he is working at home:

> So it is, it's really helpful, I don't know what I would do without them actually… and actually when she was born, we had Andrew's parents, they live in Brisbane but they were here for about a month before she was born they came. And his Mum is like a champion, she was just cooking everyday so I didn't have to do anything. So even when we came home when she was born, they were with us for another month, so it was so helpful. Because I didn't have to do anything, just look after the baby, all our meals were cooked.

Both sets of parents were helpful with the baby and both delivered advice that seemed more modern or convenient rather than traditional or cultural, as Patricia related:

> 'Drink Sustagen or a glass of milk or Milo or something like that' [her mother said], which I did do and still do. They both [her mother and mother-in-law] sort of agreed that I should take her out as little as possible for the first two months while she was really small, in terms of 'don't go out and expose her to the cold or to people', because she might catch a cold or germs and stuff like that, so they were both particular about things like that.

Patricia's mother advised her to massage Poppy to relax her, so after her bath Andrew would massage her with baby oil. Her mother would massage Patricia's back, shoulders and feet when she felt sore, and she also went to a professional masseur.

She knew that she wanted to breastfeed Poppy. She found it difficult for the first few days in terms of the baby latching on and sore nipples, but she persisted, and continued breastfeeding until Poppy was 17 months old, when she stopped due to her second pregnancy:

> Because I really didn't want to, even though she was breastfeeding still at that stage, she wasn't getting a lot of nutrition out of it, it was more like a comfort thing for her, and I didn't want to be doing that and breastfeeding a newborn together. I wanted to stop but it took a lot of convincing on her part, because she is so attached to the breast. But in the end it was okay, she just drinks normal milk out of a cup now.

She never fed her formula, breastfed on demand, introduced her to solids at the age of four months, and to cow's milk at 12 months. She also planned to breastfeed her second child, Lily.

Among the ways in which Patricia was non-traditional in her approach to infant care and rearing was her lack of modesty with regards to breastfeeding in public:

> I will do it anywhere, I have never had any issues...all the time, wherever they needed it, I just did it...no, anyone, brothers, uncles, anyone. I just do it...she was exactly the same. Mum never worried about breastfeeding anywhere.

She did not prepare most of her children's semi-solid foods at home, but fed them bottled food initially. Patricia started Lily on solids at four months as she felt that Lily wanted to start eating, even though she was aware that "WHO says exclusive breastfeeding till six months". She fed her bottled solid food until about 10 months, at which time she started feeding her what the family ate, as she did with Poppy. Lily didn't want to breastfeed as much but she ate more solid food than Poppy did. Patricia continued breastfeeding Lily until 13 months, although she noticed that her supply of breastmilk was not as plentiful as it was with Poppy. She stopped when she fell pregnant with their third child.

Both Patricia and Andrew articulate a selfless attitude towards infant care and rearing, which they feel is a cultural trait. Patricia sleeps with both the girls in her bed, with Andrew occupying a different room. The maternal and child health nurse didn't recommend that the baby be put in her bed; Patricia did not disclose that she slept with her at night. The other women in her mother's group knew that Patricia slept with her daughters; their babies all slept in cots. Patricia and Andrew felt that people in Australia thought co-sleeping was strange and so they generally didn't tell friends. On the other hand, they said that all their Indian friends slept with their children and didn't make use of the cots they had bought. Andrew felt that there were a lot of things about bringing up children in Australia that were not consistent with their own views:

> I think a lot of western attitudes are quite bizarre in terms of upbringing of children, I think that there are a lot of strange things... I think a lot of western or Australian Mums and Dads, I think that they actually feel like they have got to retain their current lifestyle without much change when a baby comes into their life...Until they are ready to have their own space, well they can be with us, it doesn't really bother us. I think that it is because we don't feel that it is

a sacrifice, I actually feel, and I think we both feel, that it is a privilege much more than a sacrifice.

Andrew identifies as Sri Lankan and Patricia as Indian, even though part of their ancestry is Anglo. They came to Australia as children, have a love for Australia and see Australia as their home. Patricia feels that her children will also not identify themselves as Australian, "because they know that their mother is Indian and their father is Sri Lankan". In terms of education, Patricia and Andrew have an appreciation for their traditional value system, but also for that of Australian society, and want to expose their children to many cultures:

> I always want our kids to know where they are from, but I don't want them to be too hooked up with it, as in I don't want them to be blind to other cultures or have a lack of appreciation for other cultures or even for the country that we live in...I don't think that you can beat an education where kids get exposed to those sorts of environments, to different cultures (Andrew).

Their plans for the near future are to live overseas, perhaps somewhere in the Mediterranean for six to twelve months, to experience another culture with their children.

CONCLUSION: MATERNITY, IDENTITY AND IMPLICATIONS FOR HEALTH AND SOCIAL CARE

The study demonstrated that among Indian immigrant women, great diversity exists in terms of their attachment to, and knowledge and practice of, traditional modes of infant and mother care. The length of time immigrants have spent in Australia, whether they have come here as a child or adult, the place where they were born, and other social, cultural and economic factors are key determinants of the extent to which such practices are employed. All the women, irrespective of background, valued Indian customs and traditions, and were proud of their heritage and identity. Many voiced the opinion that the high standard of biomedical care in Australia, combined with Indian mothering practices – even if only applied in a limited way – provided for all their medical, emotional and cultural needs, instilling confidence at this anxious time. Cultural expectations bring a degree of certainty to motherhood and cultural practices are an assertion of identity.

More recent and direct immigrants have a stronger desire to retain traditional mothering practices. Some of these women are in favour of continually visiting 'home' with their children, for the purpose of maintaining and reinforcing cultural orientations and familial ties (Bhattacharjee, 1992). This was the case with Sharmila, who was determined to hold onto her values and norms: the familiar providing comfort and security during the transition to immigrant and mother.

Those immigrants who have come from a country other than India, and have been exposed to other cultures through successive migrations, were less likely to make use of more traditional mothering practices, as with Patricia. Becoming a mother in an adopted land leads to questions surrounding identity, resulting in cultural manipulation and reconsruction (Dasgupta, 1998). Identity is asserted through the replication and renegotiation of cultural practices in Australia, just as Indian immigrants in the United States maintain "psychological" closeness by reinventing Indian culture in the host country through altered practices of religious ceremonies and rituals (Bhattacharjee, 1992).

The reproduction of culture brings a certain familiarity to the process of early mothering. Care and nurturance of the parent and child provides a smooth and comfortable transition into motherhood for women with varying degrees of exposure to and participation in the health system, as well as to the wider culture of mothering in Australia. These women do not see themselves as disadvantaged immigrants, instead, they feel fortunate to be accessing western biomedical care and a wealth of traditional knowledge from informal family and community networks. Motherhood becomes a vehicle whereby ceremony and ritual is celebrated in a manner which reveals its significance as not only custom and tradition, but as a marker of identity and cultural pride.

In a multicultural society, it is to be hoped that health professionals are sensitive to, and knowledgeable of, cross-cultural approaches to mothering. Immigrants need to feel that their beliefs, values and practices, which underpin their identity, are respected. A lack of understanding and/or questioning by service providers could leave women feeling confused and devalued, concerned that these aspects of cultural praxis and identity will be subject to censure. If immigrant women choose to utilize cultural practices during motherhood, understanding and support from health professionals will enhance the experience for mother and infant, creating positive narratives of early motherhood.

REFERENCES

Assanand, S., Dias, M., Richardson, E., & Waxler-Morrison, N., 1990, 'The South Asians', in N. Waxler-Morrison, J. Anderson & E. Richardson (eds.), *Cross-Cultural Caring: A Handbook for Health Professionals in Western Canada*, pp. 141-180. University of British Columbia Press: Vancouver.

Bhattacharjee, A., 1992, 'The Habit of Ex-Nomination: Nation, Woman, and the Indian Immigrant Bourgeoisie', *Public Culture*, 5: 19-44.

Bilimoria, P., & Ganguly-Scrase, R., 1988, *Indians in Victoria (Australia): A Historical, Social and Demographic Profile of Indian Immigrants*, Deakin University and Victorian Ethnic Affairs Commission: Geelong & East Melbourne.

Dasgupta, S.D., 1998, 'Gender Roles and Cultural Continuity in the Asian Indian Immigrant Community in the U.S.', *Sex Roles: A Journal of Research*, 38(11-12): 953-974.

Desai, J.G., 1971, 'The Religious Life Time-Cycle in Hinduism', *Journal of the University of Durban-Westville*, 3: 123-128.

Ip, D., 1993, 'Reluctant Entrepreneurs: Professionally Qualified Asian Migrants in Small Business', *Asian and Pacific Migration Journal*, 2(1): 57-74.

Kuper, H. 1960, *Indian People in Natal*, Natal University Press: Pietermaritzburg.

Mani, L., 1992, 'Gender, Class and Cultural Conflict: Indu Krishnan's "Knowing her Place"', *SAMAR: South Asian Magazine for Reflection and Action*, Winter: 11-14.

Morse, J.M., 1982, 'Feeding Patterns and Health Assessment of the Fijian and the Fiji Indian Neonate [Abstract]', *Dissertation Abstracts International*, 42(8), 3658A, No. 8202200.

Nag, M., 1994, 'Beliefs and Practices about Food during Pregnancy', *Economic and Political Weekly*, Sept. 10: 2427-2438.

Nielson, B.B., Liljestrand, J., Hedegaard, M., Thilsted, S.H., & Joseph, A., 1997, 'Reproductive Pattern, Perinatal Mortality, and Sex Preference in Rural Tamil Nadu, South India: Community Based, Cross Sectional Study', *British Medical Journal*, 314: 1521-1524.

Phinney, J.S., 1990, 'Ethnic Identity in Adolescents and Adults: Review of Research', *Psychological Bulletin*, 108: 499-514.

Rajendra, N., 1994, 'The Pioneers of Indian Immigration in Australia', *Asia Education Teacher's Journal*, 22(2): 28-29.

Reissland, N., & Burghart, R., 1987, 'The Role of Massage in South Asia: Child Health and Development', *Social Science and Medicine*, 25(3): 231-239.

Reissland, N., & Burghart, R., 1988, 'The Quality of a Mother's Milk and the Health of her Child: Beliefs and Practices of the Women of Mithila', *Social Science and Medicine*, 27(5): 461-469.

Tummala-Narra, P., 2004, 'Mothering in a Foreign Land', *The American Journal of Psychoanalysis*, 64(2): 167-182.

In: India: Economic, Political and Social Issues
Editor: Urlah B. Nissam

ISBN: 978-1-60456-509-6
© 2009 Nova Science Publishers, Inc.

Chapter 6

BALI – INDIA TRADE: MODERN AND FUTURE PERSPECTIVES

*Fr. J. Felix Raj**

St. Xavier's College, Kolkata, INDIA

Bali is the most well known of Indonesia's 13,700 islands, and it remains the number one tourist attraction in the archipelago. One of the biggest attractions of Bali is its culture which, despite the intrusion of the outside world, has been preserved in its unique arts and ceremonies. Denpasar, the island's largest town and administrative center, with a population of now over 370,000, is the capital of the island.

The island of Bali constitutes a province of Indonesia and is administrated by a governor. With a population of approximately 3 million people and a total land surface of 5,632 square kilometers (2,175 square miles) and measures just 55 miles (90 kilometers) along the north-south axis and less than about 90 miles (140 kilometers) from East to West, Bali is one of the most densely populated territories of Indonesia.

POPULATION

In Bali, the population is almost all Indonesian, with the usual small Chinese contingent in the big towns, a sprinkling of Indian merchants, plus a number of more or less permanent visitors amongst the Westerners. The overwhelming majority of Balinese people (almost 95%) are Hindu in a predominantly Muslim Indonesia. But Balinese Hinduism is a world away from that of India. At one time Hinduism was the predominant religion in Indonesia (witness the many great Hindu monuments in Java) but it died out with the spread of Islam through the archipelago. The final great Hindu Kingdom, that of the Majapahits, virtually evacuated to Bali, taking not only their religion and its rituals but also their art, literature, music and culture. They have retained their Hindu religion. It's teaching is to reach the

---

* Professor of Economics, St. Xavier's College, Kolkata-700 016, India. Tel/Fax: 91-033-2280 2800; Email: vpbcom@vsnl.net; Website: www.goethals.org

attainment of peace and harmony in life. Hindu Dharma is a special blend of Hinduism, Buddhism and ancestral worship, which has flourished over the past centuries.

Religion is inseparable from everyday life in Bali, from the simple daily rituals to the lavishly semi-annual temple festivals. Religion in Bali has two overwhelming features: it is absolutely everywhere and it is good fun! You cannot get away from religion: there are temples in every village, shrines in every field, offerings being made at every corner. However, the number of Muslims is steadily increasing through immigration of people from Java, Lombok and other areas of Indonesia who seek work in Bali.

BALI'S ECONOMY

The Nature of age-old economic relations between India and Bali underwent significant changes due to various developments in the 19th and 20th centuries. The founding of Singapore as a British free trade port in 1819 changed the volume and direction of India-Bali trade towards and through Singapore. The continued presence of the Dutch East India Company in the archipelago, its trade for profits, the subsequent colonization of Indonesia, occupation of Bali in 1904, and the massacre of 4000 Balinese had caused a trade tilt in favor of the colonizers, which affected Bali-India trade relations. After Independence of Indonesia in 1945 and its consolidation as a nation in 1950, and the killings of nearly 1,00,000 Balinese reformists and suspected communists in 1965, when the Island's population was only 2 million, opened a new chapter as India-Indonesia economic relations, overshadowing India-Bali relations.

The Trade Agreements between India and Indonesia in 1978, followed by many other Agreements between various bilateral organizations like FICCI, CII, ASSOCHAM, have strengthened the economic relations between India and Indonesia, as President Megawati had put it during her recent visit to India, " A sentimental color in the Indonesia-Indian relations is normal because of their cultural and historical relations for thousands of years which spills over to economic endeavors to achieve joint progress".

India's Trade with Indonesia.

India's trade with Indonesia	1997	1998	1999	2000	2001 (Jan-Oct)
Exports	697.41	292.93	245.82	524.63	398.37
India's exports as Percentage of global exports to Indonesia	1.67	1.07	1.15	1.56	1.46
Imports	689.50	722.89	840.90	1151.28	861.31
India's imports as percentage of global imports from Indonesia	1.29	1.48	1.90	1.85	1.78
Total trade (Ex+Imp)	1386.91	1015.82	1086.72	1675.91	1259.68
Trade Balance	(+) 7.91	(-)429.96	(-)648.48	(-)626.65	(-)250.52

Consequently, the 1970s and 1980s saw around 16 Indian manufacturing joint ventures in Indonesia (Tatas, Birlas, Bajaj, LNM, HMT Bombay Dyeing etc), almost all concentrated in

Java and Sumatra. Bali was neglected and its relation with India given less importance. Bali was, spontaneously, led to shift its emphasis on tourism. In the bilateral trade between India and Indonesia, the value of India's export was $ 697 million in 1997, 293 m in 1998, 525 m in 2000 and 398 in 2001(Jan.-Oct.); and imports 689 in 1997, 722m in 1998, 1151 m in 2000 and 861m in 2001 (Jan-Oct.).

BALI TODAY

Agriculture

Bali's economy is one of the most prosperous in Indonesia. Its economy is growing at close to 9% per year. Bali islands are very fertile and its economy is basically agrarian. About two third of its people are engaged in agriculture. Irrigated rice fields, often laid out in neat terraces carved out of mountain slopes, and other seasonal crops are found from the highlands down to the lowlands. Wet – rice cultivation is the key to Bali's agricultural success. The greatest concentration of irrigated rice fields is found in south central Bali, where water is available from spring-fed streams. There are now even vineyards near the northwest coast. Rice is planted in rotation with cash crops such as onions, soybeans, corn and beets. In the northern part of the islands, the people grow coffee, coconut, fruits and livestock, and they are major agricultural exports. The forests throughout the island are well preserved, and cover most of the mountaintop. Bali's fishing industry and seaweed farming provide other products, which are important exports.

The vast majority of the Balinese are still simple peasants working in the fields. Most of the rice produced goes to feed Bali's own teeming population. Although the Balinese are island people, their unusual tendency to focus on the mountains rather than the sea is reflected in the little importance they give to fishing. While there are many fishing villages and fish are part of the Balinese diet, fishing, as an activity is not on the scale you might expect, given how much ocean there is around the island.

With agriculture as the main occupation of the people and the basis of wealth, the ownership of land is of great significance. Bali presents the amazing spectacle where the deeply rooted agrarian communalism of the people has continued to coexist with other systems. The true Balinese village is an independent economic and social unit as we find in Indian states with predominantly tribal population. Land is not a commodity. It can never be sold to foreigners like in India where tribal people as per Government legislation, cannot sell their lands to non-tribals. In Bali the cost of living is generally low and economic inequality is not as striking as elsewhere. The main source of income in villages is the sale of cattle and pigs, and of coconuts for making copra; also from sale of coffee, rice and tobacco.

Tourism and Related Industries

Bali is fueled by a constant flow of tourism dollars, mainly from a popular tourist area located in Southern Bali, and supported by agricultural production and trade revenues. Tourism plays a considerable role in the Balinese economy, not only in providing accommodation, meals and services to many visitors but also in providing a market for all those arts and crafts! It still greatly depends on the export of raw materials in return for manufactured goods.

Bali"s Exports and Imports with India.

Period	Export Items	Import Items
Earlier period	Rice, Vegetable Oil, Agricultural products, pigs, Fish…	Opium, Textiles, guns…
Now	Textiles and garments, handicrafts, wood products, statues, furniture, Agro products, coffee, tobacco, raw materials….	Rice, groundnuts, soybeans, Iron and steel…

The southern part of Bali is where most jobs are to be found, either in the hotel and tourist industries, the textile and garment industries, or in many small scale and home industries producing handicrafts and souvenirs. Many Balinese are gifted artists. Textiles, garments, and handicrafts have become the backbone of Bali's economy providing 300,000 jobs, and exports have been increasing by around 15% per year to around US$500 million in 2001. Textiles and garments contribute about 45%, and wood products including statues, furniture and other handicrafts 22% to the province's total income from exports. Silver work is ranked third (4.65%) with 5,000 workers employed. Main buyers are the US and Europe with 38 per cent each and Japan with 9 per cent.

Almost 1.5 million tourists a year visit Bali, twice as many as a decade ago. In 2001, Indonesia earned more than $A10 billion from tourism, at least a third of it from Bali. Japan is the biggest source of Bali's tourists followed by Australia, England, Taiwan and Germany. A foreign tourist spends an average $US 62 per day in Bali; while the average wage is about $US 1.50 a day. In 2001 Bali earned $US 765.63 million from tourism. Apart from a pause when Suharto fell in 1998, and again after September 11 bombing last year, more people have kept going to the island each year. Tourists in Bali stay longer and spend more than people visiting the rest of Indonesia. Unlike the rip-them-out industries that dominate so much of Indonesia's economic activity, tourism in Bali was sustainable, and wealth from it was flowing right through the island's population.

On the eve of the financial crisis in 1997, a survey found that Balinese overwhelmingly thought their lives were good or getting better still - significantly more so than other Indonesians. Over the previous three years, 42 per cent said their general household welfare had improved, 31 per cent had improved their house, 51 per cent said they had better access to medical services, and so on. The only area in which the Balinese were becoming less confident than other Indonesians was on law and order.

Bali was evolving into a wealthier, westernized society. Balinese women generally married in their 20s, while other Indonesian girls married in their teens. They now have average just two children each, and form part of a workforce in which an extraordinary 69 per cent of all people aged over 10 have a job (compared with 57 per cent in the rest of Indonesia). Balinese live by the principle of " live and let live".

Those working as employees generally had higher incomes than those in the rest of Indonesia. In Bali, even in 1995, nearly all homes had electricity and covered floors. Most also had televisions and radio-cassette players. Most unusually for Indonesia, almost half the homes owned fast wheels: usually motorbikes or scooters, but also a significant number of cars. The Balinese were doing well. This is unusual in a country that has been going through what can only be described as a depression since 1997.

Suharto in spite of his weaknesses, generally made wise economic decisions, and, as one wit put it, the Suhartos' deals were market-friendly. They demanded a stake in return for helping new enterprises get under way, whereas in the Philippines, the Marcos family and friends simply looted the country of all the wealth that might have been used to get new enterprises under way.

By 1997 Indonesians enjoyed a real output per head three-and-a-half times its 1970 level. Growth per head had averaged almost 5 per cent a year for a generation, and most Indonesians had become much better off. Those who once walked had bikes, those who formerly had bikes now rode motorbikes, and people had become well fed, better educated and increasingly healthy. But those unheeded borrowings unhinged the economy, the president, and the whole country.

In 1998, Indonesia lost its president, 15 per cent of its gross national product, and much of its savings, which were sent abroad by the Chinese-Indonesian commercial elite, panicked by the outbreak of race-based rioting and rape. Much of that money has never come back, and many of the entrepreneurs have also left, some of them for Australia. The International Monetary Fund estimates that this year, despite growth puttering along at 3.5 per cent, real output per head will still be almost 10 per cent below its 1997 peak. The closure last week of yet another factory producing Nike shoes sums up the malaise of a country that has reformed enough to disorientate everyone, but not enough to carve out a new direction.

President Megawati's hands-off leadership style has brought political peace after years of turmoil, but not an economic new start. The courts have moved from being under the control of the government to being under the control of the highest bidder, in a country in which, as commentator Michael Bachman points out, a district court judge is paid less than a chauffeur. So investors are staying away.

The October 12 Blast and Its Aftermath

Bali"s economy was devastated after the *October 12 2002 explosion* in Kuta. Local workers feared that foreign tourists might never return. Tourists were not only fleeing from the tourist centers in the south of Bali, they were also leaving from the rest of the island, particularly Ubud, the town 20 miles north of Kuta considered to be the island's artistic and cultural soul. Sucipto, who owns the 2M restaurant five miles down the road, accepted that he would soon have to start laying off some of his staff. "I am lucky because a lot of locals come here," he said.

It was an attack on the heart of Bali's economy. As Tim Colebatch wrote, " Economically, it would harm Indonesia, particularly the island of Bali". While the debris was being cleared and the bodies identified, Balinese businesses were starting to count the economic costs of the first bomb to have ripped through South-east Asia's tourist paradise. At the Captain Haddock, a bar restaurant not far from the blast zone, the staff had already noticed a 30% fall in sales within two days after the blast.

Such concerns plague all of Indonesia, where the tourist trade earns £12.5bn per year - equivalent to 3% of national output - and accounts for 6 million jobs, or 6% of the workforce. The initial signs were extremely discouraging. The stock market crashed 10% to a four-year low while the currency, the rupiah, slumped 3.5%.

A country that once seemed to be sailing effortlessly towards becoming one of Asia's tiger economies has now suffered yet another torpedo blast, this time tearing apart one of the few bits of its economy still in perfect working order. Bali has made a big contribution to keeping Indonesia going in the past five years of economic turmoil: a financial crisis sparking a depression, the fall of President Suharto, the first free elections, war and diplomatic defeat in East Timor, the fall of President B. J. Habibie, the rise and fall of President Abdurrahman Wahid, and the fallout from September 11 and the world economic slump.

Through all this, Bali retained its magnetism for travelers around the world. Terrorist attacks in New York might stop only a few tourists going to New York. But the terrorist attack in Bali is likely to stop many tourists going to Bali, and for some years ahead. According to Bali's Chamber of Commerce, the occupancy rates in hotels and restaurants dropped from 70 per cent before October blast to 14 per cent after blast in November. Tourists' arrivals fell from 5,219 per day to 500 after September 11.

FUTURE PERSPECTIVES

Bali's economy was wounded. The October 12 bomb blast in Kuta was an attack on the heart of Bali's economy and has had a massive impact on Bali's economic relation with all countries. The effects were already noticed in terms of drastic fall in the number of tourists. Some say it is a temporary phenomenon. But there is doubt about it. The fall in tourists will adversely affect the tourism-based industries like hotels, textiles, handicrafts, wood products, and garments. Though Bali is overpopulated and every Balinese has some job or the other, this development might result in closure of some industries and unemployment problems, which add to the existing problem of influx of Muslims from other islands into Bali for employment. The insecure climate has affected the inflow of investment.

Bali bombing has affected Indonesian economy. The growth of investment expenditure in 2002 was minus 6.14 per cent compared to 2001. Almost all investment agreements were given up and investments in oil and gas sectors dropped to negative percentage. Government expenditure for 2003 as in draft budget was only 2.8 per cent of GDP (Rp 54.5 trillion), lower than 2002 level of 3.1 per cent of GDP (Rp 52.3 trillion).

The Bali bombing has raised the question of handling terrorism in Indonesia. Recall the Christmas Eve bombing in Sumatra and Java three years ago. Also the bombing in Jakarta Stock Exchange two years ago. The unfinished reform of putting the military under the civilian control, in other words, acceleration of democratic transition to stabilize its policies and maintain security comes to the foreground.

Formerly famous for its extensive rice field and its elaborate Subak traditional irrigation system, Bali now has to face the bleak reality that it has frequently sacrificed its rich agricultural resources to make way for various types of tourists related industries. Thousands of hectares of fertile land and rice fields have been transformed into glittering shopping centers, five star hotels and other symbols of luxury. Once Bali was exporting rice, but now Indonesia is importing rice from India. What Bali produces goes to feed its own teeming population. India, which has gone through agricultural revolution, could contribute towards the modernization and development of Bali's agriculture.

Of late, though tourism industry has created dramatic economic growth, it has dislocated the local people and disturbed Balinese traditional communities Javanese interests seem to dominate in all policy decisions while the local government discriminates against the locals. . The locals do not have sufficient management of tourist industrial growth. Since tourism is affected, Balinese might return to agriculture. There is a need to build close links between agriculture and tourism for sustainable development in future. The local Government should seriously think in this line and promote a policy of balanced development – both regional and Sectoral. The present situation might provide a new start and change in Bali's development paradigm.

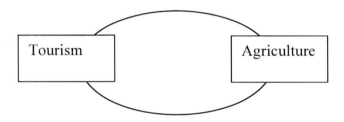

Figure 1.

As Agung Mas of Udayana University in Denpasar suggests, Bali needs to redesign and reshape its development paradigm. The Balinese people are addicted to tourism. Tourism has become their flesh and blood. They are reluctant to leave the glamorous and dollar based industry. But 80 per cent of Island's population live in villages and work as farmers. The development programmes should take into account other profitable and secure pillars including agriculture, the maritime potential and small-scale industries. Bali has to develop a modern farming system and sophisticated agro-industries to benefit from this sector like in Thailand and the Philippines.

The new free-trade regulations are creating some problems for Bali's exporters, as they do not allow employing children. Most children here work for their parents, and in handicrafts industries. They believe that this is part of the process of acquiring professional skills and kind of an informal education, which has been very important in the Balinese society for centuries. Free trade will also open these village based small-scale industries to outside competition. There is a fear whether they will be able to survive through.

One area Bali has not exploited to the maximum is fishing industry and seaweed farming. There are ample opportunities for generating of jobs, and for export revenue.

India and Bali are ancient civilizations and share lot of similarities in the field of culture and religion. Both can take steps to promote cultural, educational and religious exchanges and strengthen their bilateral relation.

Bali is Hindu, though it is not of the Indian kind, and the rest of Indonesia is Muslim. If the present immigration of Muslims continues, will it not create problems in future? Communal tensions? Yes, the recent blast was reportedly aimed at westerners particularly Americans. But why in a Hindu island? Is there a message for the Hindu world as a reaction to what is going on in Gujarat and other parts of India? There is something to reflect on.

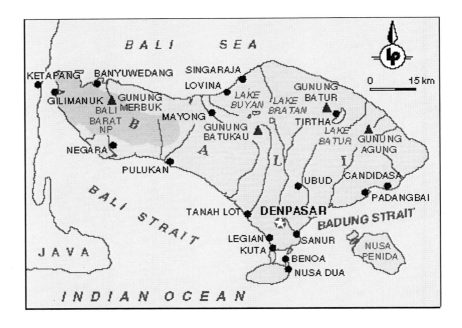

Figure 2.

In: India: Economic, Political and Social Issues
Editor: Urlah B. Nissam

ISBN: 978-1-60456-509-6
© 2009 Nova Science Publishers, Inc.

Chapter 7

EFFICIENCY IN PRODUCTION OF HEALTH: A STOCHASTIC FRONTIER ANALYSIS FOR INDIAN STATES

Anindita Chakrabarti[*]
Unit for Child and Youth Research, Tata Institute of Social Sciences
Mumbai, India
D. N. Rao
Jawaharlal Nehru University, New Delhi, India

ABSTRACT

It has been increasingly recognised that apart from medical inputs, a wide range of socio-economic factors plays an important role in determining health. The objective of the study has been to ascertain the impact of predominantly medical inputs on health status of individuals and simultaneously capture the influence of such socio-economic variables on the (in) efficiency prevalent in the production process (of health). A stochastic production frontier with inefficiency effects has been estimated based on data drawn from the fourteen major states of India over the time frame of 1986 to 1995. The frontier estimates throw light on some conflicting issues facing the policy-makers. Most importantly the results revealed that the beneficial impact of economic growth is not large enough to supersede that of medical services. Consequently greater priority ought to be given to the enhancement of health sector and utilisation of medical services. Finally the index of efficiency, generated by the frontier model, highlights the blatant regional disparity prevalent in India and draws attention to the need for pursuing policies directed towards eradication of this existing regional imbalance.

Key words: performance indicator, health production frontier, inefficiency effects, India.

---

[*] Email: anindita_ch@hotmail.com; anindita@tiss.edu

INTRODUCTION

It has been increasingly recognised that health is not produced by health care intervention alone. A wide variety of conditions and certain behaviours or exposures have also played a significant role in determining the health status of the people. Among the most important of these are tobacco & alcohol abuse, poor diet, malnutrition, occupational hazards and environmental degradation of various forms. For example, two patients treated under precisely the same quality of health care can exhibit different health outcomes because one of them is entitled to a higher level of income. Income, by increasing his access to entitlements such as food, clothing, shelter, and other general amenities, improves the health of the individual by building up the body's natural ability to heal itself.

This has been the underlying basis for the construction of the *health production function* which acknowledges that (the output) health can be produced by different inputs of which health care is just one. Consumption of the other factors described above (or abstinence as the case might be) forms the other relevant health inputs.

From a planning perspective, decisions regarding the inter-sectoral allocation of resources become significant. Policies, diverting resources from certain social sectors (e.g. education and sanitation) in favour of provision of greater health facilities will have a multiple effect. On the one hand, there is a *possibility* of improvement in health status of individuals owing to increase in public expenditures on health programmes. On the other hand, such a policy choice will have an adverse effect on health owing to reduction in the allocation of funds for education, sanitation, etc. In this regard health production functions by explicitly taking into consideration these factors plays an important role.

The rest of the paper is organised into the following sections. Section 2 gives a brief survey of the literature on health production functions with a separate subsection on the Indian scenario. Section 3 provides a discussion on the methodology and the model specification. Section 4 provides the descriptive statistics of the variables used in the analysis. The empirical results are reported in section 5. Section 6 analyses the robustness of the empirical results while section 7 concludes.

HEALTH PRODUCTION FUNCTION

Auster et al. (1969) laid the foundation for examining the efficiency of medical care inputs vis-à-vis other non-medical input, in the production of health. The tool used for this purpose was a health production function of the Cobb-Douglas form. The latter reflects the technically efficient combinations of inputs required in producing a certain level of output.

The pioneering work of Auster et al. triggered a number of similar studies. A partial list of these studies includes Stewart Jr. (1971), Meeker (1973), Cochrane et al. (1978), Hadley (1982, 1988), Brenner (1983), Jain (1985), Wolfe et al. (1987), McKinlay (1989), Tulasidhar (1989), Beenstock et al. (1990), Lopez et al. (1992), Rao et al. (1991), Gaiha et al. (1993), Reddy et al. (1994), Singh (1994) and Gerdtham et al. (1998). In the subsequent section we very briefly summarise the findings of the existing literature with particular emphasis on papers related to the Indian context.

In general, certain non-medical inputs were found to have a significant impact on the health status of the population. The channel through which such factors influence health is quite diverse. For example, literacy by increasing access to information, enhances the utilisation of existing medical services and, hence, affects health. Preventive measures, adopted by the state (increasing sanitation or supply of potable water), or by the individual (by changing his lifestyle e.g., reducing alcohol / cigarette consumption or practising safe sex), generates better health by improving hygiene and inducing protection. Of the medical inputs, health expenditure, which signifies the commitment of the state towards improving community health status, undoubtedly has a beneficial impact on health. No general consensus has been reached however regarding a) the relative importance of the latter vis-à-vis the former or b) the effectiveness of physical medical input (e.g., physicians or per capita hospitals) capturing medical infrastructure. The importance of medical inputs seems to have been undermined in some cases – by ignoring their impact on specific population sub groups or due to the non-inclusion of certain relevant inputs. Hadley (1982) analysed the impact of medical care, education and income on both general and disease specific mortality rates for different age-sex-race cohorts in the U.S.A. The elasticity estimates revealed that a unit increase in medicare expenditure would generate the maximum fall in mortality rates for the elderly black females, while the lowest fall in mortality rates was recorded for the elderly white males. In any case, the medicare expense elasticities were somewhat larger in absolute values than those suggested in previous studies. Studies undertaken by Gaiha et al. (1993) and Singh (1994)) demonstrate that births in medical institutions or under trained medical practitioner are the predominant factors explaining the determinants of mortality rates. Moreover the incorporation of such factors seems to accentuate the importance of the medical inputs vis-à-vis the non-medical inputs like income, literacy, sanitation factors etc.

The Indian Scenario

Very few studies have been made on the factors influencing health status in developing countries. The phenomenon also holds true in the Indian context. Attempts were however made by Reddy et al. (1994), Jain (1985), Beenstock et al. (1990), Tulasidhar (1989), and Rao et al. (1991). In all of the above-mentioned studies (except for Rao et al.) health was characterised in terms of mortality figures or life expectancy (population aggregates). Their findings mirrored the mixed opinion regarding the importance of medical expenditure vis-à-vis other non-medical inputs, as pointed out in the preceding section.

Reddy et al. on the basis of the OLS estimates (computed from data on 15 major states in the year 1991) concluded that income and female literacy have a statistically significant impact on life expectancy. Expenditure on health and poverty on the other hand was found to have no significant impact on health.

Jain did not share the above opinion. Based on rural data for 15 major states, obtained from the Reports of Infant and Child Mortality Survey (conducted in 1979), he determined the socio-economic factors that govern mortality (Neo-Natal, Post-Neo-Natal, Infant) rates.[1] Direct medical inputs included a) maternal health services (percentage of births in institutions

---

[1] Effort was also made to establish the linkages between the different explanatory variables by means of simple regression coefficients and OLS estimates.

or attended by trained medical personnel b) medical infrastructure (captured in terms of villages with medical facility). While the former was a predominant explanatory variable for both Infant Mortality Rate (IMR) and Neo-Natal Mortality Rate (NNMR) the latter proved to be an effective curative input only in the case of Post Neo-Natal Mortality rate (PNNMR). Preventive medical input quantified in terms of percentage of female infants that received a triple antigen vaccine was significant in reducing both IMR and PNNMR. Amongst the socio-economic variables only poverty was found to have a significant negative impact on IMR and NNMR.[2] Based on these results, Jain was of the opinion that it is the medical factors, which has a slight edge over the non-medical factors in determining mortality rates.

Two other lines of work developed (Beenstock et al. and Tulasidhar) which can be looked upon as a modification of Jain's study. Owing to a high degree of collinearity amongst the explanatory variables Jain was ultimately unable to incorporate some relevant cause variables in his model. To overcome this problem, Beenstock used factor analysis to estimate a model in which Infant Mortality Rate across Indian states is explained by socio-economic variables.[3] The result resembles that of Jain, in the sense that birth attendance, medical facilities, DPT vaccination, adult female literacy, and poverty, significantly influences infant deaths. On the other hand, unlike Jain, access to drinking water (measured in terms of tap water) and over-crowded living conditions were also found to be important.

Using a framework similar to that of Jain's, in as much as acknowledging the presence of inter-linkages between some of the explanatory variables, Tulasidhar used two-stage least square estimates to take care of the simultaneity problem. This was of course an improvement over Jain whose analysis was based on ordinary least square estimates. Results of this composite model are quite similar to that of Jain's: medical attention at birth and level of public expenditure on health continues to be significant determinants of infant mortality rates. In contrast, poverty level showed no significant impact. Literacy was found to be the single most important factor influencing the utilisation of medical facilities - an issue also pointed out by Jain.

To conclude the literature review, attention is drawn to the work of Rao et al. whereby the community health status index (CHSI) is treated as a latent unobservable variable. It manifests itself through some measurable dimensions (e.g., mortality, life expectancy etc.). On the other hand, there exists a health production function, where the output, namely CHSI is influenced by cause variables (e.g., per capita income, education etc.) that can be observed. Using these two relationships, Rao et al. derived an estimate for community health status and also captured the impact of the various inputs on community health. The estimates of the model bring back the controversy surrounding the relative importance of the medical inputs as compared to the non-medical factors. The socio-economic variables, namely net state domestic product and literacy have a positive effect on CHSI. Amongst the medical inputs, only government expenditure on health is an effective instrument for improving community health. Dubious results were obtained for the physical medical inputs such as primary health care centres and doctors.

Our paper differs from the existing literature on the following aspects:

---

[2] Astonishingly, adult female literacy was found to play no role in determining NNMR and PNNMR. For IMR it was found to have a significant impact only at 10% level. Due to the strong correlation between literacy and poverty (r=0.5), it was finally dropped from the relevant model.

[3] The data source was the same as Jain's. An additional source, namely, national sample survey, was used to incorporate calorie intake of population.

a. So far all the empirical attempts to quantify the impact of both curative and preventive measures on health status (specifically in case of a developing country like India) have been based on cross-sectional studies. The impact, however, can vary across different cross-sectional units and over time periods. More so, because policies adopted by each state to promote social development may change over time. Consequently, we need to capture the efficiency of each state unit (in promoting health status) and the differential impact of the various cause variables across states and also over time. For this, we use stochastic production frontier in our analysis.

b. The direct inputs of the production frontier are primarily medical input. The other non-medical factors affect production by increasing (or decreasing) the efficiency of the relevant inputs. Based on the above-mentioned discussion it is evident that any analysis involving the production of health must include certain non-medical factors. On the other hand, it must also be borne in mind that the latter complements the direct inputs, i.e., they are not substitutes. Advocates of integrated social programmes lend support to this kind of a framework. For example Lipton and Van der Gaag (1991) draws attention to the fact that in Narangwal, in the Indian Punjab, $1 million spent on an integrated programme of improved public health provision and extra food for children was much more effective than the same sum spent on either programmes exclusively.

METHODOLOGY AND MODEL SPECIFICATION

This section is divided into two parts: the econometric methodology used in this study is incorporated in the first part. The second part consists of the model specification throwing light on the variables used in this model

Methodology

Aigner, Lovell and Schmidt (1977) and Meeusen and Van den Broeck (1977) independently proposed the stochastic frontier production function. The original specification involved a production function specified for cross-sectional data, which had an error term with two components, one to account for random effects and another to account for (non-negative) technical inefficiency. Consequently for a given combination of inputs, it is assumed that the realised production of a firm is bounded above by the sum of a parametric function of known inputs, involving unknown parameters, and a random error term. The latter accounts for the measurement error of the level of production, or for random factors that affects the production process but could not be incorporated in the model. The further the realised production falls short of the stochastic production frontier, the greater is the level of inefficiency.

Considerable research has been done to modify and apply the stochastic frontier. One particular aspect, which has been the centre of attention, includes attempts to compute the determinants of the inefficiency effects. This issue was first raised by Pitt and Lee (1981) and Kalirajan (1981) who adopted a two-stage process to model the inefficiency effects. The first stage involved the estimation of the inefficiency effect on the basis of the stochastic production frontier described earlier. The next stage consists of (generally OLS) regression of the predicted efficiency on relevant explanatory variables. This approach contradicts the set up of the stochastic frontier model, since the latter presumes that the inefficiency effects are identical and independent (of firm specific variables).

The two-stage estimation procedure is unlikely to provide estimates, which are as efficient as that could be obtained using a single-stage estimation procedure. This issue was addressed by Kumbhakar et al. (1991) and Huang & Liu (1994). They provide a way to simultaneously estimate the parameters of the stochastic frontier model and the coefficients of the variables explaining the inefficiency effect. However such studies focus on cross-sectional data. Consequently, we have chosen the Battese and Coelli (1995) model, which allows us to do the same for panel data.[4]

Based on Battese and Coelli (1995), the following *stochastic frontier model* for panel data, has been used to ascertain the health production frontier (for major Indian States) and simultaneously determine the inefficiency effects expressed as an *explicit function of a vector of state-specific variables* and a random error:

$$Y_{it} = X_{it}\beta + V_{it} - U_{it} \qquad (1)$$

where Y_{it} is the health output of the *i*-th state at the *t*-th time period. X_{it} is a $1 \times k$ vector of input quantities of the *i*-th state at the *t*-th period. β is a $k \times 1$ vector of unknown parameters that needs to be estimated. V_{it} are random error terms, which are assumed to be i.i.d. as $N(0, \sigma_V^2)$, and independent of the U_{it}. The U_{it}'s are non-negative random variables accounting for technical inefficiency in production and are assumed to be independently distributed as truncations at zero of the $N(m_{it}, \sigma_U^2)$ distribution. Note

$$m_{it} = Z_{it}\delta$$

where Z_{it} is a $p \times 1$ vector of variables, which may influence the efficiency in the production of health. δ is a $1 \times p$ vector of parameters to be estimated.
The inefficiency model is thus specified as:

$$U_{it} = Z_{it}\delta + W_{it} \qquad (2)$$

where W_{it} are random variables, defined by the truncations of $N(0, \sigma_U^2)$ such that the point of truncation is $-Z_{it}\delta$, i.e. $W_{it} \geq -Z_{it}\delta$. This assumption is consistent with the assumption made regarding the distribution of the inefficiency effect, i.e., U_{it}.

---

[4] To the best of our knowledge the only other instance, when Battese &Coelli (1995) specification of stochastic frontier model has been used in the field of health economics, includes the estimation and determinants of technical efficiency in the Swedish public hospital system by U.G. Gerdtham, M. Lothgren, M. Tambour and C. Rehnberg (1998)

The coefficients of the frontier model along with that of the inefficiency model are estimated simultaneously on the basis of Maximum Likelihood Estimation.[5] For this purpose, fourteen major states[6] of India, over the time span of 1986 to 1995, was taken into consideration.

Model Specification

The variables used in the model described above are discussed under the following two classifications.

Variables Used in the Stochastic Production Frontier

The output in the health production frontier is quantified in terms of the "performance indicator" *(P.I.)* of the state. The performance indicator of the *i*-th state in the *t*-th time period is defined as follow:

$$PI_{it} = \frac{(IMR_{max} - IMR_{it})}{(IMR_{max} - IMR_{min})} \tag{3}$$

Table 1: Ranks of Indian States according to Infant Mortality Rates and Performance Indicator

State	I. M. R	Rank *1/*	P. I.	Rank *2/*
Kerala	19.84	1	0.943	1
Punjab	58.78	2	0.615	2
Maharashtra	59.35	3	0.611	3
Tamilnadu	64.08	4	0.571	4
West Bengal	66.54	5	0.550	5
Karnataka	71.82	6	0.506	6
Andhra Pradesh	73.48	7	0.492	7
Haryana	76.05	8	0.470	8
Gujarat	77.20	9	0.461	9
Bihar	81.70	10	0.423	10
Rajasthan	91.30	11	0.342	11
Uttar Pradesh	106.30	12	0.216	12
Madhya Pradesh	111.10	13	0.176	13
Orissa	116.90	14	0.127	14

1/ Based on the average infant mortality ranked according to the ascending order.
2/ Based on the average performance indicator ranked according to the descending order.

---

[5] For a detailed analysis of the stochastic production frontier for the panel data along with the maximum likelihood estimator of the input and the inefficiency variables, see G. E. Batesse and T. J. Coelli (1993)
[6] Andhra Pradesh (A. P.), Bihar, Gujarat, Haryana, Karnataka, Kerala, Madhya Pradesh (M. P.), Maharashtra, Orissa, Punjab, Rajasthan, Tamilnadu, Uttar Pradesh (U. P.), West Bengal (W. B.).

where IMR_{max} and IMR_{min} refer to the infant mortality rate(s) of the worst and the best performing state(s) over the entire time-period of study (1986 to 1995). IMR_{it} is the infant mortality rate of the i- th state in the t-th time period. In this study, IMR_{max} was recorded at 132 for Uttar Pradesh in the year 1986 - while IMR_{min} was recorded at 13 for Kerala in the year 1993. Consequently $P.I.$ attains the maximum value of one for Kerala at 1993 and zero for Uttar Pradesh at 1986. Note that the $P.I.$ has an inverse relationship with IMR (see Table 1).[7]

The direct inputs used in the production process are enlisted below:

1. Per capita primary health care centre (in percentage terms), hereafter referred to as *PHC,* was included to throw light on the rural infrastructure. The primary health care centres, each serving thirty thousand people, cater solely to the need of the rural sector. In a developing country like India, where a major proportion of the population resides in the rural sector and relies on state provided health facility; the inclusion of this variable seems to be important.
2. Per capita hospital (in percentage terms) hereafter referred to as *Hosp* was incorporated to capture the existing urban health facilities. Primarily located in urban areas, the hospitals (including teaching hospitals and district and sub-divisional hospitals) also serve as a referral institution for the primary health care centers.
3. Health expenditure as a percentage of current net state domestic product, hereafter referred to as HEX[8], which includes expenditure on medical institutions (viz. hospital, dispensaries etc.), family planning programme, medical education, research and administration, immunisation etc., was included to reflect on the state(s) commitment towards improving the health status of its population.
4. Births in institution (*B. I.*) was incorporated due to the following reasons: (a) it is an indicator of the access to maternal health services, (b) it captures to some degree the utilisation of the available medical care and (c) it also throws light upon the nature of pre-natal care received during pregnancies. It is unlikely that the mother received any medical care (tetanus injection etc) during pregnancy if the birth of a child was not attended by a medically trained personal.
5. Births in home by trained practitioner (*B.T.*) were incorporated due to the reasons mentioned in the case of *B. I.* However it was incorporated separately because this captures the utilisation of private medical care.
6. Per capita net state domestic product at 1980-81 prices (referred as *NSDP*) - which captures to some degree the economic well-being of its' inhabitants. This was incorporated directly in the production frontier because increase in affordability promotes the use of privately provided medical facilities - details off which could not be incorporated in this study because of lack of data.

Variables Used in the Inefficiency Model

The non-medical factors which indirectly affect health and hence the efficiency of the health production function are enlisted below:

[7] $\dfrac{dPI_{it}}{dIMR_{it}} = \dfrac{-1}{IMR_{max} - IMR_{min}} < 0$ since $IMR_{max} - IMR_{min} =$ a constant (k) > 0.

[8] This excludes expenditure on Water Supply and Sanitation.

1. Literacy rate (*Literacy*) was included because better-educated people tend to be more informed and hence have the know-how needed to use the medical (or other market) inputs more efficiently.
2. Proportion of rural population (*Rural*) was taken into consideration as an indicator of access to health facilities. In a developing country like India, with uneven regional development a pre-dominant share of the population resides in poor, backward rural areas with limited access to health care.
3. Expenditure on water supply and sanitation (as a percentage of current net state domestic product) was included because this reflects to some extent, on the general hygiene and the quality of drinking water provided. Revenue expenditure on water supply and sanitation (*REVWs&S*) and capital expenditure on water supply and sanitation (*KXWs&S*)[9] were incorporated separately to distinguish between current expenses (for maintenance etc.) and expenses incurred for building up infrastructure.

Given the importance of the above-mentioned factors, the stochastic health production frontier to be estimated takes the following form:

$$PI_{it} = \beta_0 + \beta_1(PHC) + \beta_2(Hosp) + \beta_3(NSDP) + \beta_4(HEX) + \beta_5(B.I.) + \beta_6(B.T.) \\ + \beta_7(Year) + V_{it} - U_{it} \tag{4}$$

where U_{it} is defined as:

$$U_{it} = \delta_0 + \delta_1(REVWs\&S) + \delta_2(KXWs\&S) + \delta_3(Rural) + \delta_4(Literacy) \\ + \delta_5(Trend) + W_{it} \tag{5}$$

Note in addition to the chosen variables, *Year* and *Trend* have been incorporated as additional explanatory variables in both the models to account for technical change and time-varying inefficiency effects. Battese and Coelli (1995) model allows for the simultaneous estimation of both equation (4) and (5) by the maximum likelihood estimation technique. Notes on the chosen variables and the source from which the data on these variables are drawn have been given in details in the Appendix.

Prior to discussing the empirical results of the actual heath production frontier and the inefficiency model the following section has been incorporated describing the pattern of growth and changes incurred in the chosen variables.

DESCRIPTIVE STATISTICS

Considerable discrepancy can be observed amongst the fourteen major states with respect to the output of the production frontier namely *P.I.* As shown in Table 2, the average output

---

[9] Both *REVWs&S* and *KXWs&S* (in current Rs.) are expressed in terms of percentage of current Net State Domestic Product.

for all of the fourteen major states, for the period 1986 to 1995 was recorded at 0.46. States such as Kerala with a mean *P.I.* of 0.94 and Punjab with a mean *P.I.* of 0.62 showed a much better performance than the national average.[10] On the other hand states like Orissa (mean *P.I.* of 0.13), M. P. (mean *P.I.* of 0.18) and U.P. (mean *P.I.* of 0.22) lagged far behind. However, an encouraging feature is that the rate of growth of *P.I.* was highest for U. P. (0.38) followed by Orissa (0.21) and M. P. (0.15) and relatively higher than national average of 0.09. Moreover, the inter-state inequalities in *P.I.,* showed a marked decline over the period 1986-90 to 1991-95. This is evident from the rapid fall in the average coefficient of variation across the corresponding period (see Table 2). To see how far this decline can be explained by the states expenditure on health and provision of adequate medical infrastructure, we look into the pattern of medical inputs such as *PHC*, *Hosp* and *HEX* (as shown in Table 2).

Unfortunately, the average rate of growth of *HEX* for the fourteen major states taken together was found to be negative (-0.02). This is because all the states, except for Gujarat and surprisingly the so-called backward states of Bihar, Orissa and Rajasthan, recorded a negative rate of growth of *HEX*. The highest mean *HEX* was recorded for Kerala, followed by Rajasthan and Bihar. There has also been a slight increase in the inequalities amongst the states with respect to their expenses towards improving health status (revealed by column one and two of Table 2).

When we look into the actual infrastructure captured by *PHC* or *Hosp*, the picture that emerges, is somewhat different.

As far as *Hosp* is concerned, the average growth rate across the fourteen major states over 1986 to 1995 is positive. Individually however, there is considerable variation in their performance – with six states exhibiting positive (but marginal for all but one) growth rate(s) and the rest showing corresponding negative figures. Kerala with a growth rate of 0.58 stands apart from the group. Owing to the lacklustre performance of the majority of the states, there has only been a marginal decline in inequality in provision of per capita hospitals (as is evident from column 1 and column 2 of Table 2). A somewhat dissimilar picture emerges in case of rural infrastructure, namely *PHC*. Here a majority of the states seems to be clustered around the national average (see Table 2). A positive growth rate was computed for all of the states except for Punjab. A decline in inter-state inequalities was recorded for the *PHC* (see Table 2). Considerable variation in provision of *PHC* exists for some of the states (Bihar, Gujarat, Karnataka, Kerala, Maharashtra, Punjab and Rajasthan).

---

[10] The mean for all the major fourteen states included in the study are being termed as the national average.

Table 2: Descriptive Statistics of the Variables used in Health Frontier

Variable	State														
	A.P.	Bih	Guj	Har	Kar	Ker	M.P.	Mah	Ori	Pun	Raj	Tnd	U.P.	W.B.	All
P. I.															
Mean	0.492	0.423	0.461	0.470	0.506	0.943	0.176	0.611	0.127	0.615	0.342	0.571	0.216	0.550	0.464
C. V.	12.337	27.928	30.375	16.033	8.899	5.212	41.861	7.455	57.433	7.140	24.489	13.955	66.719	9.665	23.536
Growth	0.033	0.082	0.130	0.039	0.024	0.013	0.147	0.015	0.209	0.023	0.083	0.047	0.383	0.029	0.090
PHC															
Mean	0.002	0.002	0.002	0.002	0.002	0.003	0.002	0.002	0.003	0.005	0.003	0.002	0.002	0.002	0.003
C. V.	6.657	15.784	18.788	10.106	28.391	19.159	8.342	41.505	11.191	74.175	26.429	18.676	15.402	3.839	21.317
Growth	0.013	0.068	0.084	0.035	0.117	0.083	0.029	0.112	0.037	-0.079	0.099	0.070	0.059	0.005	0.052
Hosp															
Mean	0.002	0.0004	0.005	0.0005	0.001	0.007	0.001	0.004	0.001	0.001	0.001	0.001	0.001	0.001	0.002
C. V.	48.724	3.202	18.466	5.958	4.001	32.696	6.037	60.412	8.116	14.415	14.684	4.126	6.376	7.888	16.793
Growth	0.144	-0.009	0.046	-0.017	0.002	0.579	0.001	0.173	-0.027	-0.036	-0.033	-0.011	-0.021	-0.024	0.055
NSDP															
Mean	1744	1098	2438	3320	2177	1820	1599	3487	1524	3810	1778	2262	1591	2192	2203
C. V.	7.421	5.266	9.216	9.666	13.019	14.292	9.643	16.648	7.135	8.589	14.397	15.194	6.133	8.208	10.345
Growth	0.030	-0.005	0.017	0.033	0.045	0.048	0.038	0.058	0.018	0.030	0.055	0.053	0.022	0.027	0.033
HEX															
Mean	1.018	1.218	0.930	0.704	1.132	1.510	1.023	0.849	1.179	0.853	1.315	1.194	1.153	1.066	1.082
C. V.	13.776	16.457	14.757	17.483	10.831	10.943	9.717	36.886	7.084	11.190	4.995	17.966	4.355	9.697	13.296
Growth	-0.043	0.049	0.006	-0.037	-0.020	-0.023	-0.013	-0.100	0.010	-0.040	0.011	-0.046	-0.006	-0.022	-0.019
B. I.															
Mean	35.2	11.5	23.2	19.5	36.7	88.1	12.4	34.9	9.7	7.5	4.7	53.7	4.6	30.1	26.5
C. V.	12.581	7.441	7.489	14.452	22.399	7.260	10.558	4.935	30.322	11.183	14.052	17.691	17.361	4.794	13.037
Growth	0.044	0.032	0.022	0.049	0.073	0.025	0.008	0.013	0.123	0.029	0.047	0.059	0.062	0.015	0.043
B. T.															
Mean	21.5	14.7	33.5	64.2	25.5	6.1	13.6	14.8	17.3	82.8	17.9	19.1	26.2	9.4	26.2
C. V.	15.699	11.622	6.853	1.095	4.925	19.617	9.976	12.497	15.405	11.218	17.842	2.574	14.722	23.205	11.946
Growth	0.042	0.038	0.023	0.004	-0.006	-0.043	0.031	0.037	0.050	0.035	0.068	0.005	0.045	0.076	0.029

From the point of view of medical expenses and rural infrastructure - there is no evidence to suggest why the so called BIMARU states - Bihar, M. P., Rajasthan, U. P. and Orissa - are the worst performers (among the last five) in terms of health status. Indeed contradictory evidence was found, particularly for Bihar and Rajasthan. Consequently changes and trends in other variables capturing utilisation of the existing facility (*B. I.* and *B. T.*) and general economic well-being of the state (quantified by *NSDP*) were analysed to see whether these factors can throw any light on this aspect.

In terms of utilisation of maternal services in institutions (*B.I.*) - the BIMARU states does lag behind the national average. However in the case of *B. T.* there is considerable disparity across the states. The performance of Kerala and W.B. is particularly deficient while that of Punjab is exceedingly good. The rest of the states including the BIMARU ones are more or less clustered together. There was a negligible but consistently positive growth rate for B. I. across all the states - however for B.T. negative growth rates were recorded for the South-Indian states of Karnataka and Kerala. There was a marginal decline in inequalities across the fourteen major states for both the variables (Table 2). As far as real per capita income is concerned, all states but Bihar, recorded a positive growth rate for *NSDP*. The economic performance of Punjab, Maharashtra and Haryana far surpassed that of Bihar, Orissa and U. P. (reflected by the average figures in Table 2). An encouraging feature is that while Rajasthan is economically relatively backward it shares a growth rate comparable to that of the fastest growing state, namely Maharashtra.

As mentioned earlier, the comparatively poorer performance of the BIMARU states - particularly Bihar and Rajasthan - in terms of *P. I.* could not be traced to the medical inputs (except for *B. I.* and *Hosp*). We thus briefly analyse the relative performance of the states in terms of two factors, namely literacy rate and water supply and sanitation, which exert a significant impact on health. Figures on mean literacy rate reveal that such states are substantially behind the national average (54.64). Moreover there is no sign of the gap closing (see Table 2). However, the performance of Rajasthan (with a growth rate of *Literacy* at 0.041) is encouraging because it is growing at the fastest rate. Taking account of the expenditure for promotion of water supply and sanitation, we find that the mean figures of *REVWs&S* for states like Rajasthan (0.812) and M. P. (0.746) are higher vis-à-vis the other states. Furthermore, there has been a relatively large decline in inter-state inequalities in *REVWs&S* over the time period 1986 - 90 to 1991 - 95 (see Table 2). The same holds true for capital expenditure on water supply and sanitation (*KXWs&S*).

For a better inference on how these variables affect the output of the production frontier and the inefficiency effects one needs to carefully examine the empirical results presented in the next section.

EMPIRICAL RESULTS

The Maximum Likelihood Estimates of the parameters of the model described by equations (4) and (5) have been obtained by the Frontier 4.1 software (Coelli, 1994). The estimated coefficients along with the t-values are presented in Table 4.

Table 3: Trends in Inequality of the Variables Used in the Study

Variable	Coefficient of Variation (1986- 1990)	Coefficient of Variation (1991-95)	Coefficient of Variation (1986 – 95)
P. I.	54.999	37.701	46.883
PHC	73.961	21.546	54.648
Hosp	126.401	121.247	123.872
NSDP	35.256	37.930	37.372
HEX	21.106	24.167	22.970
B. I.	86.395	83.076	85.120
B. T.	80.932	79.714	80.463
REVWs&S	55.573	50.086	53.740
KXWs&S	226.096	195.622	213.248
Rural	9.574	10.096	9.830
Literacy	20.154	21.713	21.902

Table 4: Maximum Likelihood Estimates of the Model

Variable	Parameter	Estimate	Standard Error	T – Value
Health Frontier				
Constant	β_0	0.22841	0.05962	3.831[@]
PHC	β_1	9.85451	0.99263	9.928[@]
Hosp	β_2	9.32223	0.94772	9.836[@]
NSDP	β_3	0.00002	0.000008	2.402[@]
HEX	β_4	0.11503	0.03515	3.273[@]
B. I.	β_5	0.00484	0.00043	11.256[@]
B.T.	β_6	0.00205	0.00024	8.542[@]
Year	β_7	0.00418	0.00368	1.137
Inefficiency Model				
Constant	δ_0	0.07839	0.17876	0.439
REVWs&S	δ_1	0.21186	0.04576	4.630[@]
KXWs&S	δ_2	-0.14688	0.02547	-5.767[@]
Rural	δ_3	0.55952	0.11995	4.665[@]
Literacy	δ_4	-0.00683	0.00078	-8.756[@]
Trend	δ_5	-0.01052	0.01017	-1.035
Variance Parameters				
Sigma-Square	σ^2	0.01628	0.00083	19.614[@]
Gamma	γ	0.99	0.00002	49500.00[@]

[@] Significant at 1 percent level.
Value of Log – Likelihood function = 149.957, Mean efficiency = 0.6922

The estimated coefficients of the direct inputs affecting the stochastic production frontier all have the expected positive sign and are highly significant. Consequently, the output of the stochastic health production frontier significantly rises with increase in rural infrastructure

(*PHC*), urban infrastructure (*Hosp*), expenditure incurred by the state for generating better health of its people (*HEX*), economic well-being of the state (*NSDP*) and availability and utilisation of medical attention at birth (captured by *B. I.* and *B. T.*). The *Year* variable in the stochastic health frontier was incorporated to account for Hicks-neutral technological change. The maximum likelihood estimates reveal that, ceteris paribus, there is a positive (but not significant) increase in production over time.

The variables incorporated in equation (5) explaining the inefficiency differential across states and over time have a significant impact (except for *Trend*) - although unexpected result was obtained in case of *REVWs&S*. Capital expenditures for improving sanitation and quality of potable water supplied (*KXWs&S*) and *Literacy* have a significant negative impact on inefficiency. The estimates reveal that for every rupee devoted to raising *KXWs&S* and *Literacy*, there will be a corresponding fall in inefficiency by 0.147 and 0.007 units respectively. Greater the proportion of population residing in rural areas (*Rural*) higher is the extent of inefficiency (reflected by a positive and significant coefficient of 0.559). This result is in accord with expectations because the rural population has a relatively lower access to health facilities. One plausible route through which non-accessibility enhances inefficiency (in production of health) is by increasing the transport cost incurred to get to the nearest available health facility and consequently inducing ineffective utilisation.

Surprising result was however obtained for *REVWs&S*. For every rupee devoted for increase in *REVWs&S* there would be a rise in inefficiency by 0.212 units. This may however be argued on the following grounds. A substantial share of the *REVWs&S* is used for meeting current expenses on wages and salaries of employees instead of productively using it for maintenance (the latter being the reason why *REVWs&S* was considered separately). Given the resource constraint, every additional rupee devoted for *REVWs&S* might necessitate a reallocation of resources from other productive use. Such a measure would lead to a rise in inefficiency. Over and above, the negative coefficient for the *Trend* suggests that inefficiency in production of health tends to decline over the ten - year period. Table 4 also gives us the estimates of the variances associated with this model. Both of the variance parameters were found to be significant. Note

$$\hat{\sigma}^2 = \hat{\sigma}_u^2 + \hat{\sigma}_v^2 ; \hat{\gamma} = \frac{\hat{\sigma}_u^2}{\hat{\sigma}^2} .$$

Generalised likelihood ratio tests[1] were carried out to ascertain whether it would be possible to find simpler models nested in the general model described above. The findings of the likelihood tests along with the p-values of the χ^2 statistics are given in Table 5.

The null hypothesis that the inefficiency effects are absent from the model ($H_0: \gamma = \delta_1 = \delta_2 = \delta_3 = \delta_4 = \delta_5 = 0$) is strongly rejected. The second null hypothesis in Table 5 ($H_0: \gamma = 0$) specifies that the inefficiency effect is not stochastic. This null hypothesis is also rejected (see row 2 of Table 5).[2]

---

[1] The likelihood-ratio test statistic is calculated as $\eta = -2[\log (\text{likelihood } (H_0)) - \log (\text{likelihood } (H_1))]$ and has approximately chi-square distribution with degrees of freedom equal to the number of parameters assumed to be equal to zero in the null hypothesis (H_0).

[2] If $\gamma = 0$, then this implies that the variance of the inefficiency effect is zero and consequently the model reduces to a traditional function in which the variables namely *REVWs&S*, *KXWs&S*, *Rural* and *Literacy* becomes

Table 5: Likelihood Ratio Tests for Model Selection

Null Hypothesis	Test Statistics	p- Value	Decision
$H_0: \gamma = \delta_0 = \delta_1 = \delta_2 = \delta_3 = \delta_4 = \delta_5 = 0$	46.985	0.000	Reject
$H_0: \gamma = 0$	7.601	0.055	Reject
$H_0: \delta_0 = 0$	10.316	0.001	Reject
$H_0: \delta_1 = 0$	23.716	0.000	Reject
$H_0: \delta_5 = 0$	30.260	0.000	Reject
$H_0: \delta_0 = \delta_1 = \delta_5 = 0$	24.922	0.000	Reject
$H_0: \beta_7 = \delta_5 = 0$	7.532	0.023	Reject

The inefficiency model is of particular significance in this study. Several tests were carried out to check the authenticity of the assumed inefficiency function. Firstly the likelihood test conducted to verify whether a constant term should be incorporated in equation 5 strongly rejects the null hypothesis ($H_0: \delta_0 = 0$) in favour of inclusion of the former. Secondly the associated t – value for the presence of trend in the efficiency function was not significant. Consequently, a likelihood ratio test was carried on specifically to determine whether the model could be improved by dropping this trend ($H_0: \delta_5 = 0$). We strongly reject the null hypothesis. As mentioned earlier, surprising result was obtained for *REVWs&S*. Consequently, it was also examined whether the model can be improved by excluding this variable (refer to the $H_0: \delta_1 = 0$). The latter proposition was strongly rejected. Finally the test statistics computed to ascertain whether all of the three (i.e. the constant, *REVWs&S* and the *Trend*) should be dropped from the inefficiency model strongly rejects the null hypothesis ($H_0: \delta_0 = \delta_1 = \delta_5 = 0$).

All of the explanatory variables, but the *Year* incorporated in the stochastic health frontier and the *Trend* included in the inefficiency function, were found to be highly significant. Consequently, the concluding test ($H_0: \beta_7 = \delta_5 = 0$) takes into account the above-mentioned factor. The test statistic rejects the null hypothesis that these two variables should be excluded from the specified model. The results pertaining to the conducted hypothesis tests lead to the conclusion that the functional forms specified for the health production frontier and the inefficiency effect (equations 4 and 5) are appropriate ones.

To compare the magnitude of impact of each of the variables in the production frontier over the output *P. I.* - the corresponding elasticity was computed at both mean and median value (see Table 6). This discussion, however, concentrates only on the latter in view of the large dispersion of the sample values. Contradictory to the majority of the aforementioned studies, health expenditure as a percentage of net state domestic product (*HEX*) has a positive impact on health; indeed it is found to be the single most important determinant of the performance indicator. For every rupee invested in increasing the health expenditure as a percentage of net state domestic product, the performance indicator rises by 25.4 percent. This elasticity is of much higher magnitude than that found in earlier studies. *B. I.* with an elasticity estimate of 0.212 is the next major influence in determining the output of the production frontier. As mentioned earlier, *B. I.* captures to some extent the utilisation of and

---

explanatory variables of the production function. Moreover if $\gamma=0$ then this means that δ_0 and δ_5 cannot be identified. This is because the component *Trend* has already been incorporated in the production frontier. Hence the critical value for the test statistic of $H_0: \gamma = 0$ is obtained from the χ^2 for three degrees of freedom.

access to maternal health services provided in institutions. Since such services is provided primarily through the public health system, our result highlights the importance of public programmes in improving health status. However, the analogous variable *B. T.*, incorporated separately to capture some degree of utilisation of privately supplied maternal services has a small impact on *P. I.* (elasticity = 0.079).

Table 6: Elasticity Estimates of Frontier Inputs

Frontier Variables	Elasticity at Median	Elasticity at Mean
PHC	0.045	0.054
Hosp	0.013	0.033
NSDP	0.079	0.095
HEX	0.254	0.268
B. I.	0.212	0.277
B.T.	0.079	0.116

Variables capturing the provision of medical facilities in physical terms, namely *PHC* (rural infrastructure) and *Hosp* (urban infrastructure) are found to have a positive but negligible impact on *P. I.* The elasticity of *PHC* and *Hosp* are, respectively, 0.045 and 0.013. The only non-medical input incorporated to capture economic well-being and, hence, the ability to afford privately provided medical services and other inputs is the third most influential variable: it has an elasticity of 0.079.

We conclude this empirical section with a presentation of results for the efficiency index.[3] Table 6 presents the efficiency index for each state and for each year. The mean efficiency of the fourteen states across the time span of 1986-1995 is 0.692. Table 7 ranks the state according to their mean efficiency. This yields interesting results. The state with a widely recognised commitment towards the development of its social sectors - i.e., Kerala - and the state with the fastest growing per capita real income - i.e. – Maharashtra - are the two best performers in terms of efficiency in production of health. The so-called backward states of Rajasthan, Uttar Pradesh, Madhya Pradesh, and Orissa are the four worst performing states. The case of Rajasthan is particularly disappointing: although it recorded a high mean value of *HEX* and achieved above-average rates of growth of *PHC*, *NSDP* and *Literacy*, it still features among the bottom four states. Striking result was obtained for Bihar: contrary to popular belief, it was ranked as the fifth most efficient state. However, Bihar's relatively higher rank in terms of efficiency in health production does not get reflected in its actual performance indicator. This feature is revisited, albeit to a lesser extent, in the case of Andhra Pradesh. Out of the four south-Indian states – Andhra Pradesh, Kerala, Karnataka and Tamilnadu – Andhra Pradesh follows Kerala in terms of efficiency. However, it also records the lowest mean *P.I.* in the group (refer to Table 2).

There exists one plausible explanation behind this. What might have made the difference is the efficiency with which medical services are used. In Kerala, for example, a better educated and health conscious mass not only utilise the existing medical facilities more effectively but also exerts pressure to ensure that such facilities are geared to their services. The importance

---

[3] Technical Efficiency (TE$_{it}$) of production of the *i*-th state in the *t*-th period is given by

$$TE_{it} = E(PI_i^* \mid U_i, X_i) / E(PI_i^* \mid U_i = 0, X_i)$$ where PI_i^* is the performance indicator of the *i*-th state and X_i is the vector of inputs as defined in the paper.

of the role of "effective utilisation" can, by small degree, be traced to the fact that *B. I.* has considerable impact on *P. I.* However, to explain the situation peculiar to Bihar, a more detailed data on patterns (and impact) of utilisation is required. This is beyond the scope of our study.

Table 7: Efficiency Estimates across Indian States over Time

State	Year										
	1986	1987	1988	1989	1990	1991	1992	1993	1994	1995	Mean
A. P.	0.683	0.730	0.657	0.673	0.835	0.763	0.753	0.834	0.805	0.772	0.751
Bihar	0.557	0.535	0.603	0.689	0.955	0.980	0.864	0.940	0.975	0.836	0.793
Gujarat	0.356	0.462	0.562	0.606	0.780	0.800	0.802	0.904	0.858	0.861	0.699
Haryana	0.637	0.604	0.558	0.651	0.825	0.827	0.722	0.820	0.775	0.762	0.718
Karnataka	0.799	0.753	0.750	0.662	0.792	0.674	0.698	0.747	0.731	0.765	0.737
Kerala	0.997	0.911	0.891	0.950	0.946	0.966	0.964	0.999	0.945	0.939	0.951
M. P.	0.232	0.215	0.186	0.245	0.353	0.244	0.450	0.421	0.531	0.512	0.339
Maharashtra	0.812	0.868	0.840	0.954	0.959	0.924	0.916	1.000	0.827	0.923	0.902
Orissa	0.158	0.097	0.164	0.178	0.157	0.125	0.255	0.330	0.426	0.413	0.230
Punjab	0.770	0.837	0.825	0.783	0.898	0.980	0.924	0.929	0.948	0.928	0.882
Rajasthan	0.439	0.527	0.478	0.583	0.778	0.829	0.646	0.746	0.718	0.658	0.640
Tamilnadu	0.596	0.710	0.681	0.743	0.833	0.805	0.791	0.788	0.739	0.768	0.745
U. P.	0.000	0.086	0.134	0.229	0.542	0.555	0.538	0.589	0.658	0.700	0.403
W. B.	0.882	0.879	0.897	0.764	0.956	0.802	0.906	0.999	0.916	0.988	0.899
Mean	0.566	0.587	0.588	0.622	0.758	0.734	0.731	0.789	0.775	0.773	*0.692*

Table 8: Ranks of States in Terms of Mean Efficiency (1986 - 1995)

State	Mean Efficiency	Ranks
Kerala	0.951	1
Maharashtra	0.902	2
W. B.	0.899	3
Punjab	0.882	4
Bihar	0.793	5
A.P.	0.750	6
Tamilnadu	0.745	7
Karnataka	0.737	8
Haryana	0.718	9
Gujarat	0.699	10
Rajasthan	0.640	11
U. P.	0.403	12
M. P.	0.339	13
Orissa	0.230	14

Robustness of Empirical Results

This section explores the sensitivity of the results discussed in the preceding section to changes in the data and model specification.

Table 9: Sensitivity of Results Using Alternative Specifications

Variable	Parameter	Jain Model	Dummy	Without Kerala
Frontier Model				
Constant	β_0	0.045 (0.751)	0.275 $(1.681)^{\#}$	0.311 $(5.223)^{@}$
PHC	β_1	6.500 (1.125)	13.520 $(2.549)^{@}$	2.930 (0.917)
Hosp	β_2	22.109 $(5.139)^{@}$	7.207 $(1.489)^{\$}$	-3.861 (-1.262)
NSDP	β_3	0.00006 $(7.068)^{@}$	0.00004 $(1.771)^{\#}$	0.0001 $(5.535)^{@}$
HEX	β_4	0.179 $(5.189)^{@}$	0.200 $(3.080)^{@}$	0.055 $(1.687)^{@}$
B. I.	β_5	0.005 $(13.954)^{@}$	0.004 $(5.555)^{@}$	0.001 $(2.420)^{@}$
B.T.	β_6	0.003 $(8.526)^{@}$	0.001 $(2.361)^{@}$	0.0001 (0.302)
Year	β_7	-0.011 $(-2.674)^{@}$	-0.011 (-0.918)	0.011 $(4.150)^{@}$
Dummy	β_8	--	-0.185 $(-6.158)^{@}$	--
Inefficiency Model				
Constant	δ_0	-0.343 $(-1.919)^{\#}$	0.411 $(2.195)^{\#}$	-1.490 $(-3.749)^{@}$
REVWs&S	δ_1	0.009 (0.159)	0.053 (0.963)	0.470 $(4.981)^{@}$
KXWs&S	δ_2	-0.103 $(-1.948)^{\#}$	-0.157 $(-3.183)^{@}$	-0.187 $(-2.294)^{@}$
Rural	δ_3	0.983 $(4.760)^{@}$	0.091 (0.569)	2.049 $(5.236)^{@}$
Literacy	δ_4	-0.0015 (-1.131)	-0.003 $(-2.258)^{\#}$	-0.002 (-0.704)
Trend	δ_5	-0.034 $(-4.684)^{@}$	-0.031 $(-2.636)^{@}$	-0.005 (-0.672)
Variance Parameters				
Sigma-Square	σ^2	0.007 $(4.654)^{@}$	0.006 $(6.389)^{@}$	0.017 $(4.338)^{@}$
Gamma	γ	0.963 $(31.546)^{@}$	0.931 $(7.615)^{@}$	0.984 $(92.179)^{@}$

Numbers in parenthesis are the T-statistics. [@] Significant at the1 percent level, [#] Significant at The 5 percent level, [$] Significant at the 10 percent level.

Note: DUMMY takes the value of one for M. P., Orissa, Rajasthan and U. P. for all observations.

    As pointed out by Jain (1985), the data on vital events collected through the Sample Registration System for Bihar and West Bengal are particularly deficient. Their performance indicator (computed on the basis of infant mortality rates obtained from Sample Registration System) is, however included in the original study. Consequently, for the first check on the robustness of the original results, we drop Bihar and West Bengal from the list of states. The new maximum likelihood estimates (MLE) along with associated t – values are reported in the third column of Table 9. All of the major variables of the stochastic production frontier, namely, *PHC*, *Hosp*, *NSDP*, *HEX*, *B. I.* and *B. T.*, continue to have a positive impact on the performance indicator although the first two lose significance. Similarly, the coefficients of the factors explaining the inefficiency effect in general do not change their signs and significance. The only exception is *REVWs&S* and *Trend*. They continue to yield the same sign, but while the former loses its significance the latter gains it.

Traditionally the five states of Bihar, Madhya Pradesh, Orissa, Rajasthan and Uttar Pradesh have been identified as backward states. Thus, they have been classified as the 'BIMARU' states. The question is whether it is prudent to control for these states. At first sight, the answer appears to be "no" given the fact that Bihar proved to be the fifth most efficient state with a mean efficiency 0.793 (the national average equalled 0.692). Hence, we assign a dummy variable (*Dummy*) for only four of the states belonging to the 'BIMARU' group (Madhya Pradesh, Orissa, Rajasthan and Uttar Pradesh). In the second check on robustness of the original model, we try to ascertain if and how the MLE of the explanatory variables are sensitive to the imposition of the dummy in the health production frontier.

Introduction of the dummy does not change the relationship of the performance indicator with the medical inputs and economic well-being of the states. The former continues to be positively and significantly influenced by the latter group of variables. The scenario for the inefficiency model is somewhat different. Although there was no reversal of sign for the explanatory variables, *REVWs&S* tends to lose its significance. Interestingly, even after controlling for the four backward states, there appears to be, a negative and significant downward trend in inefficiency over the ten year period, as evident by the coefficient of the *Trend* variable (see column 4 of Table 9).

The important issue that we set out to address was to judge whether the BIMARU states (except for Bihar) perform poorly vis-à-vis the rest of India as the original efficiency estimates suggest. The negative significant coefficient for the dummy variable incorporated in the health frontier confirms our conjecture. This conjecture is further strengthened by means of the likelihood ratio test. The test-statistics of 51.030 (following a χ^2 distribution with four degrees of freedom) strongly supports the presence of the dummy.

It is well known that among the states of India, Kerala's performance in spheres of social development outshines the others. Although, Kerala's per capita income is below the national average, its achievement in social sectors such as health and education is substantially higher. In fact, its' infant mortality rates and life expectancy figures are comparable to the corresponding figures for countries classified as having achieved "high human development" in Human Development Report (1993). Similarly, it has substantially higher literacy than that found in other major Indian states. As Table 2 tells us, this phenomenon is also true for per capita hospital and medical attention at birth provided by public institutions. Thus there is a possibility that the maximum likelihood estimates might tend to be biased owing to the influence generated by the presence of Kerala. Consequently, the concluding check for robustness drops Kerala from our sample. The new estimates are reported in the last column of Table 9. The health expenditure incurred by the state, its economic well-being and *B. I.* continue to have a positive and significant impact on output. However, while output of the stochastic production frontier that is *P. I.* is still positively but weakly influenced by *PHC* and *B. T.*, a perverse result was obtained in case of urban infrastructure. *Hosp* has a negative but insignificant impact on *P. I.* The estimated coefficients of the determinants of the inefficiency model all show the same sign as the original model. All the variables except *Literacy* and *Trend* (which is also true for the original model) are highly significant.

Finally, to conclude this section attention is drawn to one particular factor. Note the estimated value of the variance parameter (γ) is close to one in the original model and the three models designed to test for the sensitivity of the original estimates. This indicates that the inefficiency effects are likely to be highly important in the analysis of production of health for the Indian states. On the basis of the above discussion, it is fair to conclude that the maximum likelihood estimates of the original model are reasonably robust to changes in data and model specification.

CONCLUSION

Panel data on fourteen major Indian states over the period 1986 to 1995 was used to estimate a stochastic health production frontier and simultaneously estimate the parameters of the variables incorporated to explain the inefficiency effects. The output of the production frontier namely performance indicator of the state was generated on the basis of infant mortality rates of the respective states. Elasticity estimates of the inputs incorporated in the production frontier, computed on the basis of the obtained maximum likelihood estimates of the parameters, contradict the general notion that expenditure on curative services does not generate a substantial impact on health. In fact, health expenditure as a percentage of net state domestic product and births in institution with relatively higher elasticity values were found to play a dominant role. Surprisingly, per capita real net state domestic product, which is a measure of an individual's command over privately supplied medical service, has a relatively lower impact on the performance indicator. This throws light on an old debate plaguing the policy makers: should growth in real income be encouraged at the expense of development of social sectors? The present study answers this question in the negative. The beneficial impact of economic growth is certainly not large enough to obliterate the usefulness of an additional rupee spent on a social sector, for example, health.

Literacy, capturing the access to information, and capital expenditure for improving the quality of potable water supply improves the efficiency in production of the health frontier. On the other hand, revenue expenditure on water supply and sanitation is found to have a dampening effect. This draws our attention to the urgency for cutting back on non-productive current expenditure and the use of the released resources for enhancing capital infrastructure. With each region subscribing to a distinct culture, language and race, India is deemed to be a land of diversity. This diversity is revisited when we look into mean efficiency of each state in terms of production of health. On one end of the scale lies Kerala (very predictably!) with a mean efficiency as high 0.951; while in the other end of the scale lies Orissa with a mean efficiency as low as 0.230.

A striking feature underlying the ranking of states according to their efficiency index is that Bihar is found to be the fifth most efficient state. However, this does not get reflected in its' performance indicator. A natural conclusion is that efficiency in provision of health services does not produce the desired result owing to the ineffective utilisation of the available health facility. One way of motivating people to enhance utilisation is through adequate public programmes. An essential ingredient for the success of such programmes involves adequate support from the public. For example, a community can supplement a state's effort for reducing infant morbidity by means of promoting polio vaccination or by participating in the requisite programme. It would be interesting in this context to analyse the interactions between the production of health, health status and utilisation of health services. However, this is left for future research.

APPENDIX

Sources and Notes:

1. Infant mortality rates were compiled from the various issues of Sample Registration System published by Vital Statistics Division, Government of India (G.O.I.).
2. Figures on total number of primary health care centres, hospitals, births in institutions and births in home by trained medical practitioner were taken from various issues of Health Information of India published by Ministry of Health and Family Welfare, G.O.I. The above mentioned source however provided the data until 1993. Consequently, in case of primary health care centres we have supplemented the data from Rural health Statistics a publication of Ministry of Health, Govt. of India. In case of hospitals, for the missing years, we have adopted the figures same as the previous year. So far as births in institutions and in home under medically trained practitioner are concerned, we have interpolated the data by computing the average growth rate.
3. Net state domestic product at 80-81 prices, current net state domestic product and proportion of rural population were incorporated from the various issues of National Account Statistic published by the Central Statistical Organisation, G.O.I.
4. Health expenditure, revenue and capital expenditure on water supply and sanitation were collected from the various issues of Reserve Bank of India Bulletin.
5. Literacy rates were collected from two sources: Census of India and the requisite rounds of National Sample Survey conducted by the Central Statistical Organisation, G.O.I. For the years where no observation was available from either source, we have interpolated the data for the missing years by using a simple growth rate.
6. Population figures were collected from the Census of India. Census data is available only for 1981 and 1991. Data on the intermittent years were computed on the basis of the growth rates for the decades.

REFERENCES

Aigner, D. J., C. A. K. Lovell, and P. Schmidt (1977), "Formulation and Estimation of Stochastic Frontier Production Function Models", *Journal of Econometrics*, 6, 21-37.

Auster, R., I. Leveson, and D. Sarachek (1969), "The Production of Health: an Exploratory Study ", *Journal of Human Resources*, IV, Fall, 411-36.

Battese, G. E. and T. J. Coelli (1995), "A Model for Technical Inefficiency Effects in a Stochastic Frontier Production Function for Panel Data", *Empirical Economics*, 20, 325-332.

Battese, G. E. and T. J. Coelli (1993), "A Stochastic Frontier Production Function Incorporating a Model for Technical Inefficiency Effects", Working Paper 69, Department of Econometrics and Applied Statistics, University of New England.

Bauer, P.W. (1990), "Recent Developments in the Econometric Estimation of Frontiers", *Journal of Econometrics*, 46, 39-56.

Beenstock, M. and P. Sturdy (1990), "The Determinants of Infant Mortality in Regional India", *World Development*, 18, 443-453.

Brenner, H. M. (1983), "Mortality and Economic Instability: Detailed Analysis for Britain", in J. John et al.. (edited), *Influence of Economic Instability on Health*, Berlin: Springer-Verlag, 28-84.

CEHAT: Database on Health, Mumbai, India

Central Statistical Organisation, various issues, Government of India.

Cochrane, A. L., A. S. St. Leger, and F. Moore (1978), "Health Service Input and Mortality Output in Developed Countries", *Journal of Epidemiology and Community Health*, 32, 200-205.

Coelli, T. J. (1994), "A Guide to Frontier Version 4.1: A Computer Program for Stochastic Frontier Production and Cost Function Estimation", mimeo, Department of Economics, University of New England.

DasGupta, P. (1993), *An Inquiry into Well-Being and Destitution*, Clarendon Press, Oxford.

Dreze, J. and A. Sen (1989), *Hunger and Public Action*, Clarendon Press Oxford.

Duleep, H. O. (1986), "Measuring the effect of income on adult mortality using longitudinal administrative record data", *Journal of Human Resources XXI (1)*, 238-251.

Ettner, S. L. (1996), "New Evidence on the Relationship between Income and Health", *Journal of Health Economics*, 15, pp. 67-83.

Feldstein, P. J. (1988), *Health Care Economics*, Delmar Publishers Inc., U.S.A.

Forsund, F. R., C. A. K. Lovell, and P. Schmidt (1980), "A Survey of Frontier Production Functions and of their Relationship to Efficiency Measurement", *Journal of Econometrics*, 13, 5-25.

Fuchs, V. R. (1965), "Some Economic Aspects of Mortality in Developed Countries", in M. Perlman (edited), *The Economics of Health and Medical Care*, MacMillan, 174-193.

Gaiha, R. and M. Spinedi (1993), "Infant Mortality and Public Policy", *Public Finance*, 18, 63-77.

Gerdtham, U.-G., M. Lothgren, M. Tambour, C. Rehnberg (1998), "Internal Markets and Health Care Efficiency: a Multiple-Output Stochastic Frontier Analysis", Stockholm School of Economics, Working Paper Series in Economics and Finance, 222.

Greene, W. H. (1993), "The Econometric Approach to Efficiency Analysis", in Fried, H. O., C. A. K. Lovell, and S. S. Schmidt (edited), *The Measurement of Productive Efficiency*, Oxford University Press, New York, 68-119.

Hadley, J. (1988), "Medicare Spending and Mortality Rates of the Elderly", *Inquiry*, 23, 485–493.

Hadley, J. (1982), *More Medical Care, Better Health?* The Urban Institute, Washington D.C.

Health Information of India, various issues, Government of India.

Himmelblau, D. M. (1972), *Applied Non-Linear Programming*, McGraw- Hill, New York.

Huang, C. J. and J. T. Liu (1994), "Estimation of a Non-Neutral Stochastic Frontier Production Function", *Journal of Productivity Analysis*, 5, 171-180.

Hughes, M.D. (1988), "A Stochastic Frontier Cost Function for Residential Child Care Provision", *Journal of Applied Econometrics*, 3, 203-214.

Jain, A. K., (1985), "Determinants of Regional Variations in Infant Mortality in Rural India", *Population Studies*, 39, 407-424.

Jondrow, J., C. A. K. Lovell, I. S. Materov, and P. Schmidt (1982), "On estimation of Technical Inefficiency in the Stochastic Frontier Production Function Model", *Journal of Econometrics*, 19, 233-238.

Kumbhakar, S. C., S. Ghosh and J. T. McGukin (1991), "A Generalised Production Frontier Approach for Estimating Determinants of Inefficiency in U.S. Dairy Farms", *Journal of Business and Economics Statistics*, 9, 279-286.

Lipton, M. and J. Van der Gaag (1990), *The Willingness to Pay for Medical Care: Evidence from Two Developing Countries*, Baltimore: Johns Hopkins University Press.

Lovell, C. A. K. and Schmidt, S. S.(edited), *The Measurement of Productive Efficiency*, Oxford University Press, New York, 68-119.

Lopez, E., V. L. Phillips and M. Silos (1992), "Deaths from Gastro-Intenstinal Cancer in Mexico: Probable Cause for Water Sampling" in Zweifel, P. and H. E. Frech III (edited), *Health Economics Worldwide*, 331-347.

McKinlay, J. B. (1989), "A Review of the Evidence Concerning the Impact of Medical Measures on Recent Mortality and Morbidity in the United States", *International Journal of Health Services*, 19 (2), 181-208.

Meeker, E., (1973), "Allocation of Resources to Health Revisited", *Journal of Human Resources*, vol. VIII, Spring, 257-259.

Meeusen, W. and J. van den Broeck (1977), "Efficiency Estimation from Cobb-Douglas Production Functions With Composed Error", *International Economic Review*, 18, 435-444.

National Sample Survey, various issues, Government of India.

Pitt, M. M. and L. F. Lee (1981), "Measurement and Sources of Technical Inefficiency in the Indonesian Weaving Industry", *Journal of Development Economics*, 9, 43-64.

Rao, D. N. and R. L. Bhat (1991), "Estimation of A Community Health Status Index on the basis of a MIMIC Model", Indian Economic Review, XXVI, No. 1, 50-62.

Reddy, K. N. and V. Selvaraju (1994), *Health Care Expenditures by Government in India: 1974-75 to 1990-91*, Seven Hills Publication, New Delhi, India.

Reifschneider, D. and R. Stevenson (1991), "Systematic Departures from the Frontier: A Framework for the Analysis of Firm Inefficiency", *International Economic Review*, 32, 715-723.

Rural Health Statistics, various issues, Government of India.

Sample Registration System, various issues, Government of India.

Schmidt, P. (1986), "Frontier Production Functions", *Econometric Reviews*, 4, 289-328.

Schmidt, P. and C. A. K. Lovell (1979), "Estimating Technical and Allocative Inefficiency Relative to Stochastic Production and Cost Frontiers", *Journal of Econometrics*, 9, 343-366.

Singh, Ram D. (1994), "Fertility- Mortality Variations Across LDCs: Women's Education, Labour Force Participation, and Contraceptive- Use, *Kyklos*, 47, 209-229.

Stewart Jr., C. T. (1971), "The Allocation of Resources to Health", *Journal of Human Resources*, VI, Winter, 103-121.

Tulasidhar, V. B. (1989) "*Public Expenditure, Medical Care And Infant Mortality: A comparative Study of States in India*", State Finance Unit Research Paper-2, National Institute of Public Finance and Policy.

United Nations Development Programme: Human Development Report (1993), New York: Oxford University Press.

Wolfe, B. and M. Gabay (1987), "Health Status and Medical Expenditure: More Evidence of a Link", *Social Science and Medicine*, 25(8), 883-888.

Zweifel, P. and F. Breyer (1997), *Health Economics*, New York: Oxford University Press.

In: India: Economic, Political and Social Issues
Editors: Urlah B. Nissam
ISBN: 978-1-60456-509-6
© 2008 Nova Science Publishers, Inc.

Chapter 8

INDIA-U.S. RELATIONS[*]

K. Alan Kronstadt

ABSTRACT

Long considered a "strategic backwater"from Washington's perspective, South Asia has emerged in the 21st century as increasingly vital to core U.S. foreign policy interests. India, the region's dominant actor with more than one billion citizens, is now recognized as a nascent major power and "natural partner" of the United States, one that many analysts view as a potential counterweight to China's growing clout. Washington and New Delhi have since 2004 been pursuing a "strategic partnership" based on shared values such as democracy, multi-culturalism, and rule of law. Numerous economic, security, and global initiatives, including plans for "full civilian nuclear energy cooperation," are underway. This latter initiative, launched by President Bush in July 2005 and provisionally endorsed by the 109th Congress in late 2006 (P.L. 109-401), reverses three decades of U.S. nonproliferation policy. It would require, among other steps, conclusion of a peaceful nuclear agreement between the United States and India, which would itself enter into force only after a Joint Resolution of Approval by Congress. Also in 2005, the United States and India signed a ten-year defense framework agreement that calls for expanding bilateral security cooperation. Since 2002, the two countries have engaged in numerous and unprecedented combined military exercises. The issue of major U.S. arms sales to India may come before the 110th Congress. The influence of a growing and relatively wealthy Indian-American community of more than two million is reflected in Congress's largest country-specific caucus.

Further U.S. interest in South Asia focuses on ongoing tensions between India and Pakistan, a problem rooted in unfinished business from the 1947 Partition, competing claims to the Kashmir region, and, in more recent years, "cross-border terrorism" in both Kashmir and major Indian cities. In the interests of regional stability, the United States strongly encourages an ongoing India-Pakistan peace initiative and remains concerned about the potential for conflict over Kashmiri sovereignty to cause open hostilities between these two nuclear-armed countries. The United States seeks to curtail the proliferation of nuclear weapons and ballistic missiles in South Asia. Both India and Pakistan have resisted external pressure to sign the major nonproliferation treaties. In

---

[*] Excerpted from CRS Report RL33529, dated January 3, 2007.

1998, the two countries conducted nuclear tests that evoked international condemnation. Proliferation-related restrictions on U.S. aid were triggered, then later lifted through congressional-executive cooperation from 1998 to 2000. Remaining sanctions on India (and Pakistan) were removed in October 2001.

India is in the midst of major and rapid economic expansion. Many U.S. business interests view India as a lucrative market and candidate for foreign investment. The United States supports India's efforts to transform its once quasi-socialist economy through fiscal reform and market opening. Since 1991, India has taken steps in this direction, with coalition governments keeping the country on a general path of reform. Yet there is U.S. concern that such movement remains slow and inconsistent. Congress also continues to have concerns about abuses of human rights, including caste- and gender-based discrimination, and religious freedoms in India. Moreover, the spread of HIV/AIDS in India has attracted congressional attention as a serious development.

MOST RECENT DEVELOPMENTS

- On December 22, two days of India-Pakistan talks on the militarized Sir Creek dispute ended with agreement to conduct a joint survey. In mid-November, the India-Pakistan "Composite Dialogue" recommenced when the Indian and Pakistani foreign secretaries held formal meetings in New Delhi, the first such meetings since New Delhi's suspension of the peace process in the wake of July 11 terrorist bombings in Bombay. New Indian Foreign Secretary Shiv Shankar Menon called the talks "very useful and constructive" and, along with Pakistani Foreign Secretary Riaz Khan, further developed the planned joint anti-terrorism mechanism mandated by Prime Minister Singh and Pakistani President Pervez Musharraf on the sidelines of a September Nonaligned Movement summit in Cuba. The foreign secretaries also reviewed the peace process and developments in Kashmir, but made no announcements on longstanding territorial disputes or the status of investigations into the Bombay bombings (in October, Prime Minister Singh said India had "credible evidence" of Pakistan's involvement in those bombings).
- On December 18, President Bush signed into law H.R. 5682, the Henry J. Hyde United States-India Peaceful Atomic Energy Cooperation Act of 2006 (P.L. 109-401), to enable civil nuclear cooperation with India. Days earlier, a conference report (H.Rept. 109-721) had been issued to accompany the bill; congressional conferees had reconciled House and Senate versions of the legislation and provided a 30-page explanatory statement. The Indian government welcomed the developments while also claiming the legislation contained "extraneous and prescriptive provisions," and Prime Minister Singh said "clearly difficult negotiations lie ahead." Vocal critics of the initiative in its current form include India's main opposition Bharatiya Janata Party, influential Left Front leaders, and some members of the country's nuclear scientific community, who express various concerns about potentially negative effects on India's scientific and foreign policy independence. (See also CRS Report RL33016, *U.S. Nuclear Cooperation With India.*)
- On December 15, Prime Minister Singh paid a visit to Tokyo, where India and Japan inked 12 bilateral agreements to forward their "strategic partnership," including

negotiations toward a future free trade agreement. Tokyo withheld endorsement of India's entry into the civilian nuclear club.

- On December 8, day, Under Secretary of State Nicolas Burns met with Foreign Secretary Shiv Shankar Menon in New Delhi to discuss "progress in all the areas" of U.S.-India relations.

- On December 4, Pakistani President Musharraf said Pakistan is "against independence" for Kashmir, instead offering a four-point proposal that would lead to "self-governance," defined as "falling between autonomy and independence." Many analysts saw the proposal as being roughly in line with New Delhi's Kashmir position. Prime Minster Singh later welcomed Musharraf's proposals, saying they "contribute to the ongoing thought process."

- On November 28, a delegation of 250 American business executives arrived in Bombay on a mission to explore new opportunities to invest in India and develop new partnerships with companies there. The delegation, led by Under Secretary of Commerce Franklin Lavin, represented 180 companies from a variety of sectors and is the largest-ever to visit India.

- On November 23, Chinese President Hu Jintao ended a four-day visit to India, the first such visit by a Chinese president since 1996. Two days earlier, India and China issued a Joint Declaration which outlined a "ten-pronged strategy" to boost bilateral socio-economic ties and defense cooperation, and to "reinforce their strategic partnership." The two countries, which declared themselves "partners for mutual benefit" rather than rivals or competitors, also signed 13 pacts on a variety of bilateral initiatives. The Joint Declaration notably contained an agreement to "promote cooperation in the field of nuclear energy." Outstanding border disputes, including China's continuing claim to 35,000 square miles of Indian territory, remain unresolved.

- On November 18, Agriculture Secretary Mike Johanns was in New Delhi for meetings with top Indian officials in New Delhi to discuss trade issues and to "get the Doha talks back on track." Secretary Johanns urged India to further open its farm markets to exports from other countries.

- On November 17, Iranian Foreign Minister Manouchehr Mottaki held talks with top Indian officials in New Delhi, where he said Tehran would "very soon" begin exports to India of liquid natural gas under a $21 billion, five million tons per year deal. According to New Delhi, India and Iran agreed that "the economic potential of the relationship needed to be actualized in the maximum."

- Also on November 16, a two-day meeting of the U.S.-India Defense Policy Group ended in New Delhi, where Under Secretary of Defense Eric Edelman and other U.S. officials expressed optimism about the potential for major arms sales to India in 2007.

- On November 5, a series of bombings in the northeastern Assam state left at least 15 people dead and dozens more injured. Police blamed the separatist the United Liberation Front of Assam (ULFA). A spike in violence in the region follows New Delhi's September withdrawal from a six-week-long truce with ULFA after militants shot dead a policeman and a civilian.

CONTEXT OF THE U.S.-INDIA RELATIONSHIP

Background

U.S. and congressional interests in India cover a wide spectrum of issues, ranging from the militarized dispute with Pakistan and weapons proliferation to concerns about regional security, terrorism, human rights, health, energy, and trade and investment opportunities. In the 1990s, India-U.S. relations were particularly affected by the demise of the Soviet Union — India's main trading partner and most reliable source of economic and military assistance for most of the Cold War — and New Delhi's resulting need to diversify its international relationships. Also significant were India's adoption of significant economic policy reforms beginning in 1991, a deepening bitterness between India and Pakistan over Kashmir, and signs of a growing Indian preoccupation with China as a potential long-term strategic rival. With the fading of Cold War constraints, the United States and India began exploring the possibilities for a more normalized relationship between the world's two largest democracies. Throughout the 1990s, however, regional rivalries, separatist tendencies, and sectarian tensions continued to divert India's attention and resources from economic and social development. Fallout from these unresolved problems — particularly nuclear proliferation and human rights issues — presented irritants in bilateral relations.

India's May 1998 nuclear tests were an unwelcome surprise and seen to be a policy failure in Washington, and they spurred then-Deputy Secretary of State Strobe Talbott to launch a series of meetings with Indian External Affairs Minister Jaswant Singh in an effort to bring New Delhi more in line with U.S. arms control and nonproliferation goals. While this proximate purpose went unfulfilled, the two officials soon engaged a broader agenda on the entire scope of U.S.-India relations, eventually meeting fourteen times in seven different countries over a two-year period. The Talbott-Singh talks were considered the most extensive U.S.-India engagement up to that time and likely enabled circumstances in which the United States could play a key role in defusing the 1999 Kargil crisis, as well as laying the groundwork for a landmark U.S. presidential visit in 2000.

President Bill Clinton's March 2000 visit to South Asia seemed a major U.S. initiative to improve relations with India. One outcome was a Joint Statement in which the two countries pledged to "deepen the India-American partnership in tangible ways."[1] A U.S.-India Joint Working Group on Counterterrorism was established that year and continues to meet regularly. During his subsequent visit to the United States later in 2000, Prime Minister Atal Bihari Vajpayee addressed a joint session of Congress and issued a second Joint Statement with President Clinton agreeing to cooperate on arms control, terrorism, and HIV/AIDS.[2]

In the wake of the September 2001 terrorist attacks on the United States, India took the immediate and unprecedented step of offering to the United States full cooperation and the use of India's bases for counterterrorism operations. Engagement was accelerated after a November 2001 meeting between President Bush and Prime Minister Vajpayee, when the two leaders agreed to greatly expand U.S.-India cooperation on a wide range of issues, including regional security, space and scientific collaboration, civilian nuclear safety, and broadened economic ties.[3] Notable progress has come in the area of security cooperation, with an increasing focus on counterterrorism, joint military exercises, and arms sales. In late 2001, the U.S.-India Defense Policy Group met in New Delhi for the first time since India's 1998 nuclear tests and outlined a defense partnership based on regular and high-level policy dialogue.

India in Brief

Population: 1.1 billion; *growth rate*: 1.4% (2006 est.)

Area: 3,287,590 sq. km. (slightly more than onethird the size of the United States)

Capital: New Delhi

Head of Government: Prime Minister Manmohan Singh (Congress Party)

Ethnic Groups: Indo-Aryan 72%; Dravidian 25%; other 3%

Languages: 15 official, 13 of which are the primary tongue of at least 10 million people; Hindi is primary tongue of about 30%; English widely used

Religions: Hindu 81%; Muslim 13%; Christian 2%; Sikh 2%, other 2% (2001 census)

Life Expectancy at Birth: female 65.6 years; male 63.9 years (2006 est.)

Literacy: female 48%; male 70% (2003 est.)

Gross Domestic Product (at PPP): $4.24 trillion; *per capita*: $3,870; *growth rate* 8.5% (2006 est.)

Currency: Rupee (100 = $2.27)

Inflation: 5.6% (2006 est.)

Military Expenditures: $22.8 billion (2.9% of GDP; 2005)

U.S. Trade: exports to U.S. $21.9 billion; imports from U.S. $9.9 billion (2006 est.)

Sources: CIA World Factbook; U.S. Commerce Department; Economist Intelligence Unit; Global Insight.

Prime Minister Manmohan Singh paid a landmark July 2005 visit to Washington, where what may be the most significant joint U.S.-India statement to date was issued.[4] In March 2006, President Bush spent three days in India, discussed further strengthening a bilateral "global partnership," and issued another Joint Statement.[5] Today, the Bush Administration vows to "help India become a major world power in the 21st century," and U.S.-India relations are conducted under the rubric of three major "dialogue" areas: strategic (including global issues and defense), economic (including trade, finance, commerce, and environment), and energy. President Bush's 2002 *National Security Strategy of the United States* stated that "U.S. interests require a strong relationship with India." The 2006 version claims that, "India now is poised to shoulder global obligations in cooperation with the United States in a way befitting a major power."[6] (See also CRS Report RL33072, *U.S.-India Bilateral Agreements.*)

Recognition of India's increasing stature and importance — and of the growing political influence some 2.3 million Indian-Americans — is found in the U.S. Congress, where the India and Indian-American Caucus is now the largest of all country-specific caucuses. Over the past six years, legal Indian immigrants have come to the United States at a more rapid rate than any other group. In 2005 and 2006, the Indian-American community, relatively wealthy, geographically dispersed, and well-entrenched in several U.S. business sectors, conducted a major (and apparently successful) lobbying effort to encourage congressional passage of legislation to enable U.S.-India civil nuclear cooperation.[7]

Current U.S.-India Engagement

Following President Bush's March 2006 visit to New Delhi — the first such trip by a U.S. President in six years — U.S. diplomatic engagement with India has continued to be deep and multifaceted:

- A two-day meeting of the U.S.-India Joint Working Group on Counterterrorism was held in April in Washington, where Counterterrorism Coordinator Henry Crumpton led the U.S. delegation.
- Indian Power Minister Sushil Shinde paid an April visit to Washington for meetings with top U.S. officials.
- The fourth meeting of the U.S.-India Trade Policy Forum took place in May in New Delhi, where talks focused on trade barriers, agriculture, investment, and intellectual property rights.
- In June, the Chairman of the U.S. Joint Chiefs of Staff, Gen. Peter Pace, met with top Indian officials in New Delhi to discuss expanding U.S.-India strategic ties.
- Also in June, new U.S. Trade Representative Susan Schwab met with Indian Commerce Minister Kamal Nath in Washington, agreeing on initiatives to strengthen and deepen bilateral trade.
- In July, President Bush met with Prime Minister Singh on the sidelines of the G-8 Summit in St. Petersburg, Russia, to discuss the 7/11 Bombay bombings and planned U.S.-India civil nuclear cooperation.
- In August, a delegation of U.S. officials, including President Bush's top energy and environment advisor, visited New Delhi to meet with top Indian officials and business leaders to discuss energy security and the environment.
- Also in August, a meeting of the U.S.-India Financial and Economic Forum was held in Washington, where officials discussed Indian efforts to liberalize its financial sector, among other issues.
- In September, U.S. and Indian army troops conducted joint counterinsurgency exercises in Hawaii.
- Defense Minister Pranab Mukherjee led an Indian delegation to the U.N. General Assembly session later in September and met with top U.S. officials in New York.

- In October, a meeting of the U.S.-India CEO Forum was held in New York City. Along with numerous U.S. and Indian business leaders, high-level government officials joining the session included Commerce Secretary Carlos Gutierrez and Assistant to the President for Economic Policy Allan Hubbard from the American side, and Commerce Minister Kamal Nath and Planning Commission Deputy Minister Montek Singh Ahluwalia from India.

- Assistant Secretary of State Richard Boucher made a lengthy visit to India in November for meetings with top Indian leaders.

- In mid-November, U.S. Under Secretary of Defense Edelman met with Defense Secretary Dutt in New Delhi for the eighth session of the U.S.-India Defense Policy Group, where officials discussed bolstering bilateral cooperation in military security, technology, and trade.

- Also in mid-November, the U.S. Environmental Protection Agency announced establishment of a Methane to Markets Partnership to promote development of coal bed and coal methane projects in India.

- Later in November, Agriculture Secretary Michael Johannes visited New Delhi to discuss bilateral and multilateral trade issues with top Indian leaders.

- In late November, Under Secretary of Commerce Franklin Lavin led a delegation of 250 American business executives to Bombay on a mission to explore new opportunities to invest in India and develop new partnerships with companies there.

- In December, Under Secretary of Commerce and Director of the U.S. Patent and Trademark Office Jon Dudas visited New Delhi to discuss intellectual property rights and copyright protections with India leaders.

- Also in December, Under Secretary of State Nicholas Burns met with Foreign Secretary Shiv Shankar Menon in New Delhi to discuss progress in all areas of U.S.-India relations. (See also CRS Report RL33072, *U.S.-India Bilateral Agreements*.)

India's Regional Relations

India is geographically dominant in both South Asia and the Indian Ocean region. While all of South Asia's smaller continental states (Pakistan, Bangladesh, Nepal, and Bhutan) share borders with India, none share borders with each other. The country possesses the region's largest economy and, with more than one billion inhabitants, is by far the most populous on the Asian Subcontinent. The United States has a keen interest in South Asian stability, perhaps especially with regard to the India-Pakistan nuclear weapons dyad, and so closely monitors India's regional relationships.

Pakistan

Decades of militarized tensions and territorial disputes between India and Pakistan have seriously hamstrung economic and social development in both countries while also precluding establishment of effective regional economic or security institutions. Seemingly incompatible national identities contributed to the nuclearization of the Asian Subcontinent, with the nuclear weapons capabilities of both countries becoming overt in 1998. Since that time, a central aspect of U.S. policy in South Asia has been prevention of interstate conflict that could lead to nuclear war. In 2004, New Delhi and Islamabad launched their most recent comprehensive effort to reduce tensions and resolve outstanding disputes.

Current Status

The India-Pakistan peace initiative continues, with officials from both countries (and the United States) offering a generally positive assessment of the ongoing dialogue. In May 2006, India and Pakistan agreed to open a second Kashmiri bus route and to allow new truck service to facilitate trade in Kashmir (the new bus service began in June). Subsequent "Composite Dialogue" talks were held to discuss militarized territorial disputes, terrorism and narcotics, and cultural exchanges, but high hopes for a settlement of differences over the Siachen Glacier were dashed when a May session ended without progress. June talks on the Tubal navigation project/Wullar barrage water dispute similarly ended without forward movement.

Compounding tensions, separatist-related violence spiked in Indian Kashmir in the spring and summer of 2006, and included a May massacre of 35 Hindu villagers by suspected Islamic militants. Grenade attacks on tourist buses correlated with a late May roundtable meeting of Prime Minister Singh and Kashmiri leaders, leaving at least two dozen civilians dead and devastating the Valley's recently revitalized tourist industry. Significant incidents of attempted "cross-border infiltration" of Islamic militants at the Kashmiri Line of Control continue and top Indian leaders renewed their complaints that Islamabad is taking insufficient action to quell terrorist activities on Pakistan-controlled territory.

The serial bombing of Bombay commuter trains on July 11, 2006, killed nearly 200 people and injured many hundreds more. With suspicions regarding the involvement of Pakistan-based groups, New Delhi suspended talks with Islamabad pending an investigation. However, at a September meeting on the sidelines of a Nonaligned Movement summit in Cuba, Prime Minister Singh and Pakistani President Musharraf announced a resumption of formal peace negotiations and also decided to implement a joint anti-terrorism mechanism. Weeks later, Bombay's top police official said the 7/11 train bombings were planned by Pakistan's intelligence services and, in October, Prime Minister Singh himself said India had "credible evidence" of Pakistani involvement.

To date, India is not known to have gone public with or shared with Pakistan any incriminating evidence of Pakistani government involvement in the Bombay bombings. In November 2006, Composite Dialogue resumed with its third round of foreign secretary-level talks when Foreign Secretary Shiv Shankar Menon hosted a New Delhi visit by his Pakistani counterpart, Riaz Khan. No progress was made on outstanding territorial disputes, but the two officials did give shape to a joint anti-terrorism mechanism proposed in September. Such a mechanism is controversial in India, with some analysts skeptical about the efficacy of institutional engagement with Pakistan in this issue-area even as Islamabad is suspected of complicity in anti-India terrorism. The India-Pakistan peace process is slated to continue in early 2007 when External Affairs Minister Pranab Mukherjee is to visit Pakistan.

Background

Three wars — in 1947-48, 1965, and 1971 — and a constant state of military preparedness on both sides of the border have marked six decades of bitter rivalry between India and Pakistan. The bloody and acrimonious nature of the 1947 partition of British India and continuing violence in Kashmir remain major sources of interstate tensions. Despite the existence of widespread poverty across South Asia, both India and Pakistan have built large defense establishments —including nuclear weapons capability and ballistic missile programs — at the cost of economic and social development. The nuclear weapons capabilities of the two countries became overt in May 1998, magnifying greatly the potential dangers of a fourth India-Pakistan war. Although a bilateral peace process has been underway for nearly three years, little substantive progress has been made toward resolving the Kashmir issue, and New Delhi continues to be rankled by what it calls Islamabad's insufficient effort to end Islamic militancy that affects India.

The Kashmir problem is itself rooted in claims by both countries to the former princely state, now divided by a military Line of Control (LOC) into the Indian state of Jammu and Kashmir and Pakistan-controlled Azad [Free] Kashmir (see "The Kashmir Issue," below). Normal relations between New Delhi and Islamabad were severed in December 2001 after a terrorist attack on the Indian Parliament was blamed on Pakistan-supported Islamic militants. Other lethal attacks on Indian civilians spurred Indian leaders to call for a "decisive war," but intense international diplomatic engagement, including multiple trips to the region by high-level U.S. officials, apparently persuaded India to refrain from attacking.[8] In October 2002, the two countries ended a tense, ten-month military standoff at their shared border, but there remained no high-level diplomatic dialogue between India and Pakistan (a July 2001 summit meeting in the Indian city of Agra had failed to produce any movement toward a settlement of the bilateral dispute).

In April 2003, Prime Minister Vajpayee extended a symbolic "hand of friendship" to Pakistan. The initiative resulted in slow, but perceptible progress in confidence-building, and within months full diplomatic relations between the two countries were restored. September 2003 saw an exchange of heated rhetoric by the Indian prime minister and the Pakistani president at the U.N. General Assembly; some analysts concluded that the peace initiative was moribund. Yet New Delhi soon reinvigorated the process by proposing confidence-building through people-to-people contacts. Islamabad responded positively and, in November, took its own initiatives, most significantly the offer of a cease-fire along the Kashmir LOC. A major breakthrough in bilateral relations came at the close of a January 2004 summit session of the South Asian Association for Regional Cooperation in Islamabad. After a meeting between Vajpayee and Pakistani President Musharraf — their first since July 2001 — the two leaders agreed to re-engage a "composite dialogue" to bring about "peaceful settlement of all bilateral issues, including Jammu and Kashmir, to the satisfaction of both sides."

A May 2004 change of governments in New Delhi had no effect on the expressed commitment of both sides to carry on the process of mid- and high-level discussions, and the new Indian Prime Minister, Manmohan Singh, met with President Musharraf in September 2004 in New York, where the two leaders agreed to explore possible options for a "peaceful, negotiated settlement" of the Kashmir issue "in a sincere manner and purposeful spirit." After Musharraf's April 2005 visit to New Delhi, India and Pakistan released a joint statement calling their bilateral peace process "irreversible." Some analysts believe that increased people-to-people contacts have significantly altered public perceptions in both countries and may have acquired permanent momentum. Others are less optimistic about the respective governments' long-term commitment to dispute resolution. Moreover, an apparent new U.S. embrace of India has fueled Pakistan's anxieties about the regional balance of power.

China

India and China together account for one-third of the world's population, and are seen to be rising 21st century powers and potential strategic rivals. The two countries fought a brief but intense border war in 1962 that left China in control of large swaths of territory still claimed by India. Today, India accuses China of illegitimately occupying nearly 15,000 square miles of Indian territory in Kashmir, while China lays claim to 35,000 square miles in the northeastern Indian state of Arunachal Pradesh. The 1962 clash ended a previously friendly relationship between the two leaders of the Cold War "nonaligned movement" and left many Indians feeling shocked and betrayed. While Sino-Indian relations have warmed considerably in recent years, the two countries have yet to reach a final boundary agreement. Adding to New Delhi's sense of insecurity have been suspicions regarding China's long-term nuclear weapons capabilities and strategic intentions in South and Southeast Asia. In fact, a strategic orientation focused on China appears to have affected the course and scope of New Delhi's own nuclear weapons and ballistic missile programs. Beijing's military and economic support for Pakistan —support that is widely understood to have included WMD-related transfers — is a major and ongoing source of friction; past Chinese support for Pakistan's Kashmir position has added to the discomfort of Indian leaders. New Delhi takes note of Beijing's security relations with neighboring Burma and the construction of military facilities on the Indian Ocean. The two countries also have competed for energy resources to feed their rapidly growing economies; India's relative poverty puts New Delhi at a significant disadvantage in such competition.

Analysts taking a realist perspective view China as an external balancer in the South Asian subsystem, with Beijing's material support for Islamabad allowing Pakistan to challenge the aspiring regional hegemony of a more powerful India. Many observers, especially in India, see Chinese support for Pakistan as a key aspect of Beijing's perceived policy of "encirclement" or constraint of India as a means of preventing or delaying New Delhi's ability to challenge Beijing's region-wide influence.

Despite historic and strategic frictions, high-level exchanges between India and China regularly include statements that there exists no fundamental conflict of interest between the two countries. During a landmark 1993 visit to Beijing, Prime Minister Narasimha Rao signed an agreement to reduce troops and maintain peace along the Line of Actual Control that divides the two countries' forces at the disputed border. A total of 30 rounds of border talks and joint working group meetings aimed at reaching a final settlement have been held since 1981, with New Delhi and Beijing agreeing to move forward in other issue-areas even as territorial claims remain unresolved.

A 2003 visit to Beijing by Prime Minister Vajpayee was viewed as marking a period of much improved relations. In late 2004, India's army chief visited Beijing to discuss deepening bilateral defense cooperation and a first-ever India-China strategic dialogue was later held in New Delhi. Military-to-military contacts have included modest but unprecedented combined naval and army exercises. During Chinese Prime Minister Wen Jiabao's April 2005 visit to New Delhi, India and China inked 11 new agreements and vowed to launch a "strategic partnership" that will include broadened defense links and efforts to expand economic relations.[9] In a move that eased border tensions, China formally recognized Indian sovereignty over the former kingdom of Sikkim, and India reiterated its view that Tibet is a part of China. Moreover, in 2006, dubbed the "Year of India-China Friendship," the two countries formally agreed to cooperate in securing overseas oil resources. In July of that year,

India and China reopened the Nathu La border crossing for local trade. The Himalayan pass had been closed since the 1962 war. Sino-India trade relations are blossoming — bilateral commerce was worth nearly $19 billion in 2005, almost an eight-fold increase over the 1999 value. In fact, China may soon supplant the United States as India's largest trading partner.

Indo-Chinese relations further warmed in November 2006, when Chinese President Hu Jintao made a trip to India., the first such visit by a Chinese president since 1996. There India and China issued a Joint Declaration outlining a "ten-pronged strategy" to boost bilateral socio-economic ties and defense cooperation, and to "reinforce their strategic partnership." The two countries, which declared themselves "partners for mutual benefit" rather than rivals or competitors, also signed 13 new pacts on a variety of bilateral initiatives. The Joint Declaration notably contained an agreement to "promote cooperation in the field of nuclear energy," although no details have been provided on what form such cooperation might take.

Other Countries

India takes an active role in assisting reconstruction efforts in Afghanistan, having committed $650 million to this cause, as well as contributing personnel and opening numerous consulates there (much to the dismay of Pakistan, which fears strategic encirclement and takes note of India's past support for Afghan Tajik and Uzbek militias). Among Indian assistance to Afghanistan are funding for a new $111 million power station, an $84 million road-building project, a $77 million damn project, and construction of Kabul's new $67 Parliament building, to be completed in 2010. The United States has welcomed India's role in Afghanistan.

To the north, New Delhi called King Gyanendra's February 2005 power seizure in Nepal "a serious setback for the cause of democracy," but India renewed nonlethal military aid to the Royal Nepali Army only months later. India remains seriously concerned about political instability in Kathmandu and the cross-border infiltration of Maoist militants from Nepal. The United States seeks continued Indian attention to the need for a restoration of democracy in Nepal.

To the east, and despite India's key role in the creation of neighboring Bangladesh in 1971, New Delhi's relations with Dhaka have been fraught with tensions related mainly to the cross-border infiltration of Islamic and separatist militants, and huge numbers of illegal migrants into India. The two countries' border forces engage in periodic gunbattles and India is completing construction of a fence along the entire shared border. Still, New Delhi and Dhaka have cooperated on counterterrorism efforts and talks on energy cooperation continue.

Further to the east, India is pursuing closer relations with the repressive regime in neighboring Burma, with an interest in energy cooperation and to counterbalance China's influence there. Such engagement seeks to achieve economic integration of India's northeast region and western Burma, as well as bolstering energy security. International human rights groups have criticized New Delhi's military interactions with Rangoon. The Bush Administration has urged India to be more active in pressing for democracy in Burma.

In the island nation of Sri Lanka off India's southeastern coast, a Tamil Hindu minority has been fighting a separatist war against the Sinhalese Buddhist majority since 1983. The violent conflict has again become serious in 2006, causing some three thousand deaths. More than 60 million Indian Tamils live in southern India. India's 1987 intervention to assist in enforcing a peace accord resulted in the deaths of more than 1,200 Indian troops and led to the 1991 assassination of former Indian Prime Minister Rajiv Gandhi by Tamil militants.

Since that time, New Delhi has maintained friendly relations with Colombo while refraining from any deep engagement in third-party peace efforts. The Indian Navy played a key role in providing disaster relief to Sri Lanka following the catastrophic December 2004 Indian Ocean tsunami.

POLITICAL SETTING

India is the world's most populous democracy and remains firmly committed to representative government and rule of law. U.S. policymakers commonly identify in the Indian political system shared core values, and this has facilitated increasingly friendly relations between the U.S. and Indian governments.

National Elections

India, with a robust and working democratic system, is a federal republic where the bulk of executive power rests with the prime minister and his or her cabinet (the Indian president is a ceremonial chief of state with limited executive powers). As a nation-state, India presents a vast mosaic of hundreds of different ethnic groups, religious sects, and social castes. Most of India's prime ministers have come from the country's Hindi-speaking northern regions and all but two have been upper-caste Hindus. The 543-seat Lok Sabha (People's House) is the locus of national power, with directly elected representatives from each of the country's 28 states and 7 union territories. A smaller upper house, the Rajya Sabha (Council of States), may review, but not veto, most legislation, and has no power over the prime minister or the cabinet. National and state legislators are elected to five-year terms.

National elections in October 1999 had secured ruling power for a Bharatiya Janata Party (BJP)-led coalition government headed by Prime Minister Vajpayee. That outcome decisively ended the historic dominance of the Nehru-Gandhi-led Congress Party, which was relegated to sitting in opposition at the national level (its members continued to lead many state governments). However, a surprise Congress resurgence under Sonia Gandhi in May 2004 national elections brought to power a new left-leaning coalition government led by former finance minister and Oxford-educated economist Manmohan Singh, a Sikh and India's first-ever non-Hindu prime minister. Many analysts attributed Congress's 2004 resurgence to the resentment of rural and poverty-stricken urban voters who felt left out of the "India shining" campaign of a BJP more associated with urban, middle-class interests. Others saw in the results a rejection of the Hindu nationalism associated with the BJP. (See CRS Report RL32465, *India's 2004 National Elections.*)

The Congress Party

Congress's electoral strength reached a nadir in 1999, when the party won only 110 Lok Sabha seats. Observers attributed the poor showing to a number of factors, including perceptions that party leader Sonia Gandhi lacked the experience to lead the country and the failure of Congress to make strong pre-election alliances (as had the BJP). Support for Congress had been in fairly steady decline following the 1984 assassination of Prime Minister Indira Gandhi and the 1991 assassination of her son, Prime Minister Rajiv Gandhi. Sonia Gandhi, Rajiv's Italian-born, Catholic widow, refrained from active politics until the 1998 elections. She later made efforts to revitalize the party by phasing out older leaders and attracting more women and lower castes — efforts that appear to have paid off in 2004. Today, Congress again occupies more parliamentary seats (145) than any other party and, through unprecedented alliances with powerful regional parties, it again leads India's government under the United Progressive Alliance (UPA) coalition. As party chief and UPA chair, Sonia Gandhi is believed to wield considerable influence over the ruling coalition's policy decision-making process.[10]

The Bharatiya Janata Party (BJP)

With the rise of Hindu nationalism, the BJP rapidly increased its parliamentary strength during the 1980s. In 1993, the party's image was tarnished among some, burnished for others, by its alleged complicity in serious communal violence in Bombay and elsewhere. Some hold elements of the BJP, as the political arm of extremist Hindu groups, responsible for the incidents (the party has advocated "Hindutva," or an India based on Hindu culture, and views this as key to nation-building). While leading a national coalition from 1998-2004, the BJP worked — with only limited success — to change its image from right-wing Hindu fundamentalist to conservative and secular, although 2002 communal rioting in Gujarat again damaged the party's credentials as a moderate organization. The BJP-led National Democratic Alliance was overseen by party notable Prime Minister Atal Vajpayee, whose widespread personal popularity helped to keep the BJP in power. Since 2004, the BJP has been weakened by leadership disputes, criticism from Hindu nationalists, and controversy involving party president Lal Advani (in December 2005, Advani ceded his leadership post and Vajpayee announced his retirement from politics). In 2006, senior BJP leader Pramod Mahajan was shot and killed in a family dispute.[11]

Regional Parties

The influence of regional and caste-based parties has become an increasingly important variable in Indian politics; the May 2004 national elections saw such parties receiving nearly half of all votes cast. Never before 2004 had the Congress Party entered into pre-poll alliances at the national level, and numerous analysts attributed Congress's success to precisely this new tack, especially thorough arrangements with the Bihar-based Rashtriya Janata Dal and Tamil Nadu's Dravida Munnetra Kazhagam. The newfound power of both large and smaller regional parties, alike, is seen to be reflected in the UPA's ministerial appointments, and in the Congress-led coalition's professed attention to rural issues and center-state relations. Two significant regional parties currently independent of both the ruling coalition and the BJP-led opposition are the Samajwadi Party, a largely Muslim- and lower caste-based organization highly influential in Uttar Pradesh, and the Bahujan Samaj Party of Bihar, which also represents mainly lower-caste constituents. State assembly elections in Uttar Pradesh — home to more than 170 million Indians — are slated for February 2007 and may be an important indicator of national political trends, especially in gauging satisfaction with the current center coalition.

BILATERAL ISSUES

"Next Steps in Strategic Partnership" and Beyond

The now-concluded Next Steps in Strategic Partnership (NSSP) initiative encompassed several major issues in India-U.S. relations. The Indian government has long pressed the United States to ease restrictions on the export to India of dual-use high-technology goods (those with military applications), as well as to increase civilian nuclear and civilian space cooperation. These three key issues came to be known as the "trinity," and top Indian officials insisted that progress in these areas was necessary to provide tangible evidence of a changed U.S.-India relationship. There were later references to a "quartet" when the issue of missile defense was included. In January 2004, President Bush and Prime Minister Vajpayee issued a joint statement declaring that the U.S.-India "strategic partnership" included expanding cooperation in the "trinity" areas, as well as expanding dialogue on missile defense.[12] This initiative was dubbed as the NSSP and involved a series of reciprocal steps.

In July 2005, the State Department announced successful completion of the NSSP, allowing for expanded bilateral commercial satellite cooperation, removal/revision of some U.S. export license requirements for certain dual-use and civil nuclear items. Taken together, the July 2005 U.S.-India Joint Statement and a June 2005 U.S.-India Defense Framework Agreement include provisions for moving forward in all four NSSP issue-areas.[13] Many observers saw in the NSSP evidence of a major and positive shift in the U.S. strategic orientation toward India, a shift later illuminated more starkly with the Bush Administration's intention to initiate full civil nuclear cooperation with India. (See also CRS Report RL33072, *U.S.-India Bilateral Agreements and 'Global Partnership.'*)

Civil Nuclear Cooperation

India's status as a non-signatory to the 1968 Nuclear Nonproliferation Treaty (NPT) has kept it from accessing most nuclear-related materials and fuels on the international market for more than three decades. New Delhi's 1974 "peaceful nuclear explosion" spurred the U.S.-led creation of the Nuclear Suppliers Group (NSG) — an international export control regime for nuclear-related trade — and the U.S. government further tightened its own export laws with the Nuclear Nonproliferation Act of 1978. New Delhi has long railed at a "nuclear apartheid" created by apparent double standards inherent in the NPT, which allows certain states to legitimately employ nuclear deterrents while other states cannot.

The Bush Administration Policy Shift

Differences over nuclear policy bedeviled U.S.-India ties for decades and — given New Delhi's lingering resentments — have presented a major psychological obstacle to more expansive bilateral relations. In a major policy shift, the July 2005 U.S.-India Joint Statement notably asserted that, "as a responsible state with advanced nuclear technology, India should acquire the same benefits and advantages as other such states," and President Bush vowed to work on achieving "full civilian nuclear energy cooperation with India." As a reversal of three decades of U.S. nonproliferation policy, such proposed cooperation stirred controversy and required changes in both U.S. law and in NSG guidelines. India reciprocally agreed to take its own steps, including identifying and separating its civilian and military nuclear facilities in a phased manner and placing the former under international safeguards. Some in Congress express concern that civil nuclear cooperation with India might allow that country to advance its military nuclear projects and be harmful to broader U.S. nonproliferation efforts. While the Bush Administration previously had insisted that such cooperation would take place only within the limits set by multilateral nonproliferation regimes, the Administration later actively sought adjustments to U.S. laws and policies, and has approached the NSG in an effort to adjust that regime's guidelines, which are set by member consensus.

In March 2006, President Bush and Prime Minister Singh issued a Joint Statement that included an announcement of "successful completion of India's [nuclear facility] separation plan."[14] After months of complex and difficult negotiations, the Indian government had presented a plan to separate its civilian and military nuclear facilities as per the July 2005 Joint Statement. The separation plan would require India to move 14 of its 22 reactors into permanent international oversight by the year 2014 and place all future civilian reactors under permanent safeguards. Shortly thereafter, legislation to waive the application of certain requirements under the Atomic Energy Act of 1954 with respect to India was, at the President's request, introduced in the U.S. Congress.

Potential Benefits and Costs

Secretary of State Rice appeared before key Senate and House committees in April 2006 to press the Bush Administration's case for civil nuclear cooperation with India. The Administration offered five main justifications for making changes in U.S. law to allow for such cooperation, contending that doing so would

- benefit U.S. security by bringing India "into the nonproliferation mainstream;"
- benefit U.S. consumers by reducing pressures on global energy markets, especially carbon-based fuels;
- benefit the environment by reducing carbon emissions/greenhouse gases;
- benefit U.S. business interests through sales to India of nuclear reactors, fuel, and support services; and
- benefit progress of the broader U.S.-India "global partnership."[15]

Many leading American experts on South Asian affairs joined the Administration in urging Congress to support the new policy, placing particular emphasis on the "necessary" role it would play in promoting a U.S.-India global partnership.[16]

Further hearings in the Senate (April 26) and House (May 11) saw a total of fifteen independent analysts weigh in on the potential benefits and/or problems that might accrue from such cooperation. Some experts opined that the Administration's optimism, perhaps especially as related to the potential effects on global energy markets and carbon emissions, could not be supported through realistic projections. Numerous nonproliferation experts, scientists, and former U.S. government officials warned that the Bush Administration's initiative was ill-considered, arguing that it would facilitate an increase in the size of India's nuclear arsenal, potentially leading to a nuclear arms race in Asia, and would undermine the global nonproliferation regime and cause significant damage to key U.S. security interests.[17]

The U.S. Chamber of Commerce, which, along with the U.S.-India Business Council, lobbied vigorously in favor of President Bush's initiative, speculated that civil nuclear cooperation with India could generate contracts for American businesses worth up to $100 billion, as well as generate up to 27,000 new American jobs each year for a decade.[18] However, foreign companies such as Russia's Atomstroyexport and France's Areva may be better poised to take advantage of the Indian market. Moreover, U.S. nuclear suppliers will likely balk at entering the Indian market in the absence of nuclear liability protection, which New Delhi does not offer at present.

Geopolitical Motives

In the realm of geopolitics, much of the Administration's argument for moving forward with the U.S.-India nuclear initiative appears rooted in an anticipation/expectation that New Delhi will in coming years and decades make policy choices that are more congruent with U.S. regional and global interests (a desire for such congruence is, in fact, written into P.L. 109-401). Proponents suggest that this U.S. "gesture" will have significant and lasting psychological and symbolic effects in addition to the strictly material ones, and that Indian leaders require such a gesture in order to feel confident in the United States as a reliable partner on the world stage.[19] Skeptics aver that the potential strategic benefits of the nuclear initiative are being over-sold. Indeed, centuries of Indian anti-colonial sentiments and oftentimes prickly, independent foreign policy choices are unlikely to be set aside in the short run, meaning that the anticipated geopolitical benefits of civil nuclear cooperation with India remain speculative and at least somewhat dependent upon unknowable global political developments.

Congressional Action

After months of consideration, the House International Relations Committee and Senate Foreign Affairs Committee both took action on relevant legislation in late June 2006, passing modified versions of the Administration's proposals by wide margins. The new House and

Senate bills (H.R. 5682 and S. 3709) made significant procedural changes to the Administration's proposal, changes that sought to retain congressional oversight of the negotiation process, in part by requiring the Administration to gain future congressional approval of a completed peaceful nuclear cooperation agreement with India (this is often referred to as a "123 Agreement," as it is negotiated under the conditions set forth in Section 123 of the Atomic Energy Act).

During the final months of its tenure, the 109th Congress demonstrated widespread bipartisan support for the Administration's new policy initiative by passing enabling legislation through both chambers (in July 2006, the House passed H.R. 5682 by a vote of 359-68; in November, the Senate passed an amended version of the same bill by a vote of 85-12). Numerous so-called "killer amendments" were rejected by both chambers (Indian government and Bush Administration officials had warned that certain proposed new provisions, such as those requiring that India halt its fissile material production or end its military relations with Iran, would trigger New Delhi's withdrawal from the entire negotiation).

In a December 2006 "lame duck" session, congressional conferees reconciled the House and Senate versions of the legislation and provided a 30-page explanatory statement (H. Rept. 109-721). On December 18, President Bush signed the Henry J. Hyde United States-India Peaceful Atomic Energy Cooperation Act of 2006 into law (P.L. 109-401), calling it a "historic agreement" that would help the United States and India meet the energy and security challenges of the 21st century. The President also issued a signing statement asserting that his approval of the Act "does not constitute [his] adoption of the statements of policy as U.S. foreign policy" and that he will construe such policy statements as "advisory." Some Members of Congress later expressed concern that President Bush would seek to disregard Congress's will.[20]

Civil nuclear cooperation with India cannot commence until Washington and New Delhi finalize a peaceful nuclear cooperation agreement, until the NSG allows for such cooperation, and until New Delhi concludes its own safeguards agreement with the International Atomic Energy Agency. (See CRS Report RL33016, *U.S. Nuclear Cooperation With India.*)

Indian Concerns

Almost immediately upon the release of the July 2005 Joint Statement, key Indian political figures and members of the country's insular nuclear scientific community issued strong criticisms of the U.S.-India civil nuclear initiative; critics continue to be vocal to this day. Former Prime Minister Vajpayee, along with many leading figures in his Bharatiya Janata Party (BJP), insisted that the deal as envisioned would place unreasonable and unduly expensive demands on India, particularly with regard to the separation of nuclear facilities. In reaction to the U.S. Congress's passage of enabling legislation in late 2006, the BJP listed numerous continuing objections, and went so far as to call the deal "unacceptable" and aimed at "capping, rolling back, and eventually eliminating India's nuclear weapons capability."[21] Many analysts view the BJP's opposition as political rather than substantive, especially in light of the fact that the 2004 NSSP initiative was launched during the BJP's tenure.

India's influential communist parties, whose Left Front provides crucial support to the Congress-led ruling coalition in New Delhi, have focused their ire on geopolitical aspects of the civil nuclear initiative. In December 2006, the leader of India's main communist party said the U.S.-India civil nuclear deal was "not acceptable" as it would "seriously undermine India's independent foreign policy." Previously, the Left Front had called India's two IAEA votes on Iran a "capitulation" to U.S. pressure. Indian leftists thus have been at the forefront of political resistance to India's becoming a "junior partner" of the United States.

Equally stinging and perhaps more substantive criticism has come from several key Indian scientists, whose perspectives on the technical details of the civil nuclear initiative are considered highly credible. India's nuclear scientific community, mostly barred from collaboration with international civil nuclear enterprises as well as direct access to key technologies, has worked for decades in relative isolation, making its members both proud of their singular accomplishments and sensitive to any signs of foreign "interference." Many view the enabling legislation passed by the U.S. Congress as being more about nonproliferation and less about energy cooperation. They consider it both intrusive on and preclusive of their activities.

The seven major criticisms of existing plans for U.S.-India civil nuclear cooperation made by Indian commentators may be summarized as follows:

- Intra-U.S. government certification and reporting requirements are overly rigorous;
- India's unilateral moratorium on nuclear tests is being codified into a bilateral obligation;
- India is being denied nuclear reprocessing technologies warranted under "full cooperation;"
- India has not been given assurances that it will receive uninterrupted fuel supplies in perpetuity;
- The United States is retaining the right to carry out its own "intrusive" end-use verifications;
- India is being expected to adhere to multilateral protocols, including the Proliferation Security Initiative, the Missile Technology Control Regime, and the Waasenaar Arrangement, which it has declined to accept in the past; and
- Language on securing India's assistance with U.S. efforts to prevent Iran from obtaining weapons of mass destruction limits New Delhi's foreign policy independence.[22]

Prime Minister Singh has stood firm against such wide-ranging and high-profile criticisms, repeatedly assuring his Parliament that relevant negotiations with the United States have not altered basic Indian policies or affected New Delhi's independence on matters of national interest. Within this context, however, Singh has expressed serious concern about the points listed above.[23] Regardless of the legally binding or non-binding nature of certain controversial sections of the U.S. legislation, New Delhi has found many of them to be either "prescriptive" in ways incompatible with the provisions of the July 2005 and March 2006 Joint Statements, or "extraneous" and inappropriate to engagements "among friends."[24]

Civil Space Cooperation

India has long sought access to American space technology; such access has since the 1980s been limited by U.S. and international "red lines" meant to prevent assistance that could benefit India's military missile programs. India's space-launch vehicle technology was obtained largely from foreign sources, including the United States, and forms the basis of its intermediate-range Agni ballistic missile booster, as well as its suspected Surya intercontinental ballistic missile program. The NSSP called for enhanced U.S.-India cooperation on the peaceful uses of space technology, and the July 2005 Joint Statement called for closer ties in space exploration, satellite navigation and launch, and in the commercial space arena. Conferences on India-U.S. space science and commerce were held in Bangalore (headquarters of the Indian Space Research Organization) in 2004 and 2005. During President Bush's March 2006 visit to India, the two countries committed to move forward with agreements that will permit the launch of U.S. satellites and satellites containing U.S. components by Indian space launch vehicles and, two months later, they agreed to include two U.S. scientific instruments on India's Chandrayaan lunar mission planned for 2007.

High-Technology Trade

U.S. Commerce Department officials have sought to dispel "trade-deterring myths" about limits on dual-use trade by noting that only about 1% of total U.S. trade value with India is subject to licensing requirements and that the great majority of dual-use licensing applications for India are approved (more than 90% in FY2005). July 2003 saw the inaugural session of the U.S.-India High-Technology Cooperation Group (HTCG), where officials discussed a wide range of issues relevant to creating the conditions for more robust bilateral high technology commerce; the fourth HTCG meeting was held in New Delhi in November 2005 (in early 2005, the inaugural session of the U.S.-India High-Technology Defense Working Group was held under HTCG auspices).[25]

Since 1998, a number of Indian entities have been subjected to case-by-case licensing requirements and appear on the U.S. export control "Entity List" of foreign end users involved in weapons proliferation activities. In September 2004, as part of NSSP implementation, the United States modified some export licensing policies and removed the Indian Space Research Organization (ISRO) headquarters from the Entity List. Further adjustments came in August 2005 when six more subordinate entities were removed. Indian entities remaining on the Entity List are four subordinates of the ISRO, four subordinates of the Defense Research and Development Organization, one Department of Atomic Energy entity, and Bharat Dynamics Limited, a missile production agency.[26]

Security Issues

U.S.-India Security Cooperation

Defense cooperation between the United States and India is in the early stages of development (unlike U.S.-Pakistan military ties, which date back to the 1950s). Since September 2001, and despite a concurrent U.S. rapprochement with Pakistan, U.S.-India security cooperation has flourished. The India-U.S. Defense Policy Group (DPG) — moribund since India's 1998 nuclear tests and ensuing U.S. sanctions — was revived in late 2001 and meets annually; U.S. diplomats call military cooperation among the most important aspects of transformed bilateral relations. In June 2005, the United States and India signed a ten-year defense pact outlining planned collaboration in multilateral operations, expanded two-way defense trade, increasing opportunities for technology transfers and co-production, expanded collaboration related to missile defense, and establishment of a bilateral Defense Procurement and Production Group. The United States views defense cooperation with India in the context of "common principles and shared national interests" such as defeating terrorism, preventing weapons proliferation, and maintaining regional stability. Many analysts laud increased U.S.-India security ties as providing an alleged "hedge" against or "counterbalance" to growing Chinese influence in Asia.

Since early 2002, the United States and India have held a series of unprecedented and increasingly substantive combined exercises involving all military services. "Cope India" air exercises have provided the U.S. military with its first look at Russian-built Su-30MKIs; in 2004, mock air combat saw Indian pilots in late-model Russian-built fighters hold off American pilots flying older F-15Cs, and Indian successes were repeated versus U.S. F-16s in 2005. U.S. and Indian special forces soldiers have held joint exercises near the India-China border, and major annual "Malabar" joint naval exercises are held off the Indian coast (the sixth and most recent in October 2006). Despite these developments, there remain indications that the perceptions and expectations of top U.S. and Indian military leaders are divergent on several key issues, including India's regional role, approaches to countering terrorism, and U.S.-Pakistan relations.

Along with increasing military-to-military ties, the issue of U.S. arms sales to India has taken a higher profile. In 2002, the Pentagon negotiated a sale to India of 12 counter-battery radar sets (or "Firefinder" radars) worth a total of $190 million. India also purchased $29 million worth of counterterrorism equipment for its special forces and has received sophisticated U.S.-made electronic ground sensors to help stem the tide of militant infiltration in the Kashmir region. In 2004, Congress was notified of a possible sale to India involving up to $40 million worth of aircraft self-protection systems to be mounted on the Boeing 737s that carry the Indian head of state. The State Department has authorized Israel to sell to India the jointly developed U.S.-Israeli Phalcon airborne early warning system, an expensive asset that some analysts believe may tilt the regional strategic balance even further in India's favor. In August 2006, New Delhi approved a $44 million plan to purchase the USS Trenton, a decommissioned American amphibious transport dock. The ship, which will become the second largest in the Indian navy, is set to fly the Indian flag in early 2007, possibly carrying six surplus Sikorsky UH-3H Sea King helicopters India seeks to purchase for another $39 million.

The Indian government reportedly possesses an extensive list of desired U.S.-made weapons, including PAC-3 anti-missile systems, electronic warfare systems, and possibly even combat aircraft. The March 2005 unveiling of the Bush Administration's "new strategy for South Asia" included assertions that the United States welcomed Indian requests for information on the possible purchase of F-16 or F/A-18 multi-role fighters, and indicated that Washington is "ready to discuss the sale of transformative systems in areas such as command and control, early warning, and missile defense." American defense firms eagerly pursue new and expanded business ties with India. Still, some top Indian officials express concern that the United States is a "fickle" partner that may not always be relied upon to provide the reciprocity, sensitivity, and high-technology transfers sought by New Delhi.[27] (In February 2006, the Indian Navy declined an offer to lease two U.S. P-3C maritime reconnaissance aircraft, calling the arrangements "expensive.")

In a controversial turn, the Indian government has sought to purchase a sophisticated anti-missile platform, the Arrow Weapon System, from Israel. Because the United States took the lead in the system's development, the U.S. government has veto power over any Israeli exports of the Arrow. Although Defense Department officials are seen to support the sale as meshing with President Bush's policy of cooperating with friendly countries on missile defense, State Department officials are reported to opposed the transfer, believing that it would send the wrong signal to other weapons-exporting states at a time when the U.S. is seeking to discourage international weapons proliferation. Indications are that a U.S. interest in maintaining a strategic balance on the subcontinent, along with U.S. obligations under the Missile Technology Control Regime, may preclude any approval of the Arrow sale.

Joint U.S.-India military exercises and arms sales negotiations can cause disquiet in Pakistan, where there is concern that induction of advanced weapons systems into the region could disrupt the "strategic balance" there. Islamabad worries that its already disadvantageous conventional military status vis-à-vis New Delhi will be further eroded by India's acquisition of sophisticated "force multipliers." In fact, numerous observers identify a pro-India drift in the U.S. government's strategic orientation in South Asia. Yet Washington regularly lauds Islamabad's role as a key ally in the U.S.-led counterterrorism coalition and assures Pakistan that it will take no actions to disrupt strategic balance on the subcontinent. (See also CRS Report RL33072, *U.S.-India Bilateral Agreements*, and CRS Report RL33515, *Combat Aircraft Sales to South Asia: Potential Implications*.)

Nuclear Weapons and Missile Proliferation

Some policy analysts consider the apparent arms race between India and Pakistan as posing perhaps the most likely prospect for the future use of nuclear weapons by states. In May 1998, India conducted five underground nuclear tests, breaking a self-imposed, 24-year moratorium on such testing. Despite international efforts to dissuade it, Pakistan quickly followed. The tests created a global storm of criticism and represented a serious setback for two decades of U.S. nuclear nonproliferation efforts in South Asia. Following the tests, President Clinton imposed full restrictions on non-humanitarian aid to both India and Pakistan as mandated under Section 102 of the Arms Export Control Act. India currently is believed to have enough fissile material, mainly plutonium, for 55-115 nuclear weapons; Pakistan, with a program focused on enriched uranium, may be capable of building a similar number. Both countries have aircraft capable of delivering nuclear bombs. India's military has inducted short- and intermediate-range ballistic missiles, while Pakistan itself possesses short- and medium-range missiles (allegedly acquired from China and North Korea). All are assumed to be capable of delivering nuclear warheads over significant distances.

Proliferation in South Asia is part of a chain of rivalries — India seeking to achieve deterrence against China, and Pakistan seeking to gain an "equalizer" against a conventionally stronger India. In 1999, a quasi-governmental Indian body released a Draft Nuclear Doctrine for India calling for a "minimum credible deterrent" (MCD) based upon a triad of delivery systems and pledging that India will not be the first to use nuclear weapons in a conflict. In January 2003, New Delhi announced creation of a Nuclear Command Authority. After the body's first session in September 2003, participants vowed to "consolidate India's nuclear deterrent." India thus appears to be taking the next steps toward operationalizing its nuclear weapons capability. (See also CRS Report RL32115, *Missile Proliferation and the Strategic Balance in South Asia*, and CRS Report RS21237, *Indian and Pakistani Nuclear Weapons*.)

U.S. Nonproliferation Efforts and Congressional Action

Soon after the May 1998 nuclear tests in South Asia, Congress acted to ease aid sanctions through a series of legislative measures.[28] In September 2001, President Bush waived remaining sanctions on India pursuant to P.L. 106-79. During the 1990s, the U.S. security focus in South Asia sought to minimize damage to the nonproliferation regime, prevent escalation of an arms race, and promote Indo-Pakistani bilateral dialogue. In light of these goals, the Clinton Administration set out "benchmarks" for India and Pakistan based on the contents of U.N. Security Council Resolution 1172, which condemned the two countries' nuclear tests. These included signing and ratifying the Comprehensive Nuclear Test Ban Treaty (CTBT); halting all further production of fissile material and participating in Fissile Material Cutoff Treaty negotiations; limiting development and deployment of WMD delivery vehicles; and implementing strict export controls on sensitive WMD materials and technologies.

Progress in each of these areas has been limited, and the Bush Administration quickly set aside the benchmark framework. Along with security concerns, the governments of both India and Pakistan faced the prestige factor attached to their nuclear programs and domestic resistance to relinquishing what are perceived to be potent symbols of national power. Neither has signed the CTBT, and both appear to be producing weapons-grade fissile materials. (India has consistently rejected the CTBT, as well as the Nuclear Nonproliferation Treaty, as discriminatory, calling instead for a global nuclear disarmament regime. Although both India and Pakistan currently observe self-imposed moratoria on nuclear testing, they continue to resist signing the CTBT — a position made more tenable by U.S. Senate's rejection of the treaty in 1999.) The status of weaponization and deployment is unclear, though there are indications that this is occurring at a slow but steady pace. Section 1601 of P.L. 107-228 outlined U.S. nonproliferation objectives for South Asia. Some Members of Congress identify "contradictions" in U.S. nonproliferation policy toward South Asia, particularly as related to the Senate's rejection of the CTBT and U.S. plans to build new nuclear weapons. In May 2006, the United States presented in Geneva a draft global treaty to ban future production of fissile material (a Fissile Material Cutoff Treaty) that it hopes will be supported by India. Some analysts speculated that the move was meant to bolster U.S. congressional support for proposed U.S.-India civil nuclear cooperation.

India-Iran Relations

India's relations with Iran traditionally have been positive and, in 2003, the two countries launched a bilateral "strategic partnership."[29] Many in the U.S. Congress have voiced concern that New Delhi's policies toward Tehran's controversial nuclear program may not be congruent with those of Washington, although these concerns were eased when India voted with the United States (and the majority) at the International Atomic Energy Agency sessions of September 2005 and February 2006. In each of the past three years, the United States has sanctioned Indian scientists and chemical companies for transferring to Iran WMD-related equipment and/or technology (most sanctions have been chemical-related, but one scientist was alleged to have aided Iran's nuclear program); New Delhi called the moves unjustified. Included in legislation to enable U.S.-India civil nuclear cooperation (P.L. 109-141) was a non-binding assertion that U.S. policy should "secure India's full and active participation" in U.S. efforts to prevent Iran from acquiring weapons of mass destruction.[30] Some in Congress also have noted with alarm reports of contacts between the Indian and Iranian militaries, although such contacts may be insubstantial.[31]

There are further U.S. concerns that India will seek energy resources from Iran, thus benefitting financially a country the United States is seeking to isolate. Indian firms have in recent years taken long-term contracts for purchase of Iranian gas and oil. Purchases could be worth many billions of dollars, but thus far differences over pricing have precluded sales. Building upon growing energy ties is the proposed construction of a pipeline to deliver Iranian natural gas to India through Pakistan. The Bush Administration has expressed strong opposition to any gas pipeline projects involving Iran, but top Indian officials insist the project is in India's national interest and they remain "fully committed" to the multi-billion-dollar venture, which may begin construction in 2007. The Iran-Libya Sanctions Act (P.L. 107-24) required the President to impose sanctions on foreign companies that make an "investment" of more than $20 million in one year in Iran's energy sector. The 109th Congress extended this provision in the Iran Freedom Support Act (P.L. 109-293). To date, no firms have been sanctioned under these Acts. (See also CRS Report RS22486, *India-Iran Relations and U.S. Interests*, and CRS Report RS20871, *The Iran-Libya Sanctions Act*.)

India's Economy and U.S. Concerns

Overview

India is in the midst of a major and rapid economic expansion, with an economy projected to be the world's third largest in coming decades. Although there is widespread and serious poverty in the country, observers believe long-term economic potential is tremendous, and recent strides in the technology sector have brought international attention to such high-tech centers as Bangalore and Hyderabad. However, many analysts and business leaders, along with U.S. government officials, point to excessive regulatory and bureaucratic structures as a hindrance to the realization of India's full economic potential. The high cost of capital (rooted in large government budget deficits) and an "abysmal" infrastructure also draw negative appraisals as obstacles to growth. Constant comparisons with the progress of the Chinese economy show India lagging in rates of growth and foreign investment, and in the removal of trade barriers.

India's per capita GDP is still less than $800 ($3,510 when accounting for purchasing power parity). The highly-touted information technology and business processing industries only employ about one-third of one percent of India's work force and, while optimists vaunt an Indian "middle class" of some 300 million people, a roughly equal number of Indians subsist on less than $1 per day.[32] Yet, even with the existence of ongoing problems, the current growth rate of India's increasingly service-driven economy is among the highest in the world and has brought the benefits of development to many millions of citizens. The U.N. Development Program ranked India 126th out of 177 countries on its 2006 human development index, up from 127th in both 2004 and 2005.

After enjoying an average growth rate above 6% for the 1990s, India's economy cooled with the global economic downturn after 2000. Yet sluggish Cold War-era "Hindu rates of growth" became a thing of the past. For the fiscal year ending March 2006, real change in GDP was 8.5%, the second-fastest rate of growth among the world's 20 largest economies. Robust growth in the services and industry sectors continues, but is moderated by a fluctuating agricultural sector (low productivity levels in this sector, which accounts for about one-fifth of the country's GDP, are a drag on overall growth). Estimated growth for the current fiscal year is about 8.7% and short-term estimates are encouraging, predicting expansion well above 7% for the next two years. A major upswing in services is expected to lead; this sector now accounts for more than half of India's GDP. Consumer price inflation has risen (a year-on-year rate above 7% in October 2006), but is predicted to again drop to between 5% and 6% in 2007. As of June 2006, India's foreign exchange reserves were at a record $163 billion. The soaring Bombay Stock Exchange tripled in value from 2001-2006, then apparently overheated with the worst-ever daily decline of its benchmark Sensex index on May 22, 2006, when almost 11% of its total value was lost. The market has since stabilized and apparently recovered, reaching new highs in the closing months of 2006.

A major U.S. concern with regard to India is the scope and pace of reforms in what has been that country's quasi-socialist economy. Economic reforms begun in 1991, under the Congress-led government of Prime Minister Rao and his finance minister, current Prime Minister Manmohan Singh, boosted growth and led to major new inbound foreign investment in the mid-1990s. Reform efforts stagnated, however, under weak coalition governments later in the decade, and combined with the 1997 Asian financial crisis and international sanctions on India (as a result of its 1998 nuclear tests) to further dampen the economic outlook. Following the 1999 parliamentary elections, the BJP-led government launched second-generation economic reforms, including major deregulation, privatization, and tariff-reducing measures.

Once seen as favoring domestic business and diffident about foreign involvement, New Delhi appears to gradually be embracing globalization and has sought to reassure foreign investors with promises of transparent and nondiscriminatory policies. In February 2006, a top International Monetary Fund official said that India's continued rapid economic growth will be facilitated only by enhanced Indian integration with the global economy through continued reforms and infrastructure improvements. A November 2006 World Bank report identified the country's main economic challenges as

- improving the delivery of core public services such as healthcare, education, power and water supply for all India's citizens;
- making growth more inclusive by diminishing existing disparities, accelerating agricultural growth, improving th job market, and helping lagging states grow faster;
- sustaining growth by addressing its fiscal and trade deficits, and pushing ahead with reforms that facilitate growth, and;
- addressing HIV/AIDS before the epidemic spreads to the general public.

Trade and Investment

As India's largest trade and investment partner, the United States strongly supports New Delhi's continuing economic reform policies; a U.S.-India Trade Policy Forum was created in November 2005 to expand bilateral economic engagement and provide a venue for discussing multilateral trade issues. India was the 22nd largest export market for U.S. goods in 2005 (up from 24th the previous year). Levels of U.S.-India trade, while relatively low, are blossoming; the total value of bilateral trade has doubled since 2001 and the two governments intend to see it doubled again by 2009. U.S. exports to India in 2006 had an estimated value of $9.9 billion (up 24% over 2005), with aircraft; business and telecommunications equipment; pearls, gemstones, and jewelry; fertilizer; and chemicals as leading categories. Imports from India in 2006 totaled an estimated $21.9 billion (up 17% over 2005). Leading imports included cotton apparel; textiles; and pearls, gemstones, and jewelry. Annual foreign direct investment to India from all countries rose from about $100 million in 1990 to an estimated $7.4 billion for 2005 and more than $11 billion in 2006. About one-third of these investments was made by U.S. firms; in recent months and years, the major U.S.-based companies Microsoft, Dell, Oracle, and IBM announced plans for multi-billion-dollar investments in India. Strong portfolio investment added another $10 billion in 2005. India has moved to raise limits on foreign investment in several key sectors, although U.S. officials prod New Delhi to make more rapid and more substantial changes to foreign investment ceilings, especially in the retail, financial services, and banking sectors.

During his March 2006 visit to Delhi, President Bush noted India's "dramatic progress" in economic reform while insisting "there's more work to be done," especially in lifting caps on foreign investment, making regulations more transparent, and continuing to lower tariffs. That same month, the U.S.-India CEO Forum —composed of ten chief executives from each country representing a cross-section of key industrial sectors — issued a report identifying India's poor infrastructure and dense bureaucracy as key impediments to increased bilateral trade and investment relations.[33]

Barriers to Trade and Investment

Despite significant tariff reductions and other measures taken by India to improve market access, according to the 2006 report of the United States Trade Representative (USTR), a number of foreign trade barriers remain, including high tariffs, especially in the agricultural sector. The USTR asserts that "substantial expansion of U.S.-India trade will depend on continued and significant additional Indian liberalization."[34] The Commerce Department likewise encourages New Delhi to continue lowering tariffs as a means of fostering trade and development.

India's extensive trade and investment barriers have been criticized by U.S. government officials and business leaders as an impediment to its own economic development, as well as to stronger U.S.-India ties. For example, in 2004, the U.S. Ambassador to India told a Delhi audience that "the U.S. is one of the world's most open economies and India is one of the most closed." Later that year, U.S. Under Secretary of State Alan Larson opined that "trade and investment flows between the U.S. and India are far below where they should and can be," adding that "the picture for U.S. investment is also lackluster." He identified the primary reason for the suboptimal situation as "the slow pace of economic reform in India."[35]

Inadequate intellectual property rights protection is another long-standing issue between the United States and India. The USTR places India on its Special 301 Priority Watch List for "inadequate laws and ineffective enforcement" in this area. The International Intellectual Property Alliance, a coalition of U.S. copyright-based industries, estimated U.S. losses of $443 million due to trade piracy in India in 2005, three-quarters of this in the categories of business and entertainment software (estimated loss amounts for 2005 do not include motion picture piracy, which in 2004 was estimated to have cost some $80 million).[36] In December 2006, Under Secretary of Commerce and Director of the U.S. Patent and Trademark Office Jon Dudas told a New Delhi audience that "further modifications are necessary" in India's intellectual property rights protection regime and that India's copyright laws are "insufficient in many aspects." He also warned that "piracy and counterfeiting rates will continue to rise without effective enforcement."[37]

While the past two decades have seen a major transformation of the Indian economy, it remains relatively closed in many aspects. The Heritage Foundation's *2006 Index of Economic Freedom* — which may overemphasize the value of absolute growth and downplay broader quality-of-life measurements — again rated India as being "mostly unfree," highlighting especially restrictive trade policies, heavy government involvement in the banking and finance sector, demanding regulatory structures, and a high level of "black market" activity.[38] The Vancouver-based Fraser Institute provides a more positive assessment of economic freedom in India, while also faulting excessive restrictions on capital markets and regulations on business.[39] Corruption also plays a role: Berlin-based Transparency International placed India 70th out of 163 countries in its 2006 "corruption perceptions index." The group's 2006 "bribery index" found India to be the worst offender among the world's top 30 exporting countries.[40] (See also CRS Report RS21502, *India-U.S. Economic Relations*.)

Multilateral Trade Negotiations

In July 2006, the World Trade Organization's "Doha Round" of multilateral trade negotiations were suspended indefinitely due to disagreement among the WTO's six core group members —which include the United States and India — over methods to reduce trade-distorting domestic subsidies, eliminate export subsidies, and increase market access for agricultural products. The United States and other developed countries seek substantial tariff reductions in the developing world. India, like other members of the "G-20" group of developing states, has sought more market access for its goods and services in the developed countries, while claiming that developing countries should be given additional time to liberalize their own markets. In particular, India is resistant to opening its markets to subsidized agricultural products from developed countries, claiming this would result in further depopulation of the countryside. India's Commerce Minister, Kamal Nath, blamed U.S. intransigence for the Doha Round's collapse. In November 2006, during a visit to New Delhi to discuss trade issues with top Indian leaders, U.S. Agriculture Secretary Mike Johanns urged India to match "ambitious" U.S. offers and "lead the way toward unlocking the Doha negotiations by offering real market access."[41] (See also CRS Report RL32060, *World Trade Organization Negotiations: The Doha Development Agenda*, and CRS Report RL33144, *WTO Doha Round: The Agricultural Negotiations*.)

The Energy Sector

India's continued economic growth and security are intimately linked to the supply of energy resources. Indeed, Indian leaders insist that energy security is an essential component of the country's development agenda, calling for an integrated national energy policy, diversification of energy supplies, greater energy efficiency, and rationalization of pricing mechanisms. The country's relatively poor natural energy resource endowment and poorly functioning energy market are widely viewed as major constraints on the country's continued rapid economic growth. Estimates indicate that maintaining recent rates of growth will require that India increase its commercial energy supplies by 4%-6% annually in coming years.[42] The U.S. government has committed to assist India in promoting the development of stable and efficient energy markets there; a U.S.-India Energy Dialogue was launched in July 2005 to provide a forum for bolstering bilateral energy cooperation.[43]

India is the world's fifth largest energy consumer and may become third by the middle of this century. Overall power generation in the country more than doubled from 1991 to 2005.[44] Coal is the country's leading commercial energy source, accounting for more than half of national demand. India is the world's third most productive coal producer, and domestic supplies satisfy most demand (however, most of India's coal is a low-grade, high-ash variety of low efficiency). Oil consumption accounts for some one-third of India's total energy consumption; about 70% of this oil is imported (at a rate of 1.7 million barrels per day in 2005), mostly from the West Asia/Middle East region. India's domestic natural gas supply is not likely to keep pace with demand, and the country will have to import much of its natural gas, either via pipeline or as liquefied natural gas. Hydropower, especially abundant in the country's northeast and near the border with Nepal, supplies about 5% of energy needs. Nuclear power, which Indian government officials and some experts say is a sector in dire need of expansion, currently accounts for only 1% of the country's energy supplies and less than 3% of total electricity generation.[45] Even optimistic projections suggest that nuclear power will provide less than 10% of India's generation capacity in 25 years.[46] One-fifth of the country's power is consumed by farmers' irrigation systems, making the farm lobby a powerful obstacle to curtailing subsidies provided by State Electricity Boards, which collectively lose $4.5 billion annually. Moreover, as much as 42% of India's electricity is said to disappear though "transmission losses," i.e., theft.[47]

Regional Dissidence and Human Rights

The United States maintains an ongoing interest in India's domestic stability and the respect for internationally recognized human rights there. The U.S. Congress has held hearings in which such issues are discussed. As a vast mosaic of ethnicities, languages, cultures, and religions, India can be difficult to govern. Internal instability resulting from diversity is further complicated by colonial legacies such as international borders that separate members of the same ethnic groups, creating flashpoints for regional dissidence and separatism. Beyond the Kashmir problem, separatist insurgents in remote and underdeveloped northeast regions confound New Delhi and create international tensions by operating out of neighboring Bangladesh, Burma, Bhutan, and Nepal. Maoist rebels continue to operate in numerous states. India also has suffered outbreaks of serious communal violence between

Hindus and Muslims, especially in the western Gujarat state. (See also CRS Report RL32259, *Terrorism in South Asia*.)

India's domestic security is a serious issue beyond the Jammu and Kashmir state: in April 2006, Prime Minister Singh identified a worsening Maoist insurgency as "the single biggest internal security challenge" ever faced by India. Lethal attacks by these "Naxalites" continue and have included June and December landmine explosions that left a total of 26 policemen dead in the eastern Jharkhand state. Three days of communal rioting followed the demolition of a Muslim shrine in the Gujarat state in May and left six people dead and dozens more injured. More than 1,000 Indian army troops were deployed to quell the violence. Later communal clashes between Hindus and Muslims in the Uttar Pradesh state left two children dead and more than 100 homes destroyed by fire. As for militant separatism in the northeast, serious violence has flared anew in the Assam state following the collapse of negotiations with the United Liberation Front of Assam, which is designated as a "group of concern" by the U.S. State Department.

The Kashmir Issue

Although India suffers from several militant regional separatist movements, the Kashmir issue has proven the most lethal and intractable. Conflict over Kashmiri sovereignty also has brought global attention to a potential "flashpoint" for interstate war between nuclear-armed powers. The problem is rooted in competing claims to the former princely state, divided since 1948 by a military Line of Control (LOC) separating India's Jammu and Kashmir and Pakistan-controlled Azad [Free] Kashmir. India and Pakistan fought full-scale wars over Kashmir in 1947-48 and 1965. Some Kashmiris seek independence from both countries. Spurred by a perception of rigged state elections in 1989, an ongoing separatist war between Islamic militants and their supporters and Indian security forces in Indian-held Kashmir has claimed perhaps 66,000 lives.

Some separatist groups, such as the Jammu and Kashmir Liberation Front (JKLF), continue to seek an independent or autonomous Kashmir. Others, including the militant Hizbul Mujahideen (HuM), seek union with Pakistan. In 1993, the All Parties Hurriyat [Freedom] Conference was formed as an umbrella organization for groups opposed to Indian rule in Kashmir. The Hurriyat membership of more than 20 political and religious groups has included the JKLF (now a political group) and Jamaat-e-Islami (the political wing of the HuM). The Hurriyat Conference, which states that it is committed to seeking dialogue with the Indian government on a broad range of issues, calls for a tripartite conference on Kashmir, including Pakistan, India, and representatives of the Kashmiri people. Hurriyat leaders demand Kashmiri representation at any talks between India and Pakistan on Kashmir. The Hurriyat formally split in 2003 after a dispute between hardliners allied with Islamabad and those favoring negotiation with New Delhi. Subsequent efforts to reunify the group failed. In September 2005, the Congress-led government renewed high-level contact with moderate Hurriyat leaders begun by the previous BJP-led coalition. New Delhi vowed to pull troops out of Kashmir if militant infiltrations and violence there cease, but to date only nominal troop withdrawals have come in response to a somewhat improved security situation in the region.

India blames Pakistan for supporting "cross-border terrorism" and for fueling a separatist rebellion in the Muslim-majority Kashmir Valley with arms, training, and militants. Islamabad, for its part, claims to provide only diplomatic and moral support to what it calls "freedom fighters" who resist Indian rule and suffer alleged human rights abuses in the region. New Delhi insists that the dispute should not be "internationalized" through involvement by third-party mediators and India is widely believed to be satisfied with the territorial status quo. In 1999, a bloody, six-week-long battle near the LOC at Kargil cost more than one thousand lives and included Pakistani army troops crossing into Indian-controlled territory. Islamabad has sought to bring external major power persuasion to bear on India, especially from the United States. The longstanding U.S. position on Kashmir is that the issue must be resolved through negotiations between India and Pakistan while taking into account the wishes of the Kashmiri people.

The Northeast

Since the time of India's foundation, numerous militant groups have fought for greater ethnic autonomy, tribal rights, or independence in the country's northeast region. Some of the tribal struggles in the small states known as the Seven Sisters are centuries old. It is estimated that more than 50,000 people have been killed in such fighting since 1948, including some 10,000 deaths in 15 years of fighting in the Assam state. The United Liberation Front of Assam (ULFA), the National Liberation Front of Tripura, the National Democratic Front of Bodoland (NDFB), and the United National Liberation Front (seeking an independent Manipur) are among the groups at war with the central government. In April 2005, the U.S. State Department's Counterterrorism Office named ULFA in its list of "other groups of concern," the first time an Indian separatist group outside Kashmir was so named.[48] A series of bombings left at least 15 people dead and dozens more injured in Assam in November 2006; police blamed ULFA rebels for the attacks.

New Delhi has at times blamed Bangladesh, Burma, Nepal, and Bhutan for "sheltering" one or more of these groups beyond the reach of Indian security forces, and New Delhi has launched joint counter-insurgency operations with some of its neighbors. India also has accused Pakistan's intelligence agency of training and equipping militants. Bhutan launched major military operations against suspected rebel camps on Bhutanese territory in 2003 and appeared to have routed the ULFA and NDFB. In 2004, five leading separatist groups from the region rejected New Delhi's offer of unconditional talks, saying talks can only take place under U.N. mediation and if the sovereignty issue was on the table. Later, in what seemed a blow to the new Congress-led government's domestic security policies, a spate of lethal violence in Assam and Nagaland was blamed on ULFA and NDFB militants who had re-established their bases in Bhutan. Major Indian army operations in late 2004 may have overrun Manipur separatist bases near the Burmese border. New Delhi's hesitant year-long efforts at negotiation with ULFA rebels and a six-week-old cease-fire in Assam collapsed in October 2006, leading to a spike of lethal violence that included multiple bombings the final months of 2006.

Maoist Insurgency

Also operating in India are "Naxalites" — Maoist insurgents ostensibly engaged in violent struggle on behalf of landless laborers and tribals. These groups, most active in inland areas of east-central India, claim to be battling oppression and exploitation in order to create a classless society. Their opponents call them terrorists and extortionists. The groups get their name from Naxalbari, a West Bengal village and site of a militant peasant uprising in 1967. In April 2006, Prime Minister Singh identified a worsening Maoist insurgency as "the single biggest internal security challenge" ever faced by India, saying it threatened India's democracy and "way of life." The U.S. State Department's *Country Reports on Terrorism 2005* warned that attacks by Maoist terrorists in India are "growing in sophistication and lethality and may pose a long-term threat."[49] Naxalites now operate in half of India's 28 states and related violence caused nearly 1,000 deaths in 2005.

The most notable of these outfits are the People's War Group (PWG), mainly active in the southern Andhra Pradesh state, and the Maoist Communist Center of West Bengal and Bihar. In 2004, the two groups merged to form the Communist Party of India (Maoist). Both appear on the U.S. State Department's list of "groups of concern" and both are designated as terrorist groups by New Delhi, which claims there are nearly 10,000 Maoist militants active in the country. PWG fighters were behind a 2003 landmine attack that nearly killed the chief minster of Andhra Pradesh. In 2004, that state's government lifted an 11-year-old ban on the PWG, but the Maoists soon withdrew from ensuing peace talks, accusing the state government of breaking a cease-fire agreement. Violent attacks on government forces then escalated in 2005 and continued with even greater frequency in 2006.

The Indian government has since May 2005 sponsored a grassroots anti-Maoist effort. This "Salwa Jundum" ("Campaign for Peace" or, literally, "purification hunt") militia, especially active in the Chhattisgarh state, is viewed by some as an effective countervailing people's movement, but others label it a vigilante group that has engaged in its own coercive and violent tactics against innocent tribals. New Delhi has also expressed concern that indigenous Maoists are increasing their links with Nepali communists that recently ended their war with the Kathmandu government. Many analysts see abundant evidence that Naxalite activity is spreading and becoming more audacious in the face of incoherent and insufficient Indian government policies to halt it.

Hindu-Muslim Tensions

Some elements of India's Hindu majority have at times engaged in violent conflict with the country's Muslim minority. In late 1992, a huge mob of Hindu activists in the western city of Ayodhya demolished a 16th century mosque said to have been built at the birth site of the Hindu god Rama. Ensuing communal riots in cities across India left many hundreds dead. Bombay was especially hard hit and was the site of coordinated 1993 terrorist bombings believed to have been a retaliatory strike by Muslims. In early 2002, another group of Hindu activists returning by train to the western state of Gujarat after a visit to the site of the now razed Babri Mosque (and a proposed Hindu temple) were attacked by a Muslim mob in the town of Godhra; 58 were killed. Up to 2,000 people died in the fearsome communal rioting that followed, most of them Muslims. The BJP-led state and national governments came under fire for inaction; some observers saw evidence of state government complicity in anti-Muslim attacks.

The U.S. State Department and human rights groups have been critical of New Delhi's largely ineffectual efforts to bring those responsible to justice; some of these criticisms were echoed by the Indian Supreme Court in 2003. In March 2005, the State Department made a controversial decision to deny a U.S. visa to Gujarat Chief Minster Narendra Modi under a U.S. law barring entry for foreign government officials found to be complicit in severe violations of religious freedom. The decision was strongly criticized in India. Sporadic incidents of communal violence continued to destroy both lives and property in 2006.

Human Rights

According to the U.S. State Department's *India: Country Report on Human Rights Practices, 2005*, the Indian government "generally respected the human rights of its citizens; however, numerous serious problems remained." These included extensive societal violence against women; extrajudicial killings, including faked encounter killings; excessive use of force by security forces, arbitrary arrests, and incommunicado detentions in Kashmir and several northeastern states; torture and rape by agents of the government; poor prison conditions and lengthy pretrial detentions without charge; forced prostitution; child prostitution and female infanticide; human trafficking; and caste-based discrimination and violence, among others. Terrorist attacks and kidnapings also remained grievous problems, especially in Kashmir and the northeastern states.[50] New York-based Human Rights Watch's latest annual report noted "important positive steps" by the Indian government in 2005 with respect to human rights, but also reviewed the persistence of problems such as abuses by security forces and a failure to contain violent religious extremism.[51]

The State Department's Bureau of Democracy, Human Rights, and Labor has claimed that India's human right abuses "are generated by a traditionally hierarchical social structure, deeply rooted tensions among the country's many ethnic and religious communities, violent secessionist movements and the authorities' attempts to repress them, and deficient police methods and training."[52] India's 1958 Armed Forces Special Powers Act, which gives security forces wide leeway to act with impunity in conflict zones, has been called a facilitator of "grave human rights abuses" in several Indian states. India generally denies international human rights groups official access to Kashmir and other sensitive areas. State's 2005-2006 report on *Supporting Human Rights and Democracy* calls India "a vibrant democracy with strong constitutional human rights protections," but also asserts that "poor enforcement of laws, widespread corruption, a lack of accountability, and the severely overburdened court system weakened the delivery of justice."[53]

Human Trafficking

The State Department's June 2006 report on trafficking in persons said that New Delhi "does not fully comply with the minimum standards for the elimination of trafficking; however, it is making significant efforts to do so" and it placed India on the "Tier 2 Watch List" for the third consecutive year "due to its failure to show evidence of increasing efforts to address trafficking in persons." New Delhi later downplayed the claims and said the report was "not helpful." The trafficking of women and children is identified as a serious problem in India.[54]

Religious Freedom

An officially secular nation, India has a long tradition of religious tolerance (with occasional lapses), which is protected under its constitution. The population includes a Hindu majority of 82% as well as a large Muslim minority of some 150 million (14%). Christians, Sikhs, Buddhists, Jains, and others total less than 4%. Although freedom of religion is protected by the Indian government, human rights groups have noted that India's religious tolerance is susceptible to attack by religious extremists.

In its annual report on international religious freedom released in November 2005, the State Department found that the status of religious freedom in India had "improved in a number of ways ... yet serious problems remained." It lauded the New Delhi government for demonstrating a commitment to policies of religious inclusion, while claiming that "the government sometimes in the recent past did not act swiftly enough to counter societal attacks against religious minorities and attempts by some leaders of state and local governments to limit religious freedom."[55] A May 2006 report of the U.S. Commission on International Religious Freedom lauds continued improvements since the May 2004 election of the Congress-led coalition, but warns that concerns about religious freedom in India remain. These include ongoing attacks against religious minorities, perpetrated mainly by Hindu activists and most often in states with BJP-led governments. The Commission also continues to criticize allegedly insufficient state efforts to pursue justice in cases related to 2002 communal rioting in Gujarat.[56]

HIV/AIDS

The United Nations estimates that 5.7 million Indians are infected with HIV/AIDS, giving India the largest such population worldwide (India overtook South Africa in this category in 2006). Due to the country's large population, prevalence rates among adults remain below 1%. India's AIDS epidemic has become generalized in four states in the country's south (Andhra Pradesh, Tamil Nadu, Karnataka, and Maharashtra) and two in the northeast (Manipur and Nagaland). According to USAID, these six states account for 80% of the country's reported AIDS cases.[57] India first launched its AIDS control program in 1992; New Delhi boosted related funding to about $120 million in the most recent fiscal year. As part of its foreign assistance program in India, the U.S. government supports integrated HIV/AIDS prevention, treatment, and support services in high prevalence states. Stigma, gender inequalities, and discrimination present major obstacles to controlling India's HIV/AIDS epidemic. In the country's traditional society, open discussion of sexuality and risk of infection is rare, making education and awareness difficult. Analysts have said substantially greater resources are needed to address HIV/AIDS in India than are currently available.[58] (See also CRS Report RL33771, *Trends in U.S. Global AIDS Spending: FY2000-FY2007*.)

U.S. Assistance

Economic

According to the U.S. Agency for International Development (USAID), India has more people living in abject poverty (some 385 million) than do Latin America and Africa combined. From 1947 through 2005, the United States provided nearly $15 billion in economic loans and grants to India. USAID programs in India, budgeted at about $68 million in FY2006, concentrate on five areas: (1) *economic growth* (increased transparency and efficiency in the mobilization and allocation of resources); (2) *health* (improved overall health with a greater integration of food assistance, reproductive services, and the prevention of

HIV/AIDS and other infectious diseases); (3) *disaster management*; (4) *energy and environment* (improved access to clean energy and water; the reduction of public subsidies through improved cost recovery); and (5) *opportunity and equity* (improved access to elementary education, and justice and other social and economic services for vulnerable groups, especially women and children).[59]

Table 1. U.S. Assistance to India, FY2001-FY2007
(in millions of dollars)

Program or Account	FY2001 Actual	FY2002 Actual	FY2003 Actual	FY2004 Actual	FY2005 Actual	FY2006 Est.	FY2007 Request
CSH	24.6	41.7	47.4	47.8	53.2	47.7	48.4
DA	28.8	29.2	34.5	22.5	24.9	10.9	10.0
ESF	5.0	7.0	10.5	14.9	14.9	5.0	6.5
IMET	0.5	1.0	1.0	1.4	1.5	1.2	1.5
NADR	0.9	0.9	1.0	0.7	4.2	2.4	1.5
Subtotal	$59.8	$79.8	$94.4	$106.2	$98.7	$67.2	$67.9
Food Aid*	78.3	105.7	44.8	30.8	26.1	43.0	—
Total	$138.1	$185.5	$139.2	$137.0	$124.8	$110.2	$67.9

Sources: U.S. Departments of State and Agriculture; U.S. Agency for International Development.

Abbreviations: CSH: Child Survival and Health; DA: Development Assistance; ESF: Economic Support Fund; IMET: International Military Education and Training; NADR: Nonproliferation, Anti-Terrorism, Demining, and Related (mainly export control assistance, but includes anti-terrorism assistance for FY2007)

* P.L.480 Title II (grants) and Section 416(b) of the Agricultural Act of 1949, as amended (surplus donations). Food aid totals do not include freight costs.

Security

The United States has provided about $161 million in military assistance to India since 1947, more than 90% of it distributed from 1962-1966. In recent years, modest security-related assistance has emphasized export control enhancements and military training. Earlier Bush Administration requests for Foreign Military Financing were later withdrawn, with the two countries agreeing to pursue commercial sales programs. The Pentagon reports military sales agreements with India worth $288 million in FY2002-FY2005.

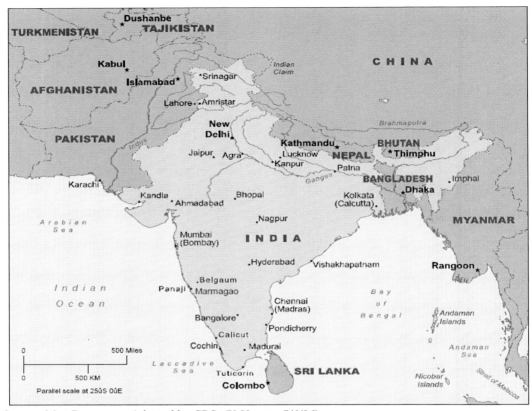

Source: Map Resources. Adapted by CRS. (K.Yancey 7/6/06).

Figure 1. Map of India.

REFERENCES

[1]   See [http://www.usindiafriendship.net/archives/usindiavision/delhideclaration.htm].
[2]   See [http://clinton4.nara.gov/WH/new/html/Wed_Oct_4_105959_2000.html].
[3]   See [http://www.state.gov/p/sca/rls/rm/6057.htm].
[4]   See [http://www.whitehouse.gov/news/releases/2005/07/20050718-6.html].
[5]   See [http://www.whitehouse.gov/news/releases/2006/03/20060302-5.html].
[6]   See [http://www.comw.org/qdr/fulltext/nss2002.pdf] and [http://www.comw.org/qdr/fulltext/nss2006.pdf].
[7]   Walter Andersen, "The Indian-American Community Comes Into Its Political Own," *India Abroad*, Sep. 1, 2006; "Indian Community Burgeoning in America," Associated Press, Oct. 22, 2006.
[8]   See Polly Nayak and Michael Krepon, "US Crisis Management in South Asia's Twin Peaks Crisis" at [http://www.stimson.org/southasia/pdf/USCrisisManagement.pdf].
[9]   See John Lancaster, "India, China Hoping to 'Reshape the World Order' Together," *Washington Post*, Apr. 12, 2005, at [http://www.washingtonpost.com/wp-dyn/articles/A43053-2005Apr11.html].
[10]   See Indian National Congress at [http://www.congress.org.in].
[11]   See Bharatiya Janata Party at [http://www.bjp.org].

[12] See [http://www.whitehouse.gov/news/releases/2004/01/20040112-1.html].

[13] See [http://www.whitehouse.gov/news/releases/2005/07/20050718-6.html] and [http://www.indianembassy.org/press_release/2005/June/31.htm].

[14] See [http://www.whitehouse.gov/news/releases/2006/03/20060302-5.html].

[15] See "U.S.-India Civil Nuclear Cooperation Initiative Fact Sheet," U.S. Department of State, at [http://www.state.gov/r/pa/scp/2006/62904.htm]; Condoleezza Rice, "Our Opportunity With India," *Washington Post*, Mar. 13, 2006.

[16] See, for example, an open letter Congress at [http://www.indianembassy.org/newsite/press_release/2006/Mar/30.asp].

[17] See, for example, open letters to Congress at [http://fas.org/ intt2006/ X3e_FDC01218.pdf]; [http://www. armscontrol.org/ pdf/20060912_ India_Ltr_ Congress.pdf]; and [http:// www.armscontrol. org/pdf/ 20051118_ India_ Ltr_Congress.pdf].

[18] See Sridhar Krishnaswami, "'Indo-US N-deal a Historic Opportunity,'" Rediff India Abroad, Mar. 22, 2006, at [http://www.rediff.com/news/2006/mar/22ndeal.htm].

[19] Some believe that offering U.S. support for a permanent Indian seat on the U.N. Security Council (UNSC) might have been a more appropriate and more readily delivered gesture. For example, the former Chairman of the House International Relations Subcommittee on Asia and the Pacific, Representative Jim Leach, called U.S. support for India's permanent seat on the UNSC a "self-apparent gesture" (House Committee on International Relations Hearing, "The U.S. and India: An Emerging Entente?," Sep. 8, 2005).

[20] See [http://www.whitehouse.gov/news/releases/2006/12/20061218-1.html]; [http://www.whitehouse.gov/news/releases/2006/12/20061218-12.html]; Carol Giacomo, "Bush India Statement Raises Congress Concerns," Reuters, Dec. 21, 2006).

[21] See "Press Statement of the BJP on the Indo-US Nuclear Deal," Dec. 10, 2006, at [http://www.bjp.org].

[22] Ibid.; M.R. Srinavasan, "India May Lose Control of Its Nuclear Future," *Frontline* (Madras), Dec. 14, 2006; "India's Top Scientists Oppose US Deal," Agence France Presse," Dec. 16, 2006; V. Sudarshan, "Not Much Frisson," *Outlook* (Delhi), Dec. 25, 2006.

[23] See "Excerpts from PM's Reply to Discussion in Rajya Sabha on Civil Nuclear Energy Cooperation with the United States," Aug. 17, 2006, at [http://www.carnegieendowment.org/static/npp/Singh_speech_Aug_2006.pdf].

[24] Author interview with Indian government officials, New Delhi, Sep.13, 2006.

[25] See U.S. Department of Commerce, Bureau of Industry and Security fact sheets at [http://www.bis.doc.gov/InternationalPrograms/IndiaCooperation.htm] and [http://www.bis.doc.gov/InternationalPrograms/IndialCoopPresentation.htm].

[26] See [http://www.bis.doc.gov/Entities].

[27] See, for example, "Defense Firms Seek Sales in India," *Chicago Tribune*, Dec. 21, 2006.

[28] The India-Pakistan Relief Act of 1998 (in P.L. 105-277) authorized a one-year sanctions waiver exercised by President Clinton in November 1998. The Department of Defense Appropriations Act, 2000 (P.L. 106-79) gave the President permanent authority after October 1999 to waive nuclear-test- related sanctions applied against India and Pakistan. On October 27, 1999, President Clinton waived economic sanctions

on India (Pakistan remained under sanctions as a result of an October 1999 military coup). (See CRS Report RS20995, *India and Pakistan: U.S. Economic Sanctions*.)

[29] See text of the January 2003 "New Delhi Declaration" at [http://meaindia.nic.in/declarestatement/2003/01/25jd1.htm].

[30] Although President Bush indicated he has not adopted the law's statements of policy as U.S. foreign policy, this provision has rankled many in New Delhi who view it as an "extraneous" constraint on India's foreign policy independence. In their explanatory statement accompanying P.L. 109-401, congressional conferees repeatedly emphasized their belief that securing India's assistance on this matter was "critical" (H.Rept. 109-721).

[31] See, for example, Vivek Raghuvanshi and Gopal Ratnam, "Indian Navy Trains Iranian Sailors," *Defense News*, Mar. 27, 2006; "India-Iran Military Ties Growing," *Strategic Affairs*, June 16, 2001; "Rice Downplays India's Iran Links," CNN.com, Apr. 6, 2006.

[32] A December 2006 study by the Indian Ministry of Statistics found that more than 200 million citizens in rural areas subsist on less than 12 rupees (about 27 cents) per day.

[33] See "U.S.-India Strategic Economic Partnership," U.S.-India CEO Forum, Mar. 2006 at [http://planningcommission.nic.in/reports/genrep/USIndia.pdf].

[34] See [http://www.ustr.gov/Document_Library/Reports_Publications/Section_Index.html].

[35] See [http://www.state.gov/e/rls/rm/2004/36345.htm].

[36] See [http://www.iipa.com/rbc/2006/2006SPEC301INDIA.pdf].

[37] See [http://newdelhi.usembassy.gov/pr120706.html]. Bush Administration policy is at [http://mumbai.usconsulate.gov/chris_israel.html].

[38] See [http://www.heritage.org/research/features/index/country.cfm?id=India].

[39] See [http://www.fraserinstitute.ca/admin/books/chapterfiles/3aEFW2006ch3A-K.pdf#].

[40] See [http://www.transparency.org].

[41] "India Blames U.S. for Failure of WTO Talks," *Hindu* (Madras), July 26, 2006; Secretary Johanns at [http://newdelhi.usembassy.gov/pr112106b.html].

[42] See Vibhuti Hate, "India's Energy Dilemma," Center for Strategic and International Studies, Sep. 7, 2006, at [http://www.csis.org/media/csis/pubs/sam98.pdf].

[43] See U.S. Department of State fact sheet at [http://www.state.gov/p/sca/rls/fs/2005/49724.htm]. In May 2006, the Senate Foreign Relations Committee passed S. 1950, to promote global energy security through increased cooperation between the United States and India on non-nuclear energy-related issues, but the full Senate took no action on the bill.

[44] See [http://powermin.nic.in/reports/pdf/ar05_06.pdf].

[45] Data from U.S. Department of Energy, Energy Information Administration, Dec. 2005 at [http://www.eia.doe.gov/emeu/cabs/india.html]; Tanvi Madan, "India," Brookings Institution Energy Security Series Report, Nov. 2006 at [http://www.brookings.edu/fp/research/energy/2006india.pdf].

[46] John Stephenson and Peter Tynan, "Will the U.S.-India Civil Nuclear Cooperation Initiative Light India?," Nov. 13, 2006, at [http://www.dalberg.com/npec.pdf].

[47] Mark Gregory, "India Struggles With Power Theft," BBC News, Mar. 15, 2006.

[48] See [http://www.state.gov/s/ct/rls/crt/2005/65275.htm].

[49] See [http://www.state.gov/s/ct/rls/crt/2005/64345.htm].

[50] See [http://www.state.gov/g/drl/rls/hrrpt/2005/61707.htm].

[51] See [http://hrw.org/wr2k6/wr2006.pdf].

[52] *Supporting Human Rights and Democracy: The U.S. Record 2002 -2003,"* U.S. Department of State, at [http://www.state.gov/g/drl/rls/shrd/2002/21760.htm].

[53] See [http://www.state.gov/g/drl/rls/shrd/2005/63948.htm].

[54] See [http://www.state.gov/g/tip/rls/tiprpt/2006/65989.htm].

[55] See [http://www.state.gov/g/drl/rls/irf/2006/71440.htm].

[56] See [http://www.uscirf.gov/countries/publications/currentreport/index.html].

[57] See "Health Profile: India," U.S. Agency for International Development, at [http://www.usaid.gov/our_work/global_health/aids/Countries/ane/india_05.pdf].

[58] See, for example, Pramit Mitra and Teresita Schaffer, "Public Health and International Security: The Case of India," July 2006 at [http://www.csis.org/media/csis/pubs/060731_aids_india.pdf].

[59] See USAID India at [http://www.usaid.gov/in].

In: India: Economic, Political and Social Issues   ISBN: 978-1-60456-509-6
Editors: Urlah B. Nissam   © 2008 Nova Science Publishers, Inc.

Chapter 9

U.S.-INDIA NUCLEAR COOPERATION: A SIDE-BY-SIDE COMPARISON OF CURRENT LEGISLATION[*]

Sharon Squassoni and Jill Marie Parillo

ABSTRACT

In March 2006, the Bush Administration proposed legislation to create an exception for India from certain provisions of the Atomic Energy Act to facilitate a future nuclear cooperation agreement. After hearings in April and May, the House International Relations Committee and the Senate Foreign Relations Committee considered bills in late June 2006 to provide an exception for India to certain provisions of the Atomic Energy Act related to a peaceful nuclear cooperation agreement. On July 26, 2006, the House passed its version of the legislation, H.R. 5682, by a vote of 359 to 68. On November 16, 2006, the Senate incorporated the text of S. 3709, as amended, into H.R. 5682 and passed that bill by a vote of 85 to 12. The Senate insisted on its amendment, and a conference committee produced a conference report on December 7, 2006. The House agreed to the conference report (H.Rept. 109-721) on December 8 in a 330-59 vote; the Senate agreed by unanimous consent to the conference report on December 9. The President signed the bill into law (P.L. 109-401) on December 18, 2006.

The Senate and House versions of the India bill contained similar provisions, with four differences. The Senate version contained an additional requirement for the President to execute his waiver authority, an amendment introduced by Senator Harkin and adopted by unanimous consent that the President determine that India is "fully and actively participating in U.S. and international efforts to dissuade, sanction and contain Iran for its nuclear program." This provision was watered down into a reporting requirement in the conference report. The Senate version also had two unique sections related to the cooperation agreement, Sections 106 and 107, both of which appear in the conference report. Section 106 (now Section 104 (d) (4)) prohibits exports of equipment, material or technology related for uranium enrichment, spent fuel reprocessing or heavy water production unless conducted in a multinational facility participating in a project

---

[*] Excerpted from CRS Report RL33561, December 22, 2006.

approved by the International Atomic Energy Agency (IAEA) or in a facility participating in a bilateral or multilateral project to develop a proliferation-resistant fuel cycle. Section 107 (now Section 104 (d) (5)) would establish a program to monitor that U.S. technology is being used appropriately by Indian recipients. Finally, the Senate version also contained the implementing legislation for the U.S. Additional Protocol in Title II, which was retained in the conference bill. Minor differences in reporting requirements and statements of policy are compared in table I of this report.

This article provides a thematic side-by-side comparison of the provisions of the conference report with H.R. 5682 as passed by the House and by the Senate, and compares them with the Administration's initially proposed legislation, H.R. 4974/S. 2429, and the conference report. The report concludes with a list of CRS resources that provide further discussion and more detailed analysis of the issues addressed by the legislation summarized in the table.

OVERVIEW

In July 2005, President Bush announced his intention to conclude a peaceful nuclear cooperation agreement with India. India, which is not a party to the Nuclear Nonproliferation Treaty (NPT), is considered under U.S. law to be a non-nuclear weapon state, yet has tested nuclear weapons and has an ongoing nuclear weapons program. For these reasons, the President would need to make certain waivers and determinations pursuant to the Atomic Energy Act (AEA) before nuclear cooperation with a state such as India could proceed.

The Administration proposed legislation (introduced as H.R. 4974/ S. 2429) in March 2006 that, in addition to providing waivers of relevant provisions of the AEA (Sections 123 a. (2), 128, and 129), would have allowed a nuclear cooperation agreement with India to enter into force without a vote from Congress, as though it conformed to AEA requirements. On July 26, 2006, the House passed H.R. 5682 by a vote of 359 to 68. On November 16, 2006, the Senate passed H.R. 5682 by a vote of 85 to12, substituting the text of S. 3709 as an engrossed amendment; the Senate insisted on its amendment, necessitating a conference to resolve differences between the bills. On December 7, conferrees filed a conference report, and on December 8, the House approved the conference report by a vote of 330 to 59; the Senate approved the conference report by unanimous consent in the early hours of December 9. On December 18, President Bush signed the bill into law, P.L. 109-401. His signing statement is discussed in more detail below.

H.R. 5682 in the House

Committee Actions

The House International Relations Committee met on June 27, 2006 to consider H.R. 5682, "United States and India Nuclear Cooperation Promotion Act of 2006," introduced on June 26 by Representative Hyde.[1] The Committee voted to adopt 6 of 12 amendments (one was withdrawn):

- Representative Royce offered an amendment to ensure that nothing in the act shall be interpreted as permitting any civil nuclear cooperation with India that would in any way assist, encourage, or induce India to manufacture or otherwise acquire nuclear weapons (Section 4 (d) (1));

- Representative Sherman offered an amendment to strengthen one of the determinations the President must make to implement the waivers pertaining to the Nuclear Suppliers Group (NSG), stipulating that the required NSG decision would not permit nuclear commerce with any other non-nuclear weapon state that does not have full-scope International Atomic Energy Act (IAEA) safeguards (Section 4 (b) (7)).
- Representative Schiff offered an amendment with three components: to add a provision to U.S. policy with respect to South Asia (Section 3 (b)(7)) encouraging India not to increase its production of fissile material at military facilities pending a multilateral moratorium on production of such material for nuclear weapons; to add a reporting requirement for the Presidential submission to implement the waivers (Section 4 (c) (2) (I)) on steps taken to ensure the U.S. transfers will not be replicated by India or used in its military facilities and that U.S. nuclear fuel supply does not facilitate military production of high-enriched uranium or plutonium; and to add a reporting requirement for an annual report on the same (Section 4 (o) (2) (C)).
- Representative Crowley offered an amendment to add a requirement (Section 4 (o)(3)) for an annual report on new Indian nuclear facilities.
- Representative Berkley offered two amendments related to India's spent fuel disposal: an annual report describing the disposal of spent nuclear fuel from India's civil nuclear program (Section 4 (o) (4), and a statement of policy that any spent civilian nuclear fuel in India that might be stored in the United States is considered by Congress under existing procedures of the Atomic Energy Act (Section 3 (b) (7)).

An amendment by Ms. Berkley to prohibit any Indian spent fuel from being stored in the United States was rejected by a vote of 15-19. The Committee also voted down four other amendments, including two by Representative Berman designed to place limits on U.S. cooperation until India halts production of fissile material for nuclear weapons. The first Berman amendment, rejected by a vote of 13-32, sought to condition the President's use of waiver authority (by adding a new determination by the President in Section 4 (b) of the bill) on India's adherence to a unilateral or multilateral moratorium or a multilateral treaty prohibiting the production of fissile material for nuclear weapons. The second amendment, rejected by a vote of 12-31, sought to restrict transfers of U.S. nuclear material under a cooperation agreement until such time that India halted fissile material production for weapons, either by adhering to a unilateral or multilateral moratorium, or a multilateral treaty. The Committee also rejected by a vote of 10-32 an amendment by Representative Sherman to condition the President's use of waiver authority on an additional determination, under Section 4 (b) of H.R. 5682, that India's nuclear weapons program was not using more domestic uranium than it had before July 2005.

The amendment would have attached an annual certification that required termination of nuclear cooperation if the certification could not be made. Finally, the Committee rejected, by a vote of 4-37, an amendment by Representative Lee that would have required India to join the Nuclear Nonproliferation Treaty (NPT) before the President could exercise his waiver authority.

The Committee on Rules held a hearing on July 25th to consider amendments to H.R. 5682 and procedures for handling the bill on the floor. H. Res 947 waived all points of order against the bill, specified the allowed amendments and limited floor debate to one hour. The following six amendments were allowed to be offered on the floor:[2]

- Representatives Hyde (IL)/Lantos (CA): Manager's amendment, containing technical and conforming changes to the text, as well as one substantive change: removing an amendment proposed by Representative Sherman and adopted during the full committee markup relating to subsection 4(b)(7).
- Representative Stearns (FL): Reinforces the intent of Congress that the nuclear cooperation into which the governments of the United States and India would enter is for peaceful, productive purposes, not military.
- Representatives Jackson-Lee (TX)/Burton (IN): Sense of Congress declaring the importance of the South Asia region and urging the continuation of the United States' policy of engagement, collaboration, and exchanges with and between India and Pakistan.
- Representative Sherman (CA): Requires that, before any nuclear cooperation with India can go forward, and every year thereafter, the President must certify that during the preceding year India has not increased the level of domestic uranium it sends through its weapons program. Baseline for the determination under the amendment is the 365 day period preceding the July 18, 2005, Bush-Singh declaration on nuclear cooperation.
- Representative Berman (CA): Restricts exports of uranium and other types of nuclear reactor fuel (defined as "source material" and 'special nuclear material' in the Atomic Energy Act of 1954) to India until the President determines that India has halted the production of fissile material (i.e., plutonium and highly enriched uranium) for use in nuclear weapons.
- Representative Fortenberry (NE): Provides Congress with the ability to assess, to the extent possible, whether annual levels of India's nuclear fissile production may imply a possible violation of Article I of the Nuclear Nonproliferation Treaty.

Three amendments were not allowed for consideration on the floor.[3] These were

- an amendment by Representative Woolsey that would have prohibited the export of any nuclear-related item to India until the President has implemented and observed all NPT obligations and commitments of the United States and has revised United States' policies relating to nuclear weapons accordingly;
- an amendment by Representative Barbara Lee that would have required India to place all electricity-producing reactors under safeguards, undertake a binding obligation not to transfer any nuclear-weapon-related information or technology (per Article I of the NPT) and take concrete steps toward disarmament; and
- an amendment by Representatives Markey and Upton that would have prohibited nuclear cooperation with India from commencing until the President has determined that the United States has secured India's full and active support in preventing Iran from acquiring weapons of mass destruction.

Floor Debate and Votes

The House first considered H. Res 947, which, after several objections to limits on time and the exclusion of certain amendments by Representative Markey and others, passed by a vote of 311 to 112. Of the six amendments considered, three passed by voice vote (the Managers' amendment, Representatives Jackson-Lee/Burton's amendment, and Representative Fortenberry's amendment); Representative Stearn's amendment was recorded as 414-0, and the amendments offered by Representatives Sherman and Berman were defeated (the votes, respectively, were 155 to 268, and 184 to 241).

Representative Markey made a motion to recommit the legislation back to the House International Relations Committee with instructions to include language that would require that nuclear cooperation with India could only commence after the president has determined that the United States has secured India's full support in preventing Iran from acquiring weapons of mass destruction. That motion to recommit was defeated in a vote of 192 to 235. The House passed H.R. 5682, "Henry J. Hyde United States and India Nuclear Cooperation Promotion Act of 2006," as amended, by 359 to 68 on July 26, 2006.

S. 3709/H.R. 5682 in the Senate

Committee Actions

On June 29, 2006, the Senate Foreign Relations Committee considered original legislation, S. 3709, to create an exception for India from relevant provisions of the Atomic Energy Act (See S.Rept. 109-288).[4] The Committee voted to adopt 2 of 3 amendments:

- Senator Chafee offered an amendment making it U.S. policy to ensure that exports of nuclear fuel to India did not encourage India to increase its production of fissile material (Section 103 (9));
- Senator Obama offered an amendment to ensure that the United States did not encourage other states to continue nuclear exports to India, if the United States exports to India terminated under U.S. law (Section 102 (6)).

The Committee rejected an amendment by Senator Feingold requiring an additional presidential determination in Section 105 of the bill by a vote of 5-13. The Feingold amendment would have conditioned the President's use of waiver authority on a determination that U.S. civil nuclear assistance to India would in no way assist, encourage, or induce India to manufacture nuclear weapons or nuclear devices. The amendment was identical in text to the Schiff amendment to H.R. 5682, but sought instead to require a determination rather than a report.

Floor Debate and Votes

An initial attempt to bring S. 3709 to the Senate floor in September failed to gain unanimous consent agreement. Among several issues, two apparently delayed the bill — language in Title II pertaining to implementing legislation for the U.S. Additional Protocol, and potential concern about whether the United States would accept U.S.-origin spent fuel back from Indian reactors. In the first case, concerns appeared to be mostly resolved by incorporating language into a manager's amendment, with the exception of two issues raised by Senator Ensign in two amendments he introduced on the floor on November 16th that did not pass. These are described in more detail below. In the second case, the concern about disposition of Indian spent fuel was dropped prior to the bill's reaching the floor.

On November 15, 2006, the Senate agreed by unanimous consent to consider S. 3709, at a time to be determined by the Majority Leader, in consultation with the Democratic Leader.[5] The unanimous consent agreement specified that a managers' amendment would serve as the original text for the purpose of further amendment; and that the only other amendments to be considered would include the following: Senators Ensign (considered in closed session), Reed, Levin, Obama, Dorgan (two amendments), Feingold, Boxer, Feinstein, Harkin, Bingaman (up to seven amendments), Kennedy, and Dodd. Of these, Senators Reed, Levin, Kennedy, and Dodd did not introduce amendments, and Senator Bingaman introduced three, rather than seven. All but Senator Feingold's amendment were considered to be relevant second-degree amendments and related to the subject matter of the bill. Further, the unanimous consent agreement provided that once the bill was read a third time, the Senate would begin consideration of H.R. 5682, the House-passed companion, striking all text after the enacting clause and inserting the amended text of S. 3709 in its place.

Senator Lugar introduced the bill and offered a section-by-section analysis.[6] The following amendments, in brief, were passed either by unanimous consent or voice vote without debate:

- Senator Lugar introduced a manager's amendment, which contained new language in Title II related to the Additional Protocol (S.Amdt. 5168; unanimous consent);
- Senator Obama introduced an amendment containing a statement of U.S. policy (which became Section 114) that any nuclear power reactor fuel reserve provided to the Government of India for use in safeguarded civilian nuclear facilities should be commensurate with reasonable reactor operating requirements (S.Amdt. 5169; voice vote);[7]
- Senator Harkin introduced an amendment requiring the President to determine, before executing his waiver authority, that India was supporting U.S. and international efforts to dissuade, sanction, and contain Iran's nuclear program (S.Amdt. 5173; unanimous consent);[8]
- Senator Bingaman introduced an amendment to add a reporting requirement to Section 108 (b) on the amount of uranium mined in India during the previous year; the amount of such uranium that has likely been used or allocated for the production of nuclear explosive devices; and the rate of production in India of fissile material for nuclear explosive devices and of nuclear explosive devices as well as an analysis as to whether imported uranium has affected the rate of production in India of nuclear explosive devices (S.Amdt. 5179; unanimous consent);[9]
- Senator Bingaman introduced an amendment to add a new Section in Title I (which became Section 115) requiring the Secretary of Energy to create a Cooperative Threat Reduction Program with India (S.Amdt. 5180; unanimous consent).

Senator Lugar's amendment, S.Amdt. 5168 contained minor changes in Title I of S. 3709 as reported out of Committee. One potentially significant change was the deletion of a Sense of Congress on licensing policy in Section 106. In Title II, however, which contains the implementing legislation for the U.S. Additional Protocol,[10] significant provisions were added. These included Section 202 on findings, Section 251 (3), and Sections 254, 261, 262 and 271-275. In his opening statement, Senator Lugar reported that "a compromise was reached between the Administration, the Senate Foreign Relations Committee, and those Senators who expressed concern about the IAEA Additional Protocol implementing legislation."[11] These additional provisions appear to make explicit existing U.S. rights to exclude inspectors and certain kinds of inspection activities under the Additional Protocol. Several of the modifications address the use of environmental sampling, both for specific locations and for detecting anomalies in a wide-area mode.

Other amendments were introduced, debated, and defeated. These included the following:

- Senator Bingaman introduced an amendment requiring a Presidential determination that the United States and India are taking specific steps to conclude a multilateral treaty on the cessation of fissile material for weapons before U.S. nuclear equipment or technology could be exported under the future agreement for cooperation and that no nuclear materials may be exported to India unless the President has determined that India has stopped producing fissile materials for weapons (S.Amdt. 5174; Vote 26-74);[12]
- Senator Dorgan introduced an amendment to add a declaration of U.S. policy to continue to support implementation of United Nations Security Council Resolution 1172 (S.Amdt. 5178; Vote 27-71);[13]
- Senator Ensign introduced an amendment to Title II of the bill related to the Additional Protocol that would have required any inspection equipment, materials and resources to have been purchased, owned, inspected, and controlled by the United States (S.Amdt. 5181; Vote 27-71);[14]
- Senator Dorgan introduced an amendment that would have required the President to determine, before executing his waiver authority, that India has committed to putting all electricity-producing nuclear reactors under safeguards, has undertaken an obligation not to proliferate nuclear weapons technology, has joined a legally-binding nuclear test moratorium; is verifiably reducing its nuclear weapons stockpile, and has undertaken an obligation to agree to ultimate disarmament (S.Amdt. 5182; voice vote);[15]
- Senator Feingold introduced an amendment that would have required the President to determine, before executing his waiver authority, that the scope and content of the cooperation agreement would not allow India to use U.S. technology, equipment or material in unsafe guarded facilities, would not result in India replicating U.S. technology nuclear fuel and would not facilitate the increased production by India of fissile material in unsafeguarded nuclear facilities (S.Amdt. 5183; Vote 25-71);[16]
- Senator Boxer introduced an amendment that would have required the President to determine, before he could execute his waiver authority, that India had halted military-to-military contacts with Iran (S.Amdt. 5187; Vote 38-59).[17]

Most of these amendments were characterized by Senators Lugar and Biden as "killer amendments." Senator Bingaman described his amendment as implementing a proposal by former Senator Nunn.[18] Senator Dorgan's amendment supporting U.S. implementation of U.N. Security Council 1172 sought to reaffirm U.S. support for the steps endorsed by the

U.N. Security Council following the 1998 Indian and Pakistani nuclear tests, including limits on those nuclear programs such as a ban on deployments and fissile material production for weapons, as well as a commitment on all states' parts not to sell nuclear technology to India and Pakistan. Senator Dorgan's other amendment, S.Amdt. 5182, was similar to Representative Barbara Lee's amendment to the House bill that was rejected by the House Rules Committee. That amendment attempted to commit India to undertake the same obligations as other nuclear weapon states under the NPT. Senator Feingold's amendment was similar to the one he introduced in Committee that was rejected. Although modified to address objections voiced in the mark-up, the amendment was described by Senator Lugar on the floor as requiring a certification that would have been "impossible to make."[19] Senator Ensign's amendment was debated in closed session, apparently because of the potential need to discuss classified information relating to the protection of national security information during IAEA inspections under an Additional Protocol in the United States.

H.R. 5682 Conference Report

On December 7, 2006, conferees on H.R. 5682 filed Conference Report H.Rept. 109-721. The bill essentially combines many of the provisions of both the House and Senate versions. Specific differences are highlighted in table 1, below. Of note, the Senate provisions to ban enrichment, reprocessing, and heavy water production cooperation with India (now Section 104. (d) (4)) and create an end-use monitoring program (now Section 104.(d) (5)) prevailed in the conference bill, as did Title II, which includes the implementing legislation of the U.S. Additional Protocol. The so-called Harkin amendment, which added a determination that India was fully and actively supporting U.S. and international efforts to contain, dissuade, and sanction Iran for its nuclear weapons program, did not remain as a determination, but became two reporting requirements: first, as a one-time report when the Section 123 agreement is submitted to Congress (now Section 104.(c)(2)(H)) and as an annual reporting requirement (now Section 104.(g)(2)(E)).

P.L. 109-401 Signing Statement

On December 18, 2006, President Bush signed the "Henry J. Hyde United States-India Peaceful Atomic Energy Cooperation Act of 2006" into law (P.L. 109-401). President Bush noted that the act "will strengthen the strategic relationship between the United States and India."[20] In particular, President Bush stated that the executive branch would construe two sections of the bill as "advisory" only: policy statements in Section 103 and the restriction contained in Section 104 (d) (2) on transferring items to India that would not meet NSG guidelines. On the first, the President cited the Constitution's "commitment to the presidency of the authority to conduct the Nation's foreign affairs;" on the second, the President raised the question of whether the provision "unconstitutionally delegated legislative power to an international body." In other words, the President was questioning whether Congress were ceding authority to approve U.S. exports to the Nuclear Suppliers Group. However, U.S. officials, including Secretary of State Rice, have formally told Congress multiple times that the United States government would abide by NSG guidelines. The President's signing statement also noted that the executive branch would construe "provisions of the Act that mandate, regulate, or prohibit submission of information to the Congress, an international organization, or the public, such as sections 104, 109, 261, 271, 272, 273, 274, and 275, in a manner consistent with the President's constitutional authority to protect and control information that could impair foreign relations, national security, the deliberative processes of the Executive, or the performance of the Executive's constitutional duties." This could suggest that the executive branch might limit the scope of reporting required by Congress in those sections.

ADDITIONAL RESOURCES

CRS Report RL33016, U.S. Nuclear Cooperation with India: Issues for Congress, by Sharon Squassoni.

CRS Report RL33292, India's Nuclear Separation Plan: Issues and Views, by Sharon Squassoni.

CRS Report RL33072, U.S.-India Bilateral Agreements and 'Global Partnership,' by K. Alan Kronstadt.

CRS Report RS22474, Banning Fissile Material Production for Nuclear Weapons: Prospects for a Treaty (FMCT), by Sharon Squassoni, Andrew Demkee, and Jill Marie Parillo.

Table 1. Comparison of Current Legislation on Waivers for U.S.-India Nuclear Cooperation

Issue	Description/Purpose	H.R. 4974/S. 2429 as introduced	H.R. 5682 (House version)	H.R. 5682 (Senate version)	H.R. 5682 Conference Report
Waiver authority	Provides authority for President to waive Atomic Energy Act (AEA) requirements.	*Section 1 (a)*: President may waive sections of AEA (see below) if he makes a determination.	*Section 4 (a)*: Same as H.R. 4974.	*Section 104 (a)*: Same as H.R. 4974.	*Section 104 (a)*: Same as H.R. 4974.
Section 123 a. (2) of Atomic Energy Act (AEA)	Full-scope safeguards.	*Section 1 (a) (1)*: Waived AND the future cooperation agreement enters into force as though it met all Section 123 a. requirements (does not require a Joint Resolution of Approval).	*Section 4 (a) (1)*: Waived BUT entry into force requires Joint Resolution of Approval as all other exempted agreements (See also *Section 4 (e)*).	*Section 104 (a) (1)*: Equivalent to H.R. 5682. See *Section 104 (b)*.	*Section 104 (a) (1)*: Senate version.
Section 128 of AEA	Annual review by Congress of export license for an agreement exempted from fullscope safeguards requirement.	*Section 1 (a) (2)*: Application of Section 128 waived without conditions.	*Section 4 (a) (2)*: Waiver ends if India engages in any Section 129 actions (see description below for Section 129), except for its ongoing weapons program [129 a. (1) (D)] and future reprocessing transfers to a nonnuclear weapon state [129 a. (2) (C)].	*Section 104 (a) (2)*: Section 128 waived without conditions.	*Section 104 (a) (2)*: Same as Senate version.

Table 1. (Continued).

Issue	Description/Purpose	H.R. 4974/S. 2429 as introduced	H.R. 5682 (House version)	H.R. 5682 (Senate version)	H.R. 5682 Conference Report
Section 129 of AEA	a. Terminate U.S. nuclear exports if President determines that a (1) non-nuclear weapon state: (A) Has tested a nuclear device (B) terminates or abrogates IAEA safeguards (C) materially violates IAEA safeguards (D) Has ongoing nuclear weapons program OR if President determines (2) any state (A) materially violates a cooperation agreement (B) assists non-nuclear weapon state in nwrelated activities (C) Has agreement or transfers reprocessing material, technology, or	*Section 1 (a) (3):* "Sanctions" under Section 129 waived.	*Section 4 (a) (3):* Waiver of Section 129 limited to: Indian nuclear tests before 2005 [Section 129 a. (1) (A)] and ongoing nuclear weapons activities [Section 129 a. (1) (D)].	*Section 104 (a) (3):* Equivalent to H.R. 5682 but worded differently. The language specifies waiver for sanctions under Section 129 a. (1) (D), but covers the 1998 Indian nuclear test by waiving any Section 129 sanctions regarding any actions that occurred before July 18, 2005. (There has only been one Presidential determination for India prior to 2005 that is relevant to Section 129 – for the Indian nuclear test in 1998).	*Section 104 (a) (3):* Same as Senate version.

Table 1. (Continued).

Issue	Description/Purpose	H.R. 4974/S. 2429 as introduced	H.R. 5682 (House version)	H.R. 5682 (Senate version)	H.R. 5682 Conference Report
Determination	Establishes threshold for President to use waiver authority.	*Section 1b* President must make 1 determination that 7 actions have occurred (see below).	*Section 4 (b):* Same requirements with minor changes that strengthen measures. Specifies safeguards in perpetuity.	*Section 105:* Same requirements with minor changes Specifies safeguards in perpetuity. Added determination on India and Iran (Harkin amendment)	*Section 104 (b):* Closer to House-passed version.
Separation plan	Identification of Indian civilian nuclear facilities under IAEA.	(1) India has provided to US and IAEA a credible plan to separate civil and military facilities, materials, and programs, and has filed a declaration regarding its civil facilities with the IAEA.	*Section 4 (b) (1):* Same language as H.R. 4974.	*Section 105 (1)* and *(2)* Same language as H.R. 4974 but separates the declaration provision into *Section 105 (2)*.	*Section 104 (b) (1):* Closer to House-passed version.
Safeguards plan	India committed to placing additional civilian nuclear facilities under IAEA safeguards under the July 18, 2005, Joint Statement.	(2) Entry into force of safeguards agreement in accordance with IAEA practices for India's civil nuclear facilities as declared in the plan.	*Section 4 (b) (2):* Specifies safeguards in perpetuity in accordance with IAEA standards, principles and practices. Also mentions safeguards on materials and programs, including materials used in or produced through use of civil nuclear facilities.	*Section 105 (3)* Specifies safeguards in perpetuity in accordance with IAEA standards, principles and practices. Also mentions safeguards on materials and programs.	*Section 104 (b) (2)* Change: Requires concluding "all legal steps prior to signature" (meaning Board of Governors approval of the safeguards agreement). Specifies safeguards in perpetuity with IAEA standards, etc.

Table 1. (Continued).

Issue	Description/Purpose	H.R. 4974/S. 2429 as introduced	H.R. 5682 (House version)	H.R. 5682 (Senate version)	H.R. 5682 Conference Report
Additional Protocol	An agreement with IAEA to enhance inspections, access, and declarations relevant to safeguards.	(3) Making satisfactory progress toward implementation.	*Section 4 (b)* (3) Specifies "substantial progress" consistent with IAEA principles, practices and policies.	*Section 105 (4)* Specifies "substantial progress."	*Section 104 (b) (3)* "Substantial progress toward concluding and Additional Protocol."
FMCT (Fissile Material Production Cutoff Treaty)	Future negotiations to end production of fissile material for nuclear weapons.	(4) Working with the United States for conclusion of a multilateral FMCT.	*Section 4 (b)* (4) Specifies working "actively" for the "early" conclusion.	*Section 105 (5)* Equivalent to H.R. 4974.	*Section 104 (b) (4)* House version.
Halting enrichment/ reprocessing transfers	July 18, 2005, commitment by India to support U.S. policy to restrict access to enrichment and reprocessing.	(5) Supporting international efforts to prevent the spread of enrichment and reprocessing technology.	*Section 4 (b)* (5) Specifies "working with and supporting US and international efforts."	*Section 105 (6)* Specifies preventing spread "to any state that does not already possess full-scale, functioning enrichment and reprocessing plants."	*Section 104 (b) (5)* Combines both texts.
Export controls	July 18, 2005 commitment by India to strengthen export controls and adhere to international norms, including Missile Technology Control Regime (MTCR) and Nuclear Suppliers Group (NSG) guidelines.	(6) Ensuring that necessary steps are taken to secure nuclear materials and technology through comprehensive export control legislation and regulations; and harmonization and adherence to MTCR and NSG guidelines.	*Section 4 (b) (6)* Specifies enactment and enforcement of export control laws; specifies harmonization of laws, regulations, policies and practices with the policies and practices of MTCR and NSG.	*Section 105 (7)* Specifies effective enforcement actions.	*Section 104 (b) (6)* Closer to House version.

Table 1. (Continued).

Issue	Description/Purpose	H.R. 4974/S. 2429 as introduced	H.R. 5682 (House version)	H.R. 5682 (Senate version)	H.R. 5682 Conference Report
Nuclear Suppliers Group (NSG)	NSG guidelines currently prohibit nuclear transfers to India; a decision must be taken to allow cooperation. NSG operates by consensus.	(7) Supply to India is consistent with US participation in NSG. This assumes that the NSG will agree to an exception for exports to India.	*Section 4 (b) (7)* Specifies NSG consensus decision.	*Section 105 (9)* Specifies NSG consensus decision that does not permit an exception for another non-nuclear weapon state.	*Section 104 (b) (7)* House version.
Iran	Ensure that India is supporting U.S. and international efforts to dissuade, sanction, and contain Iran's nuclear program	NONE	NONE But see *Section 3 (b) (4)* statement of policy on India's support for U.S. efforts vis-a-vis Iran.	*Section 105 (8)* Requires India's full & active participation in U.S. and international efforts to dissuade, sanction, and contain Iran for its nuclear program consistent with U.N. Security Council resolutions	Senate provision (Harkin amendment) removed and placed in reporting requirements (see Section 104.(c)(2) (H)) and Section 104.(g)(2) (E)).
Report on Determination	Notify Congress that 7 actions have occurred to allow waiver.	*Section 1 c.* Report to HIRC, SFRC that 7 actions have occurred, including basis for determination.	*Section 4 (c) (2):* Provides details about what reports to HIRC, SFRC should contain, specifically on the 7 actions. Also, two other reports are required for the determination: a description of the scope of the 123 agreement with the US and the steps taken to ensure that U.S. assistance will not aid India's nuclear weapons program (Schiff amendment).	*Section 105:* Determination must be made in writing to appropriate Committees. Similar reports are required in *Section 108 (a) (1)*, but are not tied to President's determination.	*Section 104 (c) (1) and (2)* Includes ten requirements in the report to be submitted with the 123 agreement.

Table 1. (Continued).

Issue	Description/Purpose	H.R. 4974/S. 2429 as introduced	H.R. 5682 (House version)	H.R. 5682 (Senate version)	H.R. 5682 Conference Report
Termination	Establish a threshold for halting U.S. exports to India (now contained in Section 129 of the AEA and in the proposed peaceful nuclear cooperation agreement itself, which is not yet drafted).	*Section 1d.* All waiver authorities (for Section 123 a. (2), Section 128, and Section 129) terminate if India tests a nuclear explosive device.	*Section 4 (a) (3):* All termination provisions of Section 129 of the AEA (except 129 a.(1) (D)) would be in effect (see description of sec.129 waiver above).	*Section 104 (a) (3):* All termination provisions of Section 129 of the AEA (except 129 a.(1) (D)) would be in effect (see description of sec.129 waiver above).	*Section 104 (d) (3):* All termination provisions of Section 129 of the AEA (except 129 a.(1) (D)) would be in effect (see description of sec.129 waiver above).
			ALSO *Section 4 (d) (3):* Exports would terminate if India makes a materially significant transfer of items in violation of NSG guidelines, or of items in violation of MTCR guidelines.	*No equivalent provision* to H.R. 5682 but *Section 108 (b) (3) (A)* contains a reporting reqt if India does not comply with NSG guidelines and *Section 108 (b) (4) (A)* requires an annual certification that India is in full compliance with all July 18, 2005 commitments.	*Section 104 (d) (3):* Incorporated House version Section 4 (d) (3) (Berman amendment).

Table 1. (Continued).

Issue	Description/Purpose	H.R. 4974/S. 2429 as introduced	H.R. 5682 (House version)	H.R. 5682 (Senate version)	H.R. 5682 Conference Report
Sense of Congress	To describe Congress's policy objectives with respect to nuclear cooperation with India.	NONE	*Section 2* Notes importance of nonproliferation and NPT and focuses on how the United States could strengthen its non-proliferation policy by engaging NPT outliers like India. Sets up criteria (non-proliferation record, democratic government, support for U.S. non-proliferation aims) for engagement and states India meets criteria.	*Section 102* Notes that engaging India is in the national security interest of the United States, but need to minimize proliferation risk. United States should not facilitate trade by other nations if U.S. exports terminated.	*Section 102* Combines both texts.
Statements of Policy (1)* [*President Bush has interpreted as "advisory"]	To describe U.S. policy objectives, with respect to nonproliferation.	NONE	*Section 3 (a)* *General* (1) Oppose nuclear weapons development. (2) Support peaceful uses of nuclear energy, but only with full NPT compliance. (3) Strengthen NSG implementation, including cutoff of exports for violations.	*Section 103* *Section 103 (8):* maintain support for NPT. *No equivalent* *Similar to Section 103 (6)* on support for NSG.	*Section 103 (a)* *Section 103 (a)(1)* Combines both. *Section 103 (a)(2)* House version. *Section 103 (a)(3)* and *Section 103(a) (4).*

Table 1. (Continued).

Issue	Description/Purpose	H.R. 4974/S. 2429 as introduced	H.R. 5682 (House version)	H.R. 5682 (Senate version)	H.R. 5682 Conference Report
Statements of Policy (II)	To describe U.S. policy objectives, with respect to South Asia, U.S.-India bilateral relations, and South Asian proliferation.	NONE	*Section 3 (b) South Asia* (1) Fissile material production moratorium for India, Pakistan, China.	Section 103 (1), but moratorium does not include China.	*Section 103(b)(1)* House version
			(2) FMCT	*No equivalent*	*Section 103(b)(2)* House version
			(3) Other Non-proliferation activities, like PSI, Australia Group, Wassenaar, Convention on Supplementary Compensation.	Section 103 (2), but no mention of Convention on Supplementary Compensation	*Section 103(b)(3)* House version
			(4) Support for U.S. policies to prevent Iran from acquiring nuclear weapons.	*No equivalent*, but language similar to *Section 105 (8)* determination	*Section 103(b)(4)* Modified House version
			(5) Cap, roll back and eliminate South Asian nuclear arsenals.	*No equivalent*	*Section 103(b)(5)*
			(6) No spent fuel transfer without Congressional approval.	*No equivalent*	*Section 103(b)(6)*
			(7) Encourage cap on production of fissile material for weapons, pending moratorium.	*No equivalent provision*	*Section 103(b)(7)*

Table 1. (Continued).

Issue	Description/Purpose	H.R. 4974/S. 2429 as introduced	H.R. 5682 (House version)	H.R. 5682 (Senate version)	H.R. 5682 Conference Report
Statements of Policy (III)		NONE	*No equivalent provision*	*Section 103 (3):* Full compliance with all non-proliferation obligations.	Removed. *Section 103(b)(8)*
			No equivalent provision	*Section 103 (4):* Ensure reliability of safeguards and Additional Protocol.	
			No equivalent provision	*Section 103 (5):* Agreement must meet all other Section 123 a. requirements.	*Section 103(b)(9)*
			No equivalent provision	*Section 103 (6):* Consistency with NSG guidelines.	*Section 103(a)(3)*
			No equivalent provision	*Section 103 (7):* Work with NSG members to restrict transfers of enrichment and reprocessing, also to India.	*Section 103 (a)(5)* Akin to

Table 1. (Continued).

Issue	Description/Purpose	H.R. 4974/ S. 2429 as introduced	H.R. 5682 (House version)	H.R. 5682 (Senate version)	H.R. 5682 Conference Report
			No equivalent provision	*Section 103 (8):* Maintain support for adherence & compliance with NPT.	*Section 102 (2).*
			No equivalent provision	*Section 103 (9):* Exports of nuclear fuel to India should not contribute to or encourage India to increase production of fissile material for military uses.	Removed (see reporting requirements).
			No equivalent provision	*Section 114:* Any nuclear power reactor fuel reserve provided to India should be commensurate with reasonable reactor operating requirements	*Section 103 (b)(10)*

Table 1. (Continued).

Issue	Description/Purpose	H.R. 4974/S. 2429 as introduced	H.R. 5682 (House version)	H.R. 5682 (Senate version)	H.R. 5682 Conference Report
Expedited procedures	To provide procedures for expedited consideration of Joint Resolution of Approval.	None, except as provided already in Section 130 of AEA.	*Section 4 (f) and (g)*: track with existing law (Section 130 of AEA).	None, except as provided already in Section 130 of AEA.	None, except as provided already in Section 130 of AEA.
End-Use Monitoring	To provide reasonable assurances that the recipient is complying with relevant requirements, terms and conditions of U.S. export licenses.	NONE	NONE	*Section 107* requires following measures: (1) Obtain and implement assurances and conditions regarding end-use monitoring; (2) a detailed system of reporting on technology transfers, including those authorized by Section 57 b of AEA. (3) Fall-back safeguards, should IAEA be unable to implement safeguards in India.	*Section 104 (d)(5)*

Table 1. (Continued).

Issue	Description/Purpose	H.R. 4974/S. 2429 as introduced	H.R. 5682 (House version)	H.R. 5682 (Senate version)	H.R. 5682 Conference Report
Restrictions on cooperation		NONE	*Section 4 (d)* (1) No assistance that would aid India's nuclear weapons program.	*No equivalent but similar concept behind Section 106, Section 103 (9)*	*Section 104 (d)* *Section 104 (d)(1)*
			(2) No transfers if they would violate NSG guidelines.	*Similar to Section 103 (6)*: to act in a manner fully consistent with NSG guidelines (but this is only a Statement of Policy).	*Section 104 (d)(2)** House version. [* President Bush has interpreted as "advisory"]
			(4) President should seek to prevent cooperation by other states with India if United States terminates exports.	*Section 102 (6):* United States should not seek to facilitate cooperation by other states with India if United States terminates exports.	Similar to *Section 102 (13)*.

Table 1. (Continued).

Issue	Description/Purpose	H.R. 4974/S. 2429 as introduced	H.R. 5682 (House version)	H.R. 5682 (Senate version)	H.R. 5682 Conference Report
			No equivalent provision	*Section 106* Bans cooperation on enrichment, reprocessing, and heavy water materials, equipment, and technology with exception for multilateral and bilateral fuel cycle cooperation, if President determines that the export will not improve India's ability to produce nuclear weapons. ability to produce fissile material for weapons	*Section 104 (d)(4)* Minor editing changes.
Other reporting		NONE	*Section 4 (j) (1)*: annual report on U.S. policy objectives for South Asia (i.e., steps taken by the United States and India, extent of success, and cooperation by other countries).	*No equivalent provision*	Removed

Table 1. (Continued).

Issue	Description/Purpose	H.R. 4974/S. 2429 as introduced	H.R. 5682 (House version)	H.R. 5682 (Senate version)	H.R. 5682 Conference Report
			Section 4 (j) (2) Annual report on U.S. nuclear exports to India, including estimates of Indian uranium mining, fissile material and nuclear weapons production rates; as well as impact of imported uranium on such rates. Report also to describe India's use of any U.S. nuclear equipment, material or technology in an uninspected facility; replication of anything transferred and whether imported nuclear fuel has helped to increase fissile material production	*Section 108 (b) (6)* Annual report on estimated amount of uranium mined in India during the previous year(A); amount of such uranium that has likely been used or allocated for the production of nuclear explosive devices (B); and the rate of production in India of fissile material for nuclear explosive devices(C)(I); and of nuclear explosive devices(C)(ii) Section 108 (b) (7) Analysis on whether imported uranium has affected the rate of production in India of	*Section 104 (g) (2) (H)* and *Section 104 (g) (2) (I)*

Table 1. (Continued).

Issue	Description/Purpose	H.R. 4974/S. 2429 as introduced	H.R. 5682 (House version)	H.R. 5682 (Senate version)	H.R. 5682 Conference Report
Other reporting, continued		NONE	*Section 4 (f) (3)*: annual report on new Indian nuclear facilities.	*Section 108 (b) (2)*: list of licenses approved by NRC, DOE, Commerce or any other U.S. authorizations of exports and reexports of nuclear materials and equipment.	*Section 104 (g) (2) (B)*
			Section 4 (f) (4): annual report on India's spent fuel disposal.	*No equivalent provision*	*Section 104 (g) (2) (L)*
			Section 4 (f) (5): annual report on growth in India's military fissile material production, to include information on Indian uranium mining, electricity production, domestic uranium used in civilian electricity production, & military fissile material production, etc.	*Section 108 (b) (1)*: description of additional nuclear facilities/materials India places under IAEA safeguards. *Section 108 (a) (3)*: Implementation & Compliance Report; Information on Nuclear Activities of India; "significant changes in the production by India of nuclear weapons or in the types or amounts of fissile material produced." See also *Section 108 (b) (6)*.	*Section 104 (g) (2) (A)*

Table 1. (Continued).

Issue	Description/Purpose	H.R. 4974/S. 2429 as introduced	H.R. 5682 (House version)	H.R. 5682 (Senate version)	H.R. 5682 Conference Report
			No equivalent provision	*Section 108 (b) (3):* Any significant nuclear commerce between India and other countries that does not comply with NSG guidelines, or would not meet standards applied to U.S.-origin material.	*Section 104 (g) (2) (C)*
Other Presidential certifications		NONE	NONE	*Section 108 (b) (4):* That India is in full compliance with following obligations (listed in Section 108 (a) (1):* Joint Statement commitments, separation plan, safeguards agreement, Additional Protocol, 123 agreement, terms and conditions of approved export licenses. If certification is not possible, report on steps, responses and implications.	*Section 104 (g) (2)*

Table 1. (Continued).

Issue	Description/Purpose	H.R. 4974/S. 2429 as introduced	H.R. 5682 (House version)	H.R. 5682 (Senate version)	H.R. 5682 Conference Report
Consultation with Congress		NONE	Section 4 (e (2): Requires monthly consultations with Congress on progress in 123 agreement negotiations and IAEA safeguards agreement negotiations. *No equivalent provision*	*No equivalent provision* Section 108 (a): keep Congress fully informed on India's: (1) non-compliance (2) nuclear facility construction (3) fissile material production (4) changes in operational status of nuclear facilities.	Removed *Section 104 (g) (1)*
Program for cooperative threat reduction	To further common nonproliferation goals, including scientific research and development efforts related to nuclear nonproliferation, with emphasis on nuclear safeguards.	NONE	NONE	*Section 115* Requires Secretary of Energy to establish a United States-India Scientific Cooperative Threat Reduction Program.	*Section 109*

Table 1. (Continued).

Issue	Description/Purpose	H.R. 4974/S. 2429 as introduced	H.R. 5682 (House version)	H.R. 5682 (Senate version)	H.R. 5682 Conference Report
TITLE II	Implementing Legislation for the U.S. Additional Protocol.	NONE	NONE	*Entire Title II* See. S. 2489 for comparison and S. 3709 as reported out of committee for differences between those and the version voted on by the Senate.	*Title II*

REFERENCES

[1]   The National Journal and Congressional Quarterly wrote reports of the HIRC markup, available at [http://nationaljournal.com/members/markups/ 2006/06/mr_20060627_ 5.htm] and [http://www.cq.com/display.do? dockey=/cqonline/prod/data/ docs/html/ committees/ 109/committees109-2006062700228055.html@committees and metapub= CQ-COMMITTEEMARKUPS and searchIndex=0 and seqNum=1].

[2]   See the description in H.Rept. 109-599, "Providing for Consideration of H.R. 5682, United States and India Nuclear Cooperation Promotion Act of 2006," *Congressional Record*, July 25, 2006, p. H5820.

[3]   A fourth amendment, proposed by Mr. Hyde, would have implemented a Congressional review process for arms sales and exports under the Arms Export Control Act, but this amendment was withdrawn.

[4]   Details on the mark-up are available at *Congressional Quarterly*, [http://www.cq.com/ display.do?dockey=/cqonline/prod/data/docs/html/committees/109/committees109-2006062900228090.html@committees and met apub=CQ-COMMITTEE MARKUPS and searchIndex=0 and seqNum=1] for report of the markup.

[5]   *Congressional Record*, November 15, 2006, p. S. 10941-42, daily edition.

[6]   See Senator Lugar's opening statement in the *Congressional Record,* November 16, 2006, S10982-84, daily edition.

[7]   See *Congressional Record*, November 16, 2006, S11021, daily edition, for the colloquy between Senator Obama and the managers of the bill on the subject of limiting nuclear fuel reserves to provide a disincentive for India to conduct future nuclear tests.

[8]   See *Congressional Record*, November 16, 2006, S10996, daily edition, for Senator Harkin's description of the amendment.

[9]   See *Congressional Record*, November 16, 2006, S. 11003, daily edition for the text of Senator Bingaman's amendments, S.Amdt. 5179 and S.Amdt. 5180.

[10]   The Additional Protocol is a protocol to IAEA safeguards agreements under the Nuclear Nonproliferaton Treaty (NPT) which enhances the IAEA's inspection rights, methods, and information. The model agreement is INFCIRC/540. Nuclear weapon states have modified the model to include provisions for national security exclusions, because of their weapons status. The United States signed its additional protocol in 1998, and the Senate gave its consent for ratification in 2004, but the additional protocol requires implementing legislation to enter into force. The Senate Foreign Relations Committee reported out such implementing legislation, S. 2489, in April 2006.

[11]   *Congressional Record*, November 16, 2006, S10984, daily edition.

[12]   *Congressional Record*, November 16, 2006, S. 10998-11001, daily edition, for Senator Bingaman's explanation of his amendments and responses by Senators Lugar and Biden..

[13]   *Congressional Record*, November 16, 2006, S11001, daily edition.

[14]   *Congressional Record*, November 16, 2006, S11009, daily edition, for text of Ensign amendment. The debate was held in closed session.

[15]   See *Congressional Record*, November 16, 2006, S11006, daily edition, for Senator Dorgan's introduction of the amendment and debate.

[16] See *Congressional Record*, November 16, 2006, S11011-15, daily edition, for Senator Feingold's introduction of the amendment and debate.

[17] See *Congressional Record*, November 16, 2006, S11016-11019, daily edition, for Senator Boxer's introduction of the amendment and debate.

[18] *Congressional Record*, November 16, 2006, S109998-11000, daily edition.

[19] *Congressional Record*, November 16, 2006, S11014, daily edition.

[20] See [http://www.whitehouse.gov/news/releases/2006/12/20061218-12.html].

INDEX

C

F

G

S

T

U

V